02/04.

D0688831

02/04.

Raleigh

A Living History of North Carolina's Capital

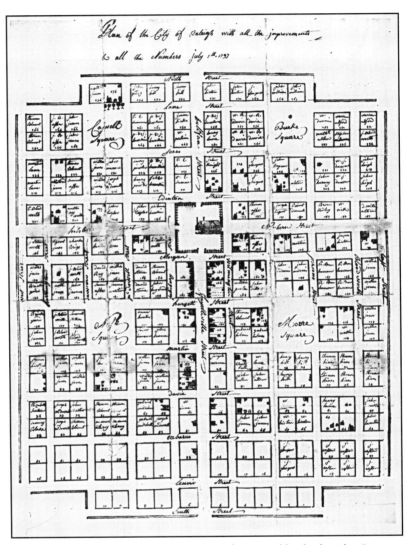

A 1797 map by an unknown draftsman shows five-year-old Raleigh with a State House and most of the city lots sold, though far fewer built upon.

Southern Historical Collection, University of North Carolina at Chapel Hill

The News & Observer's

Raleigh

A Living History of North Carolina's Capital

Edited by David Perkins

JOHN F. BLAIR, PUBLISHER
Winston-Salem, North Carolina

Library of Congress Card Catalog Number: 93–072410

Library of Congress Cataloging-in-Publication Data

The News & observer's Raleigh : a living history of North Carolina's
    capital / edited by David Perkins.

            p.   cm.
        Includes index.
        ISBN 0-89587-121-1
        1. Raleigh (N.C.)—History.   I. Perkins, David, 1954–   .
    II. News & observer.   III. Title: News and observer's Raleigh.
    IV. Title: Raleigh.
    F264.R1N38   1994
    975.6'55—dc20   94–32352

To my father, who often quotes the Middle Eastern proverb: "I would rather make a connection than be the king of Persia"

Contents

Preface   xi
Acknowledgments   xiii

PART ONE   THE NEW CAPITAL

City in the wilderness   3
Sir Walter Raleigh   *The colonizer*   10
The first family of the press   *Joseph and Winifred Gales*   13
   THE CITY'S FIRST WATERWORKS   14
An uncivil argument   *An English visitor lambastes early Raleigh;*
   the citizens rally in its defense   17
Lafayette visits Raleigh   20
The new Capitol   *'A noble monument for liberality'*   22
   THE OLD STATE HOUSE BURNS   25
Mordecai House   *A modest glory of the Old South*   26
   HOG-KILLIN' DAY   28
John Chavis   *A tutor of leaders*   29
Riding 'the Tornado'   *The railroad comes to Raleigh*   31
   'THE INGENUITY OF MAN'   32
Olmsted finds 'a pleasing town'   34
   CHRIST CHURCH: A NEW STYLE IN STONE   35
'A thorough and elegant education'   *St. Mary's College*
   and the Reverend Aldert Smedes   36
   A LETTER TO GENERAL ROBERT E. LEE FROM DR. ALBERT SMEDES   38
A freedman is tarred and feathered   *The story of Lunsford Lane*   41
'Death had passed by'   44
Sisters of charity   *Dorothea Dix Hospital and the Governor Morehead*
   School for the Blind   47

PART TWO   CIVIL WAR AND RECONSTRUCTION

Sherman's conquest   *The long march ends in Raleigh*   51
'What has befallen us?'   *From the diary of a Southern lady*   54
The newspaper war   *Recollections of a printer's devil*   58
   AN EDITORIAL FACE-OFF   59

A Yankee on the dome   *A Union soldier signals the end of the war*   60

   HAYWOOD HOUSE   63

Andrew Johnson   *A misunderstood native son*   67

Peace College   *For 'the thorough education of young ladies'*   71

Briggs and Sons, Inc.   *A memoir of a Raleigh burgher*   73

A spectacle for progress   *The North Carolina State Fair*   76

Oberlin   *The village freedom built*   79

W. W. Holden   *The career of an enigma*   81

The freedman's 'mania'   *Shaw University and St. Augustine's College*   8

   ESTEY HALL: 'THE FINEST EDIFICE'   85

Anna Cooper   *A critic of all favoritisms*   87

John Rex and R. Stanhope Pullen   *Bachelors who helped make the town*   89

   METROPOLITAN HALL   93

To wake a 'slumbering' state   *North Carolina State University*   94

   A NORTHERN VISITOR'S VIEW OF THE COLLEGE   99

PART THREE   INTO THE NEW CENTURY

Blount Street   *The very best address*   103

   A FORMAL LIFE   106

Rolling out the city   *The era of the streetcar*   108

   A BOY'S LIFE IN THE 1880S   110

The architect and the 'princess'   *The love story of A. G. Bauer and Rachel Blythe*   112

To redeem the South   *The News & Observer and partisan journalism*   118

Josephus Daniels   *Scourge of rum and Republicans*   123

'A female seminary of high order'   *Meredith College*   125

   THE GOVERNOR'S MANSION   127

   BLOOMSBURY PARK: JOYRIDE AT THE END OF THE LINE   128

   THE PULLEN PARK CAROUSEL   129

Hargett Street   *The rise and decline of the black Main Street*   130

   A SEGREGATED LIFESTYLE   133

Curtain Up!   *The founding of Raleigh Little Theater*   134

A method for education   *Berry O'Kelly*   136

Miss Blanche's salon   *Tar Heel politics at the Sir Walter Hotel*   138

The little airport that could   *Raleigh-Durham International Airport takes off*   139

   AMELIA EARHART BRINGS FIRST AUTOGYRO TO CITY   141

Clarence Poe   *An editor for the common man*   145

The City Market in the 1930s   *'Like family!'*   147

Nell Battle Lewis   *Crusader for a reformed South*   152
   INCIDENTALLY: ON THE SCOPES TRIAL   153
Jane McKimmon   *When We're Green We Grow*   154

PART FOUR   THE BOOM YEARS

Beyond the Beltline   *The rise of North Raleigh*   157
Like a 'life-size pinball machine'   *A Yankee experiences Raleigh traffic*   160
The dukes of York   *A family of builders*   162
   THE CLASSIC LINES OF MEMORIAL AUDITORIUM   165
Crossing the color line   *William Campbell integrates Raleigh's schools*   170
Sit-down strike spreads to stores   *The civil rights movement awakens*   173
Ellen Winston   *Helping others help themselves*   174
Running with the Wolfpack   *North Carolina State's sports legacy*   176
Main Street moves indoors   *The malling of Raleigh*   180
Fayetteville Street Mall   *Letting grass grow on the town's main street*   184
Dorton Arena and its designer   *An architect's lonely monument*   187
Research Triangle Park   *An engine of change*   189
The government mall   *A new home on Halifax Street*   191
Old Raleigh vs. New Raleigh   192
   FAREWELL   194

Preface

This book is a "first draft" of Raleigh history as seen by reporters of the *News & Observer*. It started out as a supplement published in December 1991 in honor of the city's two hundredth birthday. I couldn't let it stay there. As any journalist knows, the payoff of seeing one's work swiftly in print is accompanied by frustration at the compromises made along the way and the knowledge that it will all turn yellow before long. I was happy to work a little longer, to gather more photographs and write a few more articles to fill holes in the narrative.

My goal was to create a history that lived and breathed. And so, to stories from the *N&O* archives and some original articles, I have added excerpts from diaries, memoirs, letters, and oral histories.

This is not a scholarly history. I've tried to make it as accurate as possible, but there was no way to check every fact in every story. For authoritative information, the best source is still Elizabeth Reid Murray's *Wake—Capital County of North Carolina*, on which I relied heavily.

Still, Raleigh's history is dramatic, and the dramas have had something to say about the larger issues of the day—from the city's creation out of the wilderness, to its role in the middle (ideological and geographical) of the Confederacy, to its leadership in today's New South as a cornerstone of the Research Triangle.

—David Perkins

Acknowledgments

My thanks are due first of all to Frank Daniels, Jr., the *News & Observer's* publisher, to Frank Daniels III, its executive editor, and to Marion Gregory, the managing editor, for many challenging assignments over the years, including the one that started this off. Bruce Siceloff coedited the original supplement and lavished his expertise on several stories. Steve Massengill and his staff in the photography department of the North Carolina Division of Archives and History and Ed Morris and his staff in the document section were always helpful and courteous. Thanks also to Steve Adams, Jon Sanders, and Mrs. Marshall Haywood for reviewing parts of the manuscript.

Permissions

For permission to quote from works in their possession, I thank:

The Southern Historical Collection, library of the University of North Carolina at Chapel Hill; excerpts from Gales Family Papers, #2652,; "Recollections of Joseph and Winifred Gales"

The University of North Carolina Press; excerpts from Kemp P. Battle's *Memories of an Old-Time Tar-Heel* (1945)

Capital Area Preservation, Inc.; Ellen Mordecai's *Gleanings from Long Ago*

Marshall DeLancey Haywood Jr., and Margaret S. Haywood; memoirs of Richard B. Haywood and Mattie Bailey Haywood

Mrs. Evelyn Briggs Bush; memoir of T. H. Briggs, by T. H. Briggs III

Raleigh Historic Districts Commission; "Raleigh Roots" oral-history project

North Carolina Division of Archives and History; *Journal of a 'Secesh' Lady: the Diary of Catherine Ann Devereux Edmondston*

The *Saturday Evening Post*; excerpts from April 12, 1947, article on Raleigh

The articles in Part One are heavily indebted to Elizabeth Reid Murray's *Wake—Capital County of North Carolina*; William S. Powell's *North Carolina Through Four Centuries*; and David L. Swain's *Early Times in Raleigh*.

Jacob Marling, Raleigh's first resident artist of repute, rendered the State House soon after its remodeling in the 1820s. In the background is the three-story Bank of New Bern branch on Fayetteville Street.

N.C. Museum of Art

City in the wilderness

BY DAVID PERKINS

When the commissioners arrived at Joel Lane's inn on March 20, 1792, to pick out land for the state capital, they found mostly uncleared forest of oak and hickory. It was a hunter's paradise, perhaps, but not a place where dollar, or pound, signs would pop up in a tradesman's eyes. And that was one of the unspoken arguments in its favor.

There was no navigable river, no manufacturing. The few plantations were farmed for subsistence: the area was west of the cotton belt and south of the best tobacco country. Wake County had been hewed out of the surrounding counties twenty-one years earlier, but it still lacked a single incorporated town.

The nearest thing to it was the handful of houses near the log courthouse, known first as Bloomsbury (the name of Lane's estate), then as Wake Crossroads, and finally, after Lane persuaded his fellow legislators to make his neighborhood the county seat, as Wake Court House. Lane's small, gambrel-roofed house—said to be the grandest mansion for a hundred miles—doubled as a popular inn and tripled, when temperatures were too cold in the log building on the hill behind, as the courtroom.

Legislators had stayed at Lane's in 1781, and apparently had a good time of it. One Vincent Bass was reimbursed 35,720 pounds for "candles, fowls, etc." That was in inflated currency, but still it was roughly equal to the amount paid to Lane for two weeks' rent!

Perhaps they had good memories of hunting in Lane's woods, or of taverner Isaac Hunter's rum punch. But there was another, more powerful argument for the lawmakers' decision to locate the capital "within 10 miles of Isaac Hunter's tavern" in Wake County. It was near the center of the state, and at the crossroads of the state's two highways, one north-south from Petersburg, Virginia, to Charleston, South Carolina, and the other from the coast west to Hillsborough.

Wake Court House was accessible, hospitable, and neither so thickly settled nor so propitious for settlement as to offend the rival factions in the search. And, after all, American tradition shouted, "Start anew!"

Five of the nine appointed commissioners arrived by stage on March 20, 1792. They took refreshment at Hunter's tavern—a venerable establishment on the north-south highway—and then lodged at Lane's inn. A sixth arrived later. For a week and a day, including a Sunday, the men tramped over seventeen tracts offered for sale, narrowing the choices, finally, to two: a plot of a thousand acres put up by Lane, and another parcel of the Neuse River offered by his brother-in-law, John Hinton.

The commissioners voted three times. On the first two ballots, they were split, with three votes for Hinton's tract, two for Lane's, and one each for another tract. But they debated long into the night, as (I freely speculate) the claims of Lane's liquor cabinet outdid the claims of a river location, and by morning, Lane's tract came out the winner. The price was £1,378.

So, at last, ended a sectional rivalry that dated to the early days of the royal colony. The factions had shifted slightly over the years, from north-south to east-west, but were no less intense. Those who lived west of the Cape Fear River backed Fayetteville as the capital; those who lived in the Albemarle area and along the Tar, Roanoke, and Neuse rivers wanted it located farther east.

That Wake's politicians had never become tied to either camp is suggested in a March 13, 1792, letter from Lane to General William Harrington, the commissioner representing Fayetteville, urging him to make the meeting on the twentieth, "having no reason to believe that unless you are present the Eastern interests will fix it [the site] on the North Side of the Neuse River." That is, on brother-in-law Hinton's tract. Lane knew how to wrap his self-interest in the bright foil of the broader issue. Or did Harrington laugh at the obvious ploy? In any case, he was not taken in; he was one of three commissioners who didn't show.

The idea of a fixed capital was long dreamed of, but only briefly realized, in North Carolina. In the colonial era, legislatures had been "itinerant publick assemblies," in the words of Royal Governor William Tryon. Where the governor chose to live, the legislature followed, hauling its records behind it in wagons.

In 1746, the southern coastal counties made an attempt, with the royal governor's encouragement, to settle the capital in New Bern. But the effort was foiled by northern counties along the Albemarle. In 1758, Royal Governor Arthur Dobbs bought land near today's Kinston in Lenoir County and persuaded the assembly to approve his plan to build a government seat on it. But "George City," as it was to be called in honor of George II, was scuttled by disputes with Parliament and reignited sectionalism.

Dobbs's successor, Governor Tryon, tried again in 1770 and succeeded. He built a residence for himself and a chamber for the council, the upper legislative house, in New Bern. It was known as Tryon's Palace. During the Revolutionary War, assemblies continued to meet there, but westerners grew restless with the long travel and pushed for a new site. In 1777, they introduced a bill proposing Smithfield: it failed.

In 1778, as the coast became dangerous, the legislature took up its wandering again, meeting in New Bern, Bath, Wilmington, Wake Court House, Brunswick, Halifax, Smithfield, and Tarboro. Each year, lawmakers learned all over again that travel was difficult (more so during wartime) and damaging to the state's records.

Bills calling for a permanent capital became as regular a feature of the sessions as proposals for a state lottery are today. Every town wanted the honor, but to win they needed some allies, and in whose interest was it to be an ally? The stalemate favored claims from nowhere-in-particular.

Wake County was first mentioned as a possible site in 1779, in a bill along with Chatham and Johnston County. It did not pass. In 1782, a bill passed naming Hillsborough as the site, but the Cape Fear–western alliance repealed it the next year. In 1784, another bill was introduced that mentioned New Bern,

Smithfield, Hillsborough, Tarboro, Salem, Fayetteville, and "the plantation of John Abernathie" in Wake. It, too, failed.

The question couldn't be settled, it seemed, by the usual means. So the law-makers referred it to the Constitutional Convention held in Hillsborough in 1788. This was the convention that famously rejected the new federal Constitution for want of a Bill of Rights, but it did move on the question of an "unalter-able seat of government," deciding it should be settled "within 10 miles of Isaac Hunter's tavern."

That wasn't the end of it. The legislature still had to approve the action, and the Cumberland delegation continued to block it, pushing Fayetteville's virtues as a port and commercial center. But the cession of the state's western territory—later Tennessee—in 1789 had changed the balance of power, and the opposi-tion's majority grew thin. Finally, when the assembly met in New Bern in the winter of 1791–92, the convention's ordinance was approved. Nine commission-ers were appointed (one for each of the state's judicial districts and one at-large) to select and purchase land. After that, they were to lay it off, sell lots, and choose a site for a State House.

On the morning of March 21, the commissioners set out again for Lane's tract, this time in the company of state senator William Christmas, the official survey-or who had laid out the county seats of Warrenton and Louisburg. The land was more than two-thirds virgin forest, and one-third disused field. It lay on a ridge that sloped north and east toward Crabtree Creek and south toward Walnut Creek. At the high point of the southern slope, Lane surely pointed out, if he hadn't before, a famous "deer tree" near where the Capitol stands today.

Taking the peak of the slope as his center, Christmas marked off four hun-dred of the thousand acres in a large square with the north-south, east-west ori-entation customary for the time. Christmas's plan followed exactly the 1758

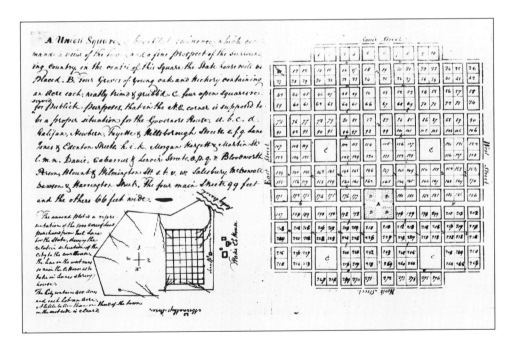

A street plan drawn in 1792, probably by surveyor state senator William Christmas of Franklin County

N.C. Division of Archives and History

State senator Joel Lane's house was praised as "the grandest house for 100 miles." It served as a popular inn and as the county courthouse when weather required. This photograph was made in the 1880s.

N.C. Division of Archives and History

specifications for Royal Governor. Dobbs's "George City," according to William Powell in *North Carolina Through Four Centuries*. What if *that* record had been lost in transit?

He then laid out a grid of streets and divided the land into 276 one-acre lots. An early map indicates that Christmas positioned the tract to take advantage of four springs, one at each corner. The spring at the southeastern corner fed Lane's own springhouse, just inside the thousand-acre survey line. Within the planned square, Christmas allowed for four "publick" parks, of four acres each, at points equidistant from a central square, called Union Square, which was reserved for the State House.

Like everything else, the naming of the streets had a clear logic. The four streets framing the square were named for the four compass directions. The four central streets (a generous ninety-nine feet wide, while the others were sixty-six) commemorated the four major court-district cities to which they pointed: Fayetteville, New Bern, Halifax, and Hillsborough. Morgan, Salisbury, Edenton, and Wilmington streets were named for the other four court seats. And the nine commissioners (Hargett, Dawson, McDowell, Bloodworth, Jones, Martin, Blount, Harrington, and Person), Senate speaker William Lenoir, House speaker Stephen Cabarrus, General William R. Davie, and, naturally, Lane got street names, too.

The commissioners' work was blessed by the General Assembly on December 31, 1792. And, showing its sense of history, the session named the new capital after the "Cittie of Ralegh" that Sir Walter had ordered built two centuries earlier on his ill-fated Roanoke Island settlement.

The public auction of lots began on June 4, 1792, and lasted five days. In all, 212 of 254 lots put up for sale were sold. Most of the commissioners bought at least 1 lot. Willie Jones, the patriot and commissioner from Halifax, bought 15.

(He later sold the lots and bought an estate near where St. Augustine's College stands today.)

With the auction's proceeds, which were almost six times what Lane had been paid, a new set of commissioners started work on the new State House in 1792. Two years later, in December 1794, legislators took their seats in a still-incomplete structure designed by an architect from Warren County, Rhoddam Atkins.

It was a simple brick building with four entrances, like the present structure, later with projecting porticoes and a cupola. In the 1820s, architect William Nichols prettied it up in the Greek Revival style, giving it a dome, false classical porticoes, and a coat of yellow stucco. For the rotunda, the legislature commissioned a marble statue of Washington from the famed Roman sculptor Antonio Canova. When it arrived, the sight of the general in a powdered wig and Roman consul's uniform struck some locals as odd, and Lafayette, who saw it in 1825, said it looked more like him.

For some years, the State House would be the hub of the young town. Kemp P. Battle, looking back in the mid-nineteenth century, described it thus: "On one day, the candidate would proclaim the pure righteousness of his cause and the diabolical mischiefs of the opposing party; on the next, men with their stomachs filled with barbecued pig, washed down with corn whiskey or apple-jack brandy, shouted defiance to Great Britain and boasted of the greatness of America. Then the floor would be swept and at night belles and beaux would walk in the stately minuet and caper in the quick-time Virginia reel. . . . And when the week was over, the people assembled in the sobered chambers and trembled as the preacher thundered forth the wrath of God."

Battle overlooked the theater troupes, puppet shows, and tightrope dancers. The hooks and lines for the latter had become such a nuisance by 1810 that the General Assembly passed a bill instructing the custodians to remove them.

It was a festive city, and never more so than on a patriotic occasion. Fourth of July celebrations brought out the entire populace for dinner at Peter Casso's inn (with as many toasts as there were states of the Union) and, finally, a ball at the State House.

Raleigh vibrated to politics, above all, and the legislators were happy for it to stay that way. They restricted its powers of self-government. While they funded an investigation of navigation on the Neuse River, they did not approve any other public works to benefit the capital until 1810, with the chartering of the State Bank of North Carolina.

Raleigh was, in fact, a capital for three years before it became a city. In 1795, the General Assembly approved the city's first charter. Seven commissioners were appointed to make such "rules, orders and regulations and ordinances as to them shall seem meet for repairing the streets, appointing a Constable or constables, city watches or patrols." From among the commissioners, an "intendant of police" was to be elected a chief law-enforcement officer—an office first filled, it is believed, by state treasurer John Haywood.

With their limited taxing power, and being beholden to the assembly rather than the voters, it's not surprising that the commissioners did little to improve the city, or even maintain it. The streets were muddy, and the stench from out-

For some years, the State House would be the hub of the young town.

houses on the public squares made them less than lovely picnic spots. The citizens complained about thefts, drunks on Fayetteville Street, and gangs of boys playing quoits on Union Square on Sundays.

In 1803, the city's charter was modified to make the commissioners subject to the voters in their districts, and they were given more money-raising powers. But streets remained the responsibility of the residents, and keeping the peace was the job of a single constable by day and a citizens' watch by night until well into the next century.

Still, they came. The 1800 census showed that Raleigh had 669 residents: 316 whites, 18 free Negroes, and 335 slaves. Perhaps thirty houses had been built, judging by an early map, mostly along Fayetteville Street south of the State House—it was the busiest trade route—and around Union Square. The county court, seeing where the action was, had moved to the street in 1795, where the present courthouse stands today.

Like anyone on paid holiday from a regular job, legislators liked to party, and in the early years, the capital's economy was built on entertaining, eating, and drinking. Peter Casso's three-story tavern on Fayetteville and East Morgan streets opened in 1795 and became the town's major hostelry. It was a big establishment, with stables for forty horses and a kitchen that could prepare food for hundreds. In the evening, Casso's cockpit drew as many as two hundred onlookers. The stage stopped at Casso's three times a week, and with it the word from the outer world. When the first town bell was built there in 1808 to signal fire, funerals, the opening of legislative sessions, and church, it gained an even more decided edge over the competition.

The official bell ringer was one Jacob Johnson, a porter for Casso. Did he ring the bell on the night of December 29, 1808, when his son, the future president Andrew Johnson, was born in an outbuilding of the inn? No one knows. But legend has it that Hannah Casso, one of Peter's daughters, came rushing from the State House, where she was attending a prenuptial ball, to name the child.

Next to the courthouse was the Indian Queen Tavern, perhaps the most popular resort after Casso's. Warren Alford had a tavern at Fayetteville and Morgan streets. And there was enough business, when the legislature was in session, for John Marshall, Lewis Green, Archibald Wills, John Porter, and Charles Parish to serve liquor and put up legislators in their homes.

Every bit as busy as most tavern keepers was Mrs. John Haywood, the wife of the state treasurer, who regularly entertained friends and legislators. Haywood had been elected in 1787 and endured in office for thirty-three years. He was a hunter and bon vivant, and it was no accident that the elegant home he built on New Bern Avenue has ornamental apples and pineapples, the signs of hospitality, in the woodwork. Wife Elizabeth testified to her exhaustion in a 1798 letter:

> Mr. H invited 30 Gentlemen to dinner, Six and Twenty at the Long Table and four at a Side Table—and that has been the number every other day since, until Saturday last, which finished the going through with the Assembly Men, but on Sunday following he had a picked set of 30: consisting of Members and Transient People, at an Elegant Dinner. . . . I am up every night till twelve or One O'Clock at Night, preparing for the next day's dinner . . . and the Federal Court meets the first of January and I shall have the same

The citizens complained about thefts, drunks on Fayetteville Street, and gangs of boys playing quoits on Union Square on Sundays.

trouble over again. Mr. Haywood is now gone to the Governor's for dinner, this is the only day our House has been still for weeks.

What she did not know was that the banquets were being bought with money that mingled with Haywood's skimmings from the state treasury. The treasurer fended off inquiries during his lifetime, but a month after his state funeral in 1827, a legislative commission reported that he had embezzled $68,631 and ⅜ cents, or roughly half the state's expenditures for one year. With the burden of making things right, Elizabeth turned her home into a boardinghouse for legislators.

Unlike the treasurer and other chief state officials, who had to take up residence right away, the governor wasn't required to reside in Raleigh until 1794. Then he had to be in town at least half the year, although he could choose which months. In 1802, the residency rule was tightened to require the governor to be in Raleigh "permanently" during his term of office.

At first, the chief executives rented houses where they could. Then the state bought a two-story frame house on the corner of Fayetteville and Hargett streets for the first official residence. The governor did his business in an outbuilding. North Carolina's legislators, never anxious to do the executive any favors, let the house fall into disrepair until it was, in the words of Governor Benjamin Smith, "not to be fit for the family of a decent tradesman. . . . The plaster is frequently falling, and the roof is so leaky that in going from the sitting room to the chambers during a rain a wetting is experienced."

The house served, however badly, until 1816, when a graceless but large structure with an imposing white-columned portico, later called the Governor's Palace, was built at the south end of Fayetteville Street.

Newspapers, the camp followers of politicians, also figured prominently in the young city. In 1799, William Boylan relocated from Fayetteville, bringing his pro-Federalist *Minerva* with him. Shortly thereafter, Joseph and Winifred Gales arrived from Philadelphia and opened a printing press on Fayetteville Street, where they published the pro-Jeffersonian *Raleigh Register*, the *Minerva's* chief rival.

Whatever their differences, Gales and Boylan had a common interest in the city's prosperity. And Raleigh did prosper, not in a flash, but slowly and steadily. Gales's hope that it would become a center of manufacturing would never be realized. It has remained what it was at the beginning, a city of lawyers and lawmakers, editors and readers, teachers and students, taverners and revelers, churchgoers and gamesters, and (especially in the 1980s and 1990s) new immigrants, who give it, once again, a cosmopolitan air.

What she did not know was that the banquets were being bought with money that mingled with Haywood's skimmings from the state treasury.

Sir Walter Raleigh

The colonizer

BY JOHN D. NEVILLE
The News & Observer
July 1985

Sir Walter Raleigh

c. 1554–1618

The man who gave his name to Raleigh never saw the town, and would probably have been suprised by the spelling.

The mystery of Sir Walter Raleigh begins with his name. Was it spelled *Rawleyghe* as he signed it once in 1578, *Rauley*, as he signed it until 1583, or *Ralegh*, as he signed it from 1584 until his death in 1618? The spelling preferred today is one he may never have used. Like the spelling and pronunciation of his name (is it Rawley or Rolly?), he was an enigma, a soldier whose failures were as notable as his successes, an adventurer whose first English-speaking colony in the New World was wiped out, a court favorite whose life ended on the scaffold.

He was born around 1554 at Hayes Barton in Devonshire. In 1569, he was in France fighting for the Huguenots. In 1572, he was at Oriel College, Oxford. And in 1575, he was at the Middle Temple, one of the Inns of Court.

Then his fabulous career began, a mixture of courtly graces, ambition, and physical danger. He fought wars in France, privateered against the Spanish with his half-brother, Sir Humphrey Gilbert, fought in Ireland, and caught the fancy of Queen Elizabeth, becoming her favorite at court.

On March 25, 1584, Raleigh received a patent from the queen granting him title to any lands he might discover and claim in the name of the crown. On April 27, 1584, he sent out on an expedition from Plymouth, commanded by Phillip Amadas and Arthur Barlowe, with the Portuguese Simón Fernández as pilot. They arrived off the coast of what is now North Carolina on July 13, 1584, took possession of the area in the name of the queen, explored the region, and returned to England, taking with them two young Indian men, Manteo and Wanchese. As a result of this expedition, Raleigh was knighted on January 6, 1585. Later in 1585, Sir Walter sent a military colony to America under Sir Richard Grenville. Captain Ralph Lane was the governor, and the company that settled on Roanoke Island included John White and Thomas Harriot.

Sir Walter Raleigh

The first family of the press

Joseph and Winifred Gales

BY DAVID PERKINS

It is tantalizing to imagine the conversation at the dinner table of Joseph and Winifred Gales. Was it about Gales's recent editorial defending Jefferson's Louisiana Purchase? Or Mrs. Gales's new novel, *Matilda Berkeley*, the first published in the state that was written by a resident? Was it Gales's game plan to make the Neuse River navigable? Or Mrs. Gales's story of how she'd shamed privateers off their ship during their journey from Hamburg to Philadelphia? ("I adjured him," she wrote in her memoirs, "to abandon a profession in which every man's hand was against his own.")

The extraordinary couple was brilliant, principled, and courageous, as well as prolific (they had twelve children). They followed the winds of democratic change from northern England to Philadelphia, and then to the young state capital of Raleigh, where they became the city's busiest founding citizens and its most cosmopolitan influence.

They arrived in Raleigh in September 1799. Six weeks later, they had set up a home, a bookstore, and a printshop on Fayetteville Street (near where the courthouse stands today) and produced the first issue of the *Raleigh Register*. It was the city's second paper—William Boylan's *Minerva* had printed its first issue a few months earlier. But the *Register* would outlast its rival and become the most important news organ in the state (perhaps the region) until the Civil War.

For thirty years, the Galeses busied themselves weaving the fabric of the young city. Joseph helped launch the Raleigh Academy, probably Raleigh's first school; he hired the city's first pastor; and he built its first paper mill. As a founder of the State Agricultural Board, he tried to persuade farmers to grow new crops, including grapes, sprigs of which he offered for sale in his bookstore.

He was an impatient civic booster with a quaint faith in new technology. After fire destroyed the State House in 1831, he instigated the "Experimental Railroad" to carry stone to build the new Capitol. The railroad's success—it worked, and it made a handsome profit for the private investors—persuaded legislators to keep Raleigh as the capital city. From 1819 to 1825, and again from 1827 to 1833, Gales was Raleigh's intendant of police, or mayor.

Sometimes, however, Gales overreached. He failed to raise money for a cotton mill, and his Neuse Navigation Project foundered in the river's shallows. He never could interest any investors in mining for plumbago (lead).

As the *Register*'s editor, Gales spoke out for penal reform, libraries, a state medical society, and an insurance company. He promoted manufacturing opportunities and the cause of Jeffersonian republicanism.

On slavery, however, Gales was no revolutionary. When a group of Greensboro

THE CITY'S FIRST WATERWORKS

FROM NOSEPH GALES'S "REMINISCENCES," T8J6

Soon after the citizens had been visited by this calamity [the fire of 1806], a Fire Engine was procured from Philadelphia and soon after an inquiry was made whether it would be practicable to obtain a supply of water from a Reservoir to be resorted to in case of Fire, from some of the Streams of Water or Springs, in the vicinity of the city. An examination was accordingly made, the result of which was that there was no source of water in the neighborhood that could, by its own gravity, be brought into a Reservoir in the State House Square. Nothing was therefore done at that time. But a suggestion was afterwards made that...[water] might easily be obtained by a little simple machinery, and that Jacob Lash, an eminent machinist at Salem, could execute the Work.

Joseph Gales

The Work was therefore immediately set about, and a number of hands employed in getting Timber for the machinery, Pipes, etc., in digging ditches, boring pipes, running levels, etc. The water of the Rocky Branch on the Western borders of the City was to be used for the moving Power and Mr. Boylan's and some other smaller springs, were to furnish the water to be conveyed to the City, through Pipes, first to a cistern raised so high, that the water would descend by its own gravity into a Reservoir dug in the State House Square, where it was to be conveyed down Fayetteville Street to a Reservoir at Mr. Coman's corner, and there to another reservoir near the Court-house at both which last mentioned places, the Water was to be kept running in a constant stream for public use.

After much labor, and at a greater expense, and in a longer time than had been anticipated, the heavy Work was effected and was for a time greatly praised and admired. But it was soon found that the Wooden pipes employed had not sufficient strength to withstand the stress that they had to bear, and that the renewal of them would be a continued expense too great to be borne by the city, so that the whole work, after the experiment of a few months, was abandoned.

Had the Commissioners obtained Iron Pipes for the distance between the Forcing Machinery and the Reservoir, the Wooden Pipes, it is not doubted, would have answered to convey the running water into Reservoir prepared to receive it, and thus the work would have been preserved and have done credit to the public spirit of the City.

Voices

from

the

Capital

Quakers asked him to publish an antislavery tract, he replied, "It will be no use to attack people's prejudices in the face." But he was not blind to what was in store. "We tremble," he wrote later, "when we reflect that this cloud may one day burst and bury so many thousands in irretrievable ruin." He saw recolonization as the best alternative to such destruction and later served as treasurer of the American Colonization Society in Washington, D.C.

Winifred Gales, when she wasn't holding listeners rapt at her table or writing novels, helped run the print shop and bookstore.

The Galeses' *Register* and Boylan's *Minerva* were formidable, occasionally vituperative rivals. What a show it was: Boylan, the native aristocrat, high churchman, and Federalist, versus Gales, the British radical, Unitarian and small *d* democrat.

Once, Boylan's attacks became personal, and the two men squared off on Fayetteville Street. Gales got the worst of it, sued Boylan for assault, and won a hundred pounds, which he turned over, minus legal fees, to the new academy.

The lesser pugilist, Gales was the better journalist and the shrewder marketer. He put out a semiweekly during legislative sessions when other papers were weeklies, and employed shorthand to record debates verbatim. He also was the first to print obituaries in North Carolina.

The *Register* benefited from its connection to the *National Intelligencer* in Washington, which Gales established with a Philadelphia associate in 1800. The Washington newspaper arrived, sometimes by special messenger, with inside news of the Jefferson and Madison administrations for Gales to extract in the *Register*.

The rivalry ended when Boylan sold his interest in the *Minerva* in 1810 and entered politics.

The Galeses' liberalism was galvanized in working-class northern England, the seedbed of the reform movement. Joseph Gales was the son of a village artisan in Gekington and got his start in the bookselling trade. In the bookstore where he was apprenticed, he met Winifred, and, although she was higher born (she was a cousin of Lord Melbourne), he won her hand and persuaded her of his political views.

They moved to Sheffield, where Gales started the Sheffield *Register* in 1787 to advocate parliamentary reform. He called for enlarging the franchise, covered disputes over enclosures, and quoted liberally Thomas Paine's *Rights of Man*.

When he became active in political organizing, however, Gales ran afoul of the British government, then nervous about the French Revolution, and avoided arrest by fleeing to Denmark and then Hamburg. Winifred joined him there, and together they set sail for Philadelphia. In the national capital, Joseph found work reporting congressional speeches for the *American Daily Advertiser*. He bought the *Independent Gazetteer* and renamed it *Galeses Independent Gazetteer*.

When war broke out between the British and French, Gales's pro-French political views once again put him at risk. And that, as well as outbreaks of yellow fever, may have inclined him once again to move.

It was Nathaniel Macon, the Warren County congressman and later House speaker, who persuaded Gales to relocate to Raleigh. Macon and other Jeffersonians

wanted a paper in North Carolina to counter the Federalists. To bait the lure, they promised Gales a shot at the state printing contract.

When the Galeses arrived in Raleigh, the seven-year-old city was barely cut out of the forest. "There were not more than 1,000 inhabitants and at least one third were slaves or free colored persons," Winifred recalled in her memoirs. "But there the Governor and Executive officers resided, the Legislature sat, and there the Federal Circuit and the Superior County courts were held.

"We were strangers to the sight and altogether unacquainted with habits and manners of that unfortunate race whose numbers are constantly increa-sing. . . . The idea of purchasing slaves was most revolting to our feelings." Gales himself added a superscript: "And yet apparently from necessity…we were indeed to purchase several."

Of their twelve children, two continued in the newspaper trade. After apprenticing at home, Joseph Jr., the eldest, was placed as editor of the *National Intelligencer*. He was enormously successful; the *Intelligencer* was Washington's leading paper for decades.

In 1833, the Galeses retired to Washington to live with Joseph Jr., and Weston, their last child, born in Raleigh in 1802, was left in charge of the *Register*. He edited it capably—if not as sharply as his father—until his death in 1848.

After Winifred's death in 1839, Joseph Sr. returned to Raleigh and was elected mayor again in 1840. He lived a year, and died at age eighty.

In the 1830s, the Galeses wrote a volume of "reminiscences" for their children and grandchildren that tells their incredible story. It includes several peephole glimpses of early Raleigh. Winifred's elegant script alternates with Joseph's crabbed hand, her vivid anecdotes and emotional appeals with his corrections and nuts-and-bolts accounts of a new city being made.

An uncivil argument

An English visitor lambastes early Raleigh; the citizens rally in its defense

An exchange in the *North Carolina Journal*, Halifax

Letter from an English gentleman, on his travels through the United States, to his friend in London:

March 12, 1798

You already are apprised that the place from which I write is the capital of North Carolina. You have with myself, I dare say, often had occasion to admire at the stupidity of princes, in founding cities in places of all others the most ineligible to ensure their future growth and importance. From the numbers in Europe and the countries of the east, which have been raised alone by the arm of power, or the superstition of the priesthood, in which commerce or national convenience had no share, you will perhaps have thought as I have done, that in despotic governments, men warred against nature. But when I shall have described to you this metropolis of one of the largest states in the American union, founded by the representatives of a free and (as they style themselves) an enlightened people . . . you may be induced to suspend your veneration of republicanism. . . .

Raleigh is situated more than an hundred miles from any seaport, and nearly thirty from any boatable waters, has no stream of water capable of making it a manufacturing town; has therefore no prospect of becoming anything more than the solitary residence of a few public officers, containing a few ordinary taverns, gaming houses and dram shops, and this is in fact what the metropolis now is. It might probably have been expected by the founders, that being in a hilly country, it would become the summer residence of many people in the eastern sickly parts of the state, but it has been found on experience not to have the degree of healthiness which its elevated situation would seem to promise. . . .

The western people are obliged to go to another state to find markets for their produce. All of the profits of trade are therefore lost to their own state, and without their deriving the least advantages from residing in the neighbourhood of the metropolis.

The plan of Raleigh (which by the bye is dignified with the name of city) would have been tolerably good, had it been situated in a place in which it could have been completed; but neither power nor superstition, as in the east, have any effect here to help its completion; for it contains neither the castle of the Lord's anointed, nor the coffin of a departed saint. The necessities of the

> *"The necessities of the government, and the groveling dissipation of a few, are its whole support."*
> —*An English visitor*

The first State House as sketched in 1811 by visiting Scottish watercolorist J. S. Glennie.

The Andre de Coppet Collection, Princeton University Library

government, and the groveling dissipation of a few, are its whole support.

The ground is divided into four quarters by as many spacious streets, which terminate in the public square, in the center of which stands the state house, a clumsy brick building, built without any regular design of architecture, and totally devoid of taste or elegance.

Disgraceful as the appearance of the state house is at best, they have contrived to place it yet in a more disadvantageous point of view, by erecting the court house, the palace of the governor, and most of the other buildings, on one of the streets which has only an end view of the statehouse, which makes but a forty appearance. . . .

At the four corners of the public square are groves which might have been made agreeable walks; I thought this was their design, and seeing a small house in two of them, I took them for summer houses, and began in my mind, to applaud the state for constructing such charming places for the recreation of the people in a warm climate, and going to visit one of them, was arrested in my progress by a terrible stench issuing from four doors, which informed me it was a temple of Cloacina.

The streets of this city are honored with the names of some of the great men who have distinguished themselves in the service of the state . . . and to do them justice the state ought, in imitation of the ancients, to place statues of them in their favorite temples.

Raleigh citizens reply

June 4, 1798

Mr. Hodge,

Your No. 295 contains much entertaining matter, particularly the curious piece pretended to have been written by the English gentleman on his tour through the United States. . . . We contend he has offered a high affront and gross indignity to the state; and if he is in fact an Englishman, in return for his civility we can but advise him through you to return to the Nabobs of his own country, where the appearance of public and private buildings is more pleasing to an English eye, and the fare of their tables better suited to an English stomach.

We are not disposed to enter into a reasoning detail with this man of the world on the subjects of his 73d . . . but you will indulge us a minute while we briefly refute a few of his statements.

He suggests that nothing short of monarchy and priestcraft (after the manner of the Eastern countries) can ever make this a place of importance independent of commerce and navigation—We will in return ask the gentleman, what the seat of government in any country has to do with commerce and navigation?—unless he could construct a state-house that should float on the water, and send it to London and show it to his correspondent there. The people of this country, in establishing a seat of government, consulted their own convenience; they fought for that purpose an eligible position in or near the centre of the state to make it equally convenient to the citizens thereof—and why should an Englishman or any other busy their brains about it?

"Raleigh has no stream of water to make it even a manufacturing town."—True, it has not much water about it; and the gentleman is right in his conclusion; because he had been raised with manufacturing animals of the amphibious kind that cannot do without water, of course Raleigh does not fit him. . . .

He approves the plan of our city, but it wants water, power and superstition to complete it, and of course it cannot be done without a cottage of the Lord's anointed, and a coffin of a departed saint. . . . The Lord's annointed [sic], and the corpse of a departed saint, we consign to the gentleman for his ingenuity and labour in writing our history—we know not his meaning by the necessities of the government, for we believe it is as well supplied here as if the metropolis had been planted on the water side, except with crabs and frogs.—It is to be lamented that there are too many dissipated people among us, but they are running away fast, and our hope is, a better race will take their place.

Were we to venture an opinion of this traveling gentleman, we should pronounce him a disappointed partisan, who had formerly struggled in the interest of that grave-yard called Fayetteville—rankling at the heart, he has assumed the character of an Englishman to vent his spleen.—That he is a natural born son, begotten by Vulcan on the body of Cloacina, at her devotion, and raised in and upon the offerings of her temples in his favourite village, where we presume the stench is not so offensive to him, as there is a material difference in the qualities of aliments that sustain human life—in one place it is mostly of the skin and bones of swine and sand-hill turkeys, in another it is very different—sound and wholesome.

Excuse scurrility—It is diamond cut diamond—and we must meet the gentleman on his own ground—we are, &c.

The Citizens of Raleigh.

"We can but advise him . . . to return to the Nabobs of his own country." —Raleigh citizens

Lafayette visits Raleigh

FROM THE WRITINGS OF R. B. HAYWOOD

Richard B. Haywood (1819–89) was the youngest son of Sherwood Haywood, one of Raleigh's first residents and a Wake County planter. He was educated at the University of North Carolina and the Jefferson Medical College in Philadelphia. After a tour of Europe, he returned to establish a medical practice in 1845.

Haywood was six years old when the Marquis de Lafayette, then on a triumphal tour of the United States in honor of his role in the American Revolution, visited Raleigh in 1825.

Voices from the Capital

Lafayette arrived at Colonel Roger's [an estate eighteen miles north of Raleigh] on the night of the 12th of March, and on the 13th was escorted to Raleigh by the Mecklenburg Cavalry and 100 gentlemen on horseback.

I have seen, since then, the Cuirassiers of Napoleon, the Hussars of Germany, and the Horse Guards of London, yet the impression made on my youthful imagination was that Polk's Mecklenburg Cavalry excelled them all. The Raleigh Blues, under Captain Griffin, received the Escort at Mr. Thomas P. Devereux's at the head of Halifax Street, where the Marquis alighted from his carriage and was introduced by his old comrade at Brandywine, Colonel William Polk, to each soldier present by name. Each man felicitated himself on hearing the sound of the General's voice in that familiar and oft-repeated expression, " 'owdy do, sair."

There was great disappointment expressed at finding him so different a man from what they expected to see. Instead of the neat, dapper Frenchman their imagination had pictured, he was an exceedingly coarse, rough-looking man over six feet in height and would have been taken on our market square for a mountain wagoneer. He wore a military overcoat of gray that reached to within six inches of the ground which did not, at all, add to the symmetry of his form. Monsieur La Vasseur, his private secretary, and George Washington Lafayette, his son, were no fraud on their nation, they acted the Frenchman and looked the Frenchman to a charm.

After the formalities of a general introduction were through, a procession was formed under the marshalship of our mercurial fellow citizen Tom Cobb and moved to the Governor's mansion. First came the Mecklenburg Cavalry, then the Raleigh Blues, and after that an open landau drawn by four iron-gray horses with Colonel Polk and the Marquis de Lafayette. This carriage was driven by Willie Harrod, who boasted of it to the day of his death. After this carriage came other carriages drawn by four horses, containing Monsieur La Vasseur, George Washington Lafayette and the state escort.

At the vestibule of the palace, they were received by the Governor and committee of arrangements and were conducted to the reception room where many

The Marquis de Lafayette visits the Canova statue of George Washington in the State House. On his arm is his guide, Betsey Haywood, daughter of state treasurer John Haywood.

N.C. Division of Archives and History

prominent citizens and the state officials were formally introduced. In the evening a grand ball was given at the Governor's mansion where "the Capital had gathered there, her beauty and her chivalry" to do honor to the nation's guest. Governor Burton introduced the ladies and Colonel Polk the gentlemen.

The rooms were handsomely decorated and in one of them hung the full-length portrait of Washington which now adorns the House of Representatives. The Marquis was very complimentary in his remarks as to the beauty of the Raleigh ladies.

The new Capitol

'A noble monument for liberality'

BY JOHN SANDERS
The News & Observer
July 1985

'The State possesses a building which for solidity & beauty of material, uniform faithfulness of execution, and for Architectural design, is not surpassed.'

North Carolina's first State House, destroyed by fire in 1831, was replaced with a grand new Capitol that must have been one of the last major buildings erected in the United States entirely by muscle power, human and animal.

No steam engines were available to aid in cutting and hoisting the heavy building stones, for example. This helps to account for the fact that the Capitol payroll at its peak carried three hundred men, then the largest construction work force in the state's history. Laborers and quarry hands were hired locally. Stone masons and carpenters, many of them natives of the British Isles, generally were hired in the North. Some of them remained in Raleigh after the Capitol was completed and today are proudly numbered among the ancestors of Raleigh residents.

Nothing in local building experience compared with the Capitol project, so it is understandable that cost estimates were consistently far too low. It is unlikely that many thought the initial 1833 legislative appropriation of $50,000 would meet the whole cost. But no one—neither building commissioners nor architects nor legislators—had any idea that the Capitol and their furnishings would cost, by the time of their completion in 1840, nearly $533,000. The general revenue of the state was then about $150,000 a year.

To get a comparative idea of the scale of financial commitment that represented and the political reaction to its cost, imagine that the General Assembly today decided to spend $30 million on a single building, chiefly for its own accommodation.

Fortunately for the state, however, the building commissioners, inspired by their ambition to raise a monument to self-government and an object of pride for all the people of the state, went first-class from the start and reckoned the cost afterward. By the time the true scale of expense became apparent, the character and size of the building were fixed and no retreat was possible. One effect of this major financial commitment, coupled with the quality and solidity of the structure that resulted, was to discourage all efforts to alter or replace the Capitol for decades. And by the time the state could afford to build a new Capitol, the 1840 building had become sufficiently invested with pride and sentiment that all thoughts were for its preservation and improvement, not its replacement.

It was conceivable, after the fire of 1831 that destroyed the first State House, that a replacement would never be built. The disaster had revived Fayetteville's

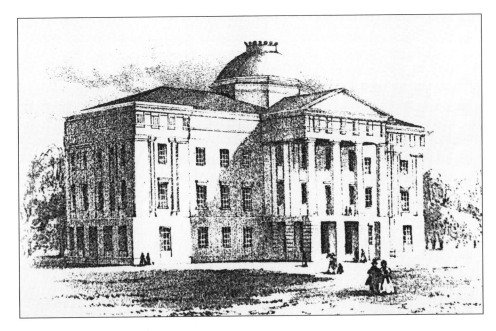

The new state Capitol was perhaps the grandest edifice in the country when it was completed.
N.C. Division of Archives and History

The statue of Henry Wyatt, the first soldier to fall in the Civil War, shrouded in early-morning mist on the Capitol grounds.
The News & Observer

hopes for displacing Wake as the site of the capital. After a year's debate, the General Assembly in 1832–33 voted funds to build a new Capitol on the old site. The legislature also determined that the structure would follow the cross-shaped plan that William Nichols had given the State House in his alterations a dozen years earlier.

Five legislators were named commissioners responsible for the design and construction of the new Capitol. Rejecting plans by other designers, the commissioners engaged, once again, William Nichols (then in Alabama) and his son, William Nichols, Jr., to design an improved version of the remodeled State House.

By mid-1833, the commissioners and the younger Nichols had agreed upon the main features of the plan: a cross-shaped three-story building of stone with a central domed rotunda, executive offices on the first floor, and legislative chambers and offices on the second floor. The Neoclassical style was adopted without question.

In August 1833, for reasons not apparent on the record, the Nicholses were superseded as the Capitol's architects by Itheil Town and Alexander Jackson Davis of New York, one of the nation's principal and earliest architectural firms. Although construction was well begun, Town and Davis made significant modifications. For example, they substituted fully developed porticoes fronting the east and west wings for the pseudo-porticoes with engaged columns that Nichols had preferred. They also gave the building a more decidedly Greek character than Nichols had contemplated.

The Capitol had been under construction for a year and a half when the commissioners were in need of a masonry superintendent. Through Itheil Town, they hired David Paton (1801–82), an architect born in Edinburgh, Scotland. Paton reached Raleigh in September 1834. He was immediately made clerk of the works, or general manager of the project, responsible to the commissioners and to Town, who continued as the architect. Within a few months, however, Paton gained the commissioners' full confidence and supplanted Town as the architect.

Paton made the interior of the Capitol more functional than it otherwise would have been. He is also due much credit for the quality of the interior workmanship and for much of the exterior construction and finish.

He described the scene in a progress report two years before completion thus: "Besides the force employed on the Square and Quarry, we have artizans [sic] employed modelling plaster enrichments; wood Carvers, carving moldings and capitols of Columns; Cabinet and Chairmakers about Furniture; Iron founders, about cast iron ornaments."

Soon after the completion of the Capitol, a legislative committee observed, "In the Capitol just erected, the State possesses a building which for solidity & beauty of material, uniform faithfulness of execution, and for Architectural design, is not surpassed, if indeed equaled, by any building in the Union. . . . And to North Carolinians it will remain for Centuries, an object of just & becoming pride, as a noble monument for the taste & liberality of the present generation." Confirmation of that early judgment is found in the observation of the noted architectural historian Wayne Andrews, made a century and a third later, that North Carolina possesses "the most distinguished of all our state capitols."

The view from the rotunda of the Capitol
The News & Observer

THE OLD STATE HOUSE BURNS

BY R. B. HAYWOOD

When fire destroyed the State House in 1831, no one was better positioned to view it than young R. B. Haywood, who lived in the home of his father, Sherwood Haywood, at the corner of Wilmington and Edenton streets, directly across from Capitol Square. Fifty years later, he recorded his impressions.

About seven o'clock in the morning of June 21st, 1831, the people were startled from their slumbers by the ringing of bells and the sad announcement that the Capitol was on fire. I ran to the east gate and discovered flames issuing from the skylight on the north east side of the dome. If it had been possible to have gotten on top of the Capitol the flames could have been extinguished with a single bucket of water, but the only mode of egress was through the skylight which was on fire.

Every one was powerless and stood motionless with fear for many minutes until the flames had spread through the roof. Many now rushed in to save such articles as could be moved and large numbers gathered around the statue of Washington and made Herculean efforts to move it out. They succeeded in moving it about four feet but when the alarm was given that the dome was about to fall in, a general stampede was made from the building.

The flames soon enveloped the whole building and the sight through the halls was perfectly magnificent. Molten glass was dropping from the beautiful French chandeliers. The red glare on the statue of Washington with its white life-like appearance gave to the scene a diabolic appearance that can better be imagined than described. The dome soon fell in with a tremendous crash, and [Antonio] Canova's great statue was broken into a hundred pieces. With this Capitol was destroyed almost entirely a valuable library, the accumulation of forty years.

Jack Bell, a tinner by trade, was the originator of the fire. He had been soldering some leaks in the zinc roofing and left his soldering furnace on the steps of the skylight and had gone to breakfast. Poor Jack, nearly scared to death, was hauled up before the Mayor next day on the charge of setting the fire intentionally . . . and not enjoying a very enviable character, the large crowd present, I think, were willing to hang him on general principles. But it was well-established that whilst there was culpable negligence, there was no criminal intent.

Voices from the Capital

Mordecai House

A modest glory of the Old South

BY DAVID PERKINS

In the 1830s, a visit to Mordecai House was a trip into the country. One took a carriage for the mile-long ride from the Capitol, down Blount Street, beyond the city line at North Street, and through fields of wood, corn, cotton, and sweet potatoes. Today, the house is in the very heart of the city, surrounded by the quiet, shady neighborhood that took its name from its owners for five generations: Mordecai (pronounced MOR-de-kee).

It is the oldest Raleigh building standing on its original foundation. Restored in 1972 and opened to the public, with many of its original furnishings, Mordecai House is a modest glory of the Old South in its first flush of prosperity.

The first house was built in about 1785 by Joel Lane—the planter who had sold the state the original thousand acres for a permanent capital—for his son, Henry. It was a simple hall-and-parlor structure, which survives as the northern, rear part of the house. In 1817, ownership was passed to a young lawyer from Warrenton, Moses Mordecai, who married Henry Lane's daughter Margaret.

Mordecai was the son of a scholarly Orthodox Jew who had moved from New York to Richmond and then to Warrenton, where he established a well-known

Mordecai House
The News & Observer

academy for girls. Moses had been taught by his parents and sisters and was self-educated in the law; he became a respected circuit-riding lawyer in eastern North Carolina. He was also an excellent farmer, and the first president of the short-lived Wake Agricultural Society. Under his supervision, the plantation prospered. At its peak, Mordecai had three thousand acres and more than fifty slaves.

Into the four-room house, Moses brought Margaret's three sisters and his younger half-brother, George. A lawyer like Moses, George became a pillar of the community, president of the Raleigh and Gaston Railroad, then president of the State Bank. He helped to bring gas lighting to the city in the late 1850s.

After Margaret's death in 1821, Moses married her sister, Ann Willis "Nancy" Lane. But the marriage was brief. Moses' health was broken by arduous travel, and he died in September 1824—nine months after the wedding to Nancy and one month before the birth of Margaret, their one child. Margaret later married John Devereux and lived in the Will's Forest mansion near today's Glenwood Avenue.

Miss Ellen Mordecai
Capitol Area Preservation, Inc.

In his will, Moses left Nancy funds for "a house fit for my family." Rather than build a new one, she hired William Nichols, the architect who had improved the old State House, to add four front rooms and a two-story portico with columns in the new Greek Revival style.

Moses Mordecai, like his father, had remained in the Jewish faith all his life. In 1833, however, Nancy and three of Moses' children were baptized in Christ Episcopal Church. George, who took care of the family after Moses' death, converted to Christianity after his father died in 1838 and became a benefactor and deacon of Christ Church.

During the Civil War, Moses' son, Henry, a successful planter and legislator, took charge of the house. In 1967, shortly before the death of Burke Haywood Little, representing the fifth generation of Mordecais, Mordecai House was bought by the city of Raleigh. It was opened to the public in 1972 as Mordecai Historic Park.

Most of the original outbuildings have disappeared, but a plantation office (now a gift shop) and a storage barn survive. The garden has been restored to the description in Ellen Mordecai's memoirs. And other buildings have been moved to the park, creating a plantation village. They include a chapel, Andrew Johnson's birthplace, the 1842 Allen kitchen, United States senator George Badger's law office, and an office building thought to have been Raleigh's post office before the Civil War.

HOG-KILLIN' DAY

BY ELLEN MORDECAI
From *Gleanings from Long Ago*, 1936,
Capital Area Preservation, Inc.

Ellen Mordecai was born in Mordecai House in 1820 and spent many of the happiest days of her childhood there. The second of Moses Mordecai's three children by his first wife, Margaret Lane, she was educated at boarding schools in Warrenton and Philadelphia. She returned to Raleigh in 1840. In 1906, she wrote her reminiscences of the plantation life in its antebellum prime. She died in 1916.

They waited for cold weather, and then we would hear the order given that hogs were to be killed next day. On that day (the day before the killing) big troughs were filled with alum salt, and all day long we would hear the heavy thud of the pestles beating the salt, ready for salting next day. Of course the little girls were never allowed nor ever wanted to go near the killing.

They would begin soon in the morning, all of the men. Huge kettles were set on the fire and the water was heated by putting in hot rocks. The first we would see of the hogs was the wagon-load coming up to the smokehouse, where they were laid in piles near the immense meat-blocks, on which the hogs were to be cut out. All day long the men were busy cutting them. They did it with admirable skill, shaping the hams nicely and the middling and the shoulders and salting them, ready to pack away in the smokehouse, where it would stay for some weeks, until time to hang it and smoke it.

While the men were busy with the meat, the women would be busy washing the lard, preparing to "try it up." That day, we children were forbidden the kitchen, and meals were a secondary consideration.

The kitchen was quite a large room and the fireplace and hearth reached halfway across it—a broad rock hearth. The andirons in the kitchen were immense and of great strength, and logs of wood, the full length, were laid on the fireplace. Then there were huge pots set along the hearth, and the women would wash and cut up the nice white lard (it was as white as snow), Aunt Nancy superintending.

There were about three large pots set on the hearth, with fires under them, all filled with lard. Then the process of "trying up" began. The cracklings were all taken out and put in barrels to themselves, then the lard taken out, strained as clear as wine and dipped and poured into barrels. The cracklings were kept separate, of course, and they were set aside in another barrel.

We would go up to Aunt Harriet's room, by a good fire, as a safe harbor, with Emily, of course, to help and enjoy with us. Every now and then during the day we would dash out to the meat-block and beg "Ung Ben," "Ung Harry," or "Ung Lewis," to give us a hog tail.

The slaves who stayed on at Mordecai plantation, from left to right: Ananias (gardener), Aunt Mittie Ann (laundress), Uncle Jerry Hinton (gardener), and Aunt Chaney (cook)

Capital Area Preservation, Inc.

John Chavis

A tutor of leaders

The News & Observer
July 1985

John Chavis fought for American independence and, for thirty years, preached and taught blacks and whites in North Carolina, including some of the state's future leaders. He ended his life a broken man, stripped like other free blacks of his right to preach and to vote.

Evidence of Chavis's early years is scanty. He was almost certainly the "indentured servant named John Chavis" mentioned in the inventory of the estate of Halifax lawyer James Milner in 1773.

Chavis enlisted in December 1778 in the Fifth Virginia Regiment and served for three years in the Revolutionary War. His commander certified in 1783 that Chavis had "faithfully fulfilled his duties and is thereby entitled to all immunities granted to three-year soldiers." He was listed as a free Negro in a 1789 tax list of Mecklenburg County, Virginia, his property consisting of a single horse.

Chavis is thought to have attended Washington Academy, a Presbyterian institution which became Washington and Lee University, and then Princeton University, under the tutelage of President David Witherspoon. From 1801 to 1807, Chavis was sent by the Lexington, Virginia, presbytery to preach to slaves in Maryland, Virginia, and North Carolina. He wrote reports about religious conditions and indicated how many attended meetings, which then included whites and blacks.

Chavis moved to Raleigh in 1807 or 1808 and opened a school for both races near where Chavis Park is today. White students attended during the day and paid $2.50 per quarter; blacks would come in the evening and stay until ten o'clock, paying $1.75 per quarter. Some white students, including children of several prominent white families, were said to have boarded in Chavis's home.

In 1830, *Raleigh Register* editor Joseph Gales was impressed with the discipline at Chavis's school and applauded the teacher's speech adjuring his students that, although they were "possessed of but limited privileges, . . . even they might become useful in their particular sphere."

John Chavis
c. 1760–1838

EDUCATION.

JOHN CHAVES takes this method of informing his Employers, and the Citizens of Raleigh in general, that the present Quarter of his School will end the 15th of September, and the next will commence on the 19th. He will, at the same time, open an EVENING SCHOOL for the purpose of instructing Children of Colour, as he intends, for the accommodation of some of his Employers, to exclude all Children of Colour from his Day School.

The Evening School will commence at an hour by Sun. When the white children leave the House, those of colour will take their places, and continue until ten o'clock

The terms of teaching the white children will be as usual, two and a half dollars per quarter; those of colour, one dollar and three quarters. In both cases, the whole of the money to be paid in advance to Mr. Benjamin S King Those who produce Certificates from him of their having paid the money, will be admitted.

Those who think proper to put their Children under his care, may rely upon the strictest attention being paid not only to their Education but to their Morals which he deems an important part of Education.   Aug 23, 1808.

He hopes to have a better School House by the commencement of the next quarter

Chavis school announcement
N.C. Division of Archives and History

Among Chavis's white pupils, in Raleigh and elsewhere, were Charles Manly, a future governor, Willie Mangum, a future senator, and Abram Rencher, later minister to Portugal and territorial governor of New Mexico.

Chavis had been accepted as a licentiate in 1809 by the Orange presbytery, which included Raleigh, and continued to preach until 1832, when, in the wake of the Nat Turner rebellion, blacks were barred from preaching. Chavis apparently received fifty dollars a year from the Orange presbytery from 1834 until his death in 1838. The Reverend William McPheeters of Raleigh's First Presbyterian Church helped raise money to alleviate the "distresses, wants [of] our old friend John Chavis."

In an effort to raise money, Chavis published *An Essay on the Atonement* in 1837. No copies are known to have survived. Chavis and Mangum, of Orange County, remained close friends and loyal correspondents after Mangum became a United States senator.

In one letter to Mangum, Chavis declared he was opposed to the abolitionists. He admitted "that Slavery is a national evil . . . , but what is to be done? . . . All that can be done is to make the best of a bad bargain. . . . For I am clearly of the opinion that immediate emancipation would be to entail the greatest earthly curse upon my brethren."

The Oxford *Torchlight* of September 28, 1880, indicated that Chavis was living between Oxford and Williamsboro at the time of his death. The editor recalled having "seen him when a short time before his death several of his white pupils, prominent gentlemen, called to see him. Chavis was then advanced in years, his white hair forming a strange contrast to his ebony face for he was of unmixed African descent. His manners were dignified yet respectful and entirely unassuming, and his conversation sprightly and interesting."

Chavis died on June 10, 1838. He had no known children.

Riding the Tornado

The railroad comes to Raleigh

BY DAVID PERKINS

The wonder was brought to town in the 1820s by an "enterprising Yankee." It was about knee-high and ran around Goneke Concert Hall at the corner of Hargett and Salisbury streets, with two or three passengers straddling it. Hundreds of Raleighites paid ten cents for six turns around the hall.

Almost two decades later, on March 21, 1840, the real thing roared into the new depot of the Raleigh and Gaston Railroad, near Halifax and North streets. It was a two-drive-wheel Virginia-made engine, with no headlight, no cab, and no cowcatcher, called the Tornado.

"Phizzz-zzz-zzz," began the *Raleigh Register's* account a few days later. "This is as near, as we can come in type, towards expressing the strange sound which greeted the ears of the assembled population of our city, on Saturday evening last." The *Standard* enthused, "We hail the rumbling of the first Locomotive, as the glad omen of future prosperity to our city and county, and feel we shall not be disappointed."

Travelers talked about the new train's "annihilating time and space"—by 1840 standards, anyway. The Tornado reached a speed of fifteen miles per hour and

The "Romulus Saunders," a locomotive on the Raleigh and Gaston Railroad, with unidentified railroad officials on board, c. 1850
N.C. Division of Archives and History

'THE INGENUITY OF MAN'

BY KEMP P. BATTLE
From *Memories of an Old-Time Tar Heel*, 1945

> *Kemp P. Battle, president of the University of North Carolina from 1876 to 1891, was born in Louisburg in 1831. His father moved the family to Raleigh in 1839, and Battle went to a private day school in the East Rock building, on the campus of what became St. Mary's College. About that time, he rode the roughshod new steam trains of the Raleigh and Gaston Railroad.*

The news that the first locomotive engine was about to enter Raleigh drew all the population from the country for many miles around. Her name was "Tornado," locomotives being regarded as feminine.

The railroad irons were flat strips, three-fourths of an inch in thickness, spiked on wooden stringers. The locomotive had no spark arrester, and as dry pine was burnt in the furnace, the sparks, although beautiful at night, kindled fires among the dry leaves near the road bed and often burnt holes in the clothes of passengers. On my first trip on a train I had a hole burnt in the sleeve of my jacket and in the skin below it.

But all defects were overlooked in the unbounded joy at the novelty. People felt that it was the beginning of great things. A journey in coaches rolling smoothly through hills and high over deep ravines seemed like magic. Although the beginnings were rude and inefficient, people were right in their prophetic boasting. There was boundless enthusiasm as "Tornado" puffed in. Many felt like the old lady in Goldsborough who said on her first sight of a locomotive, "Verily the power of God is great but the ingenuity of man is greater."

could take a passenger from Petersburg, Virginia, to Raleigh in fifteen hours—if everything went well, which it often did not. Still, it beat a carriage by several days.

In the broadest sense, Raleigh had prepared the way for all the state's railroads. In 1832, after fire had destroyed the State House, the city leaders feared that Fayetteville would steal the capital status. Mayor Joseph Gales and others proposed building an "Experimental Railroad" to haul stone from the quarry southeast of the city to Capitol Square. The horse-drawn line would facilitate the construction of a grander edifice, they argued, and prove that the state's capital was well placed.

A private company was formed, the road was built, and legislators were treated to a ride when they arrived in Raleigh later that year. Suitably impressed, they authorized funds for a new Capitol. The "Experimental Railroad" also turned a profit for its investors.

The same year, North Carolina cities began racing to join the line the Virginians had just completed from Petersburg to Weldon. A Wilmington to Weldon line was planned through Raleigh, but the hills at Goldsboro were discouraging, and it turned north. Wake County rallied behind a line to Gaston, near Weldon.

Galvanized by the prospect of larger markets, the landlocked residents put up the first $150,000, expecting Petersburg, Virginia, residents at the other end to do the same.

"My mother subscribed $2,000 in stock," R. B. Haywood recalled half a century later, "and I well remember hearing Judge [Duncan] Cameron [one of the railroad commissioners] tell her that the more she subscribed, the better she would be, for he was certain that the road would pay for itself by the time it reached Warrenton."

George Mordecai, who would become president of the Raleigh to Gaston line, wrote of the civic excitement, "The certainty of having a railroad to this place seems to have infused new life into the people and everyone estimates their property much higher than before."

Those were oversanguine hopes. The plan was, indeed, a clever one: to build the line from the northern point to Raleigh, allowing the Virginia railroad to use the line (and help pay for it) as it grew. But the terrain was rough. Hills and rivers slowed progress and pushed up costs. At Warrenton, a band of citizens with turkey rifles chased away surveyors, and the line jagged expensively west and north to Ridgeway before turning south to Henderson. Eventually, the legislature endorsed eight hundred thousand dollars in bonds to complete the project.

Despite one final hitch (the iron needed for the wooden rails failed to arrive in time), the first train rode into Raleigh on March 21.

On June 10, the two spectacular "improvements" completed in Raleigh that year—the new Capitol and the railroad—were celebrated in a great three-day "Entertainment."

On the first day, more than a thousand officers of state, judges, city authorities, stockholders, and citizens massed outside the courthouse on Fayetteville Street at 2:30 P.M. and marched to the new depot at the intersection of Halifax and North streets. In a warehouse, seven hundred sat down at five ninety-foot tables and were served a dinner of "fine fowl, delicious ham, and mellow beverage" by Hannah Stuart, innkeeper Peter Casso's daughter. Toasts came next, interspersed with the singing of "Old Virginny," "Molly Put the Kettle On," and "Oh, Say, Not Woman's Love Is Bought."

Governor E. D. Dudley spoke first, declaring the internal improvements "the distinguishing characteristic of civil from savage life. The state that neglects the one deserves the miseries of the other."

Weston Gales, editor of the *Register* and toastmaster on the occasion, exulted, "The city of Raleigh has exceeded in gallantry even its renowned namesake, Sir Walter. He but laid down his cloak for one lady to walk over. Its citizens have helped to lay down eighty-six miles of railroad for the whole sex to walk over."

In the evening, the new Capitol was showered with fireworks and citizens danced in the Senate chamber.

Prosperity, however, did not rush in on the new tracks. Growth in Raleigh was slow until after the Civil War. The railroad never gained a secure footing, and in 1848, it was bought by the state at a bankruptcy auction.

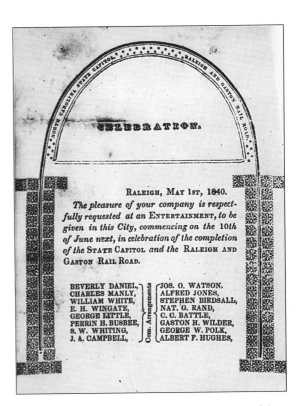

NORTH CAROLINA STATE CAPITOL · · · · · · · · · RALEIGH AND GASTON RAIL ROAD.

CELEBRATION.

RALEIGH, MAY 1st, 1840.

The pleasure of your company is respectfully requested at an ENTERTAINMENT, *to be given in this City, commencing on the 10th of June next, in celebration of the completion of the* STATE CAPITOL *and the* RALEIGH AND GASTON RAIL ROAD.

BEVERLY DANIEL,
CHARLES MANLY,
WILLIAM WHITE,
E. H. WINGATE,
GEORGE LITTLE,
PERRIN H. BUSBEE,
S. W. WHITING,
J. A. CAMPBELL,

JOS. O. WATSON,
ALFRED JONES,
STEPHEN BIRDSALL,
NAT. G. RAND,
C. C. BATTLE,
GASTON H. WILDER,
GEORGE W. POLK,
ALBERT F. HUGHES,

Com. Arrangements

Invitation to the celebration of the two great "improvements"
N.C. Division of Archives and History

Olmsted finds 'a pleasing town'

FROM THE WRITINGS OF FREDERICK LAW OLMSTED
Journey through the Seaboard Slave States, 1856

Voices

from

the

Capital

Before he became the country's foremost landscape architect (and designer of New York City's Central Park), Frederick Law Olmsted (1822–1903) was an outspoken abolitionist and traveler. His three volumes on his travels in the South and Southwest from 1852 to 1856 were influential in shaping Northern opinion before the Civil War.

In the third of these volumes, Journey through the Seaboard Slave States, *he recorded his impressions of his visit to Raleigh. He arrived at the Raleigh and Gaston Railroad depot, on Halifax Street, and found a city little landscaped but with at least one new ornament, Christ Church, that drew his admiration.*

The city of Raleigh (old Sir Walter), the capital of North Carolina, is a pleasing town—the streets wide and lined with trees, and many white wooden mansions, all having little courtyards of flowers and shrubbery around them. The State-House is, in every way, a noble building, constructed of brownish-gray granite, in Grecian style. It stands on an elevated position, near the centre of the city, in a square field, which is shaded by some tall old oaks, and could easily be made into an appropriate and beautiful little park; but which, with singular negligence, or more singular economy (while $500,000 has been spent upon the simple edifice), remains in a rude state of undressed nature, and is used as a hog pasture.

A trifle of the expense, employed with doubtful advantage, to give a smooth exterior face to the blocks of stone, if laid out in grading, smoothing, and dressing its ground base, would have added indescribably to the beauty of the edifice. An architect should always begin his work upon the ground.

There are several other public buildings and institutions of charity and education, honorable to the State. A church, near the Capitol [Christ Episcopal Church], not yet completed, is very beautiful; cruciform in ground plan, the walls of stone and the interior woodwork of oiled native pine, and with, thus far, none of the irreligious falsities in stucco and paint that so generally disenchant all expression of worship in our city meeting-houses. It is hard to admire what is common; and it is, perhaps, asking too much of the citizens of Raleigh, that they should plant for ornament, or even cause to be retained about such institutions as their Lunatic Asylum, the beautiful evergreens that crowd about the town; but can any man walk from the Capitol oaks to the pine grove, a little beyond the Deaf

Frederick Law Olmsted

CHRIST CHURCH: A NEW STYLE IN STONE

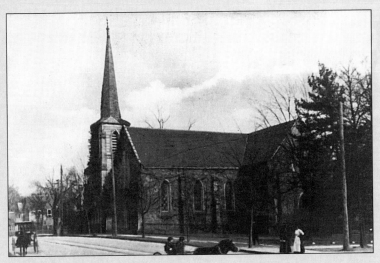

N.C. Division of Archives and History

"I am heartedly rejoiced we have gotten this far," wrote the Reverend Richard Mason, the rector of Christ Church, to the New York City architect Richard Upjohn in 1847. "And I hope the erection of our church will be the means of introducing a new style of church architecture to the South."

It was actually the second attempt by the Episcopal diocese to hire Upjohn, the leader in the Gothic Revival movement and the architect of Trinity Church in New York City. On first contact, Upjohn's fees had been too high. But by 1846, the diocese, which wanted a noble replacement for the frame church it had built at Wilmington and Edenton streets in 1829, succeeded in getting Upjohn, for five hundred dollars, to provide plans and specifications for what became the first of several Southern buildings by the architect.

An Englishman by birth, Upjohn designed Christ Church as an English parish church, with a large free-standing bell tower of locally quarried stone, a connecting cloister, and an impressive cruciform sanctuary with a hammer-beam ceiling and galleries for slaves.

Several of the Scottish stonemasons who had come to Raleigh to build the new Capitol contracted to build the church. The cornerstone was laid in 1848, and the building consecrated in 1854.

Upjohn's grandson, Hobart, designed the parish house in a conforming style. The church was designated a National Historic Landmark in 1988.

and Dumb Institution, and say that he would not far rather have the latter than the former to curtain his habitation?

If he can in summer, let him try it again, as I did, on a soft winter's day, when the evergreens fill the air with a balsamic odor, and the green light comes quivering through them, and the foot falls silently upon the elastic carpet they have spread, deluding one with all the feelings of spring.

The country, for miles about Raleigh, is nearly all pine forest, unfertile, and so little cultivated, that it is a mystery how a town of 2,500 inhabitants can obtain sufficient supplies from it to exist.

'A thorough and elegant education'

St. Mary's College and the Reverend Aldert Smedes

BY DAVID PERKINS AND TREVA JONES

The deal was struck without excess ceremony. It was the fall of 1841, and the Reverend Aldert Smedes had just been introduced to the Episcopal bishop of North Carolina, the Right Reverend Levi Silliman Ives, at a New York conference. The conversation began, as Smedes recalled it, "Bishop, what sort of place would Raleigh be for a school for girls?"

"The best in the United States."

"Have you any buildings there?"

"The best in the United States."

"Why don't you open a school there?"

"I am now looking for a man."

"Bishop, I am your man."

"The very man I want."

So was conceived St. Mary's College, Raleigh's oldest college, the only Episcopal-related women's college in the country, and one of the few surviving intermediary schools where students can take the last two years of high school and the first two of college.

It had started out as a boys' school. Bishop Ives wanted a school to train clergymen, and the Episcopal School of North Carolina in Raleigh opened in June 1834. The first buildings, known as East Rock and West Rock, were completed in 1835, built from undersize gneiss blocks that had been rejected by the builders of the new state Capitol. The buildings still stand.

Ives had hired a promising headmaster in Joseph Cogswell, a former Harvard professor who had founded a boarding school in Connecticut. But Cogswell soon found life in the new capital inelegant—a water moccasin in his bed, among other indignities. And the abolitionist movement was discussed, he said, in "language a bit too strong for Yankee pride." He left in April 1835. The school fell into financial straits and closed in 1838.

For a time, the diocese rented the buildings to private schools, and then, at its 1840 convention, ordered the property sold. Judge Duncan Cameron, a wealthy planter with a grand home near the school, and a leading Episcopal churchman and president of the State Bank, was the only bidder at a public auction. He paid the church's ten-thousand-dollar indebtedness and gave the property back to the diocese for rental.

Then Bishop Ives encountered Smedes in New York.

Smedes Hall in 1845
St. Mary's College

St. Mary's students, 1869
St. Mary's College

Smedes was born in New York City, of solid Knickerbocker stock, on April 20, 1810. He entered Columbia College at thirteen, but after his family moved to Kentucky, he completed his education at Transylvania University. He read law and was admitted to the bar, but changed course and entered the priesthood. He graduated from General Theological Seminary in 1832 and that year was ordained a deacon. From 1832 until 1836, Smedes was assistant rector to the Reverend Thomas Lyell at Christ Church in New York City. He married Sarah

A LETTER TO GENERAL ROBERT E. LEE FROM DR. ALDERT SMEDES

St. Mary's,
May 22d, 1863
General Lee,

My Dear Sir,

Amid the toils and dangers to which you are exposed for your country's welfare, you are richly entitled to every drop of comfort which it is possible to pour into your cup.

The term of your daughter's residence at this school is about to expire, and it affords me great pleasure to assure you that her diligence and proficiency as a pupil, and her conduct as a lady, have been worthy of her parentage. This is bestowing the highest praise upon her. She has been exemplary in her observance of the minutest rules of discipline, and has scarce allowed a moment to pass unemployed and unimproved.

She carries away with her the most cordial esteem and regard not only of all her teachers and young companions, but of many of our community whom her father's name had attracted towards her.

Aldert Smedes
St. Mary's College

Her modesty is not the least of her recommendations; she never betrays by look, word or gesture the least consciousness that she is the daughter of the man whom the Nation delights to honor.

While you, general, have had a daughter under my tuition, I have had two sons fighting as lieutenants, under your banner. Both were at the battle of Chancellorsville; where one, the adjutant of the 7th North Carolina, fell, mortally wounded. He was a noble, gallant, and what is infinitely better, a Christian boy. This is my consolation in so grievous a bereavement. His brother went through the same battle unhurt. He is attached to the 5th Regiment N.C.J.

But I will not intrude upon time which belongs to the country. I am, General, with the most sincere respect and esteem,

Your obedient servant,

Aldert Smedes

Lyell, the rector's daughter. In 1837, he was rector of a church in Schenectady, New York.

Forced to give up the parish in 1839 because of a chronic throat ailment, Smedes returned to New York City to help his mother, just widowed, run a day school for girls. Still worried about his health, Smedes looked farther south.

After his meeting with Ives, Smedes and his family moved to Raleigh and rented the land and buildings from Cameron. On May 12, 1842, thirteen students were welcomed to the new girls' school, which Smedes had advertised in Southern papers and church publications as aiming "to furnish a thorough and elegant education, equal to the best that can be obtained in the City of New York or in any Northern School."

From the rising bell at 5:30 A.M. until 9 P.M. prayers, St. Mary's girls led a regimented life, including required walks, study hours, chapel services, classes, recitations, and two hours of sewing every Saturday. They weren't allowed to read fiction except on Saturdays.

St. Mary's girls at the turn of the century
St. Mary's College

Smedes was the school's administrator, preacher, recruiter, and business manager. He taught the Bible, chemistry, mathematics, philosophy, astronomy, and sometimes Latin and French. He personally interviewed each of the nineteen hundred students enrolled there during his thirty-five years.

Smedes's St. Mary's aimed at a level higher than most female academies of the time. St. Mary's historian Martha Stoops quotes a student of the 1860s, who said of Smedes, "He recognized that a woman who could and would, should pursue higher studies."

In a sermon entitled "She Hath Done What She Could," he said women had the high mission of setting society's spiritual tone. A woman, he said, must be trained "in the knowledge and love of her duties towards God and man. . . . If she will do what she can . . . , she can do almost what she will for the moral and spiritual welfare of the world."

In the spring of 1862, the mayor of Raleigh got orders to seize St. Mary's buildings for use as a Confederate hospital. Smedes went to Goldsboro and discussed the matter with Confederate general Theophilus Hunter Holmes, and an unfinished building, later known as Main Hall, at the chartered but as yet unopened Peace Institute was chosen instead.

During the war, Smedes foraged for food and supplies for his students, and raised school fees from $115 to $300 for a five-month term to cover the wartime costs. St. Mary's was one of few Southern schools open throughout the war. Once closed, many never reopened.

Smedes and his wife had nine children. One son, Lyell, died at twenty-five of disease; another, Ives, died at twenty after he was wounded at Chancellorsville; and a third, Edward, died when he was shot through the heart at Spotsylvania.

When Sherman's troops entered Raleigh, Union officers camped on the St. Mary's campus. Smedes invited them inside and fed them "ham, potatoes, pickles, and everything," according to an entry from a Civil War diary.

Smedes was diagnosed with Bright's disease in 1876. On April 24, 1877, he

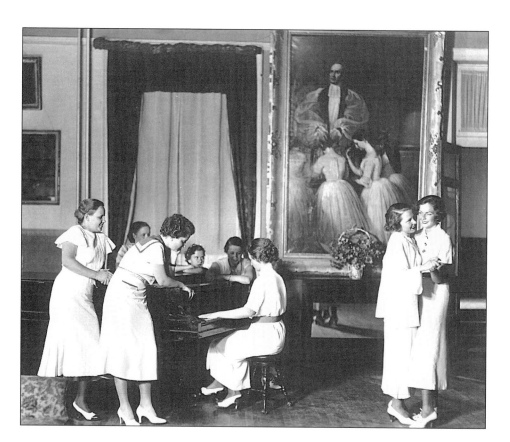

A study break in Smedes Parlor
St. Mary's College

West Rock Glee Club, pictured in the 1907 *Muse*, was one of the many hall clubs popular in the early 1900s.
St. Mary's College

taught his last class and took to his bed. He died the next day. Tributes poured in from all over the South. He was buried in Oakwood Cemetery.

In 1910, the school's remodeled main building was named Smedes Hall in his honor.

A freeman is tarred and feathered

The story of Lunsford Lane

BY DAVID PERKINS

A free black man led a dangerous life in the Raleigh of the 1830s. After the Nat Turner rebellion of 1831, many whites were jittery, and one man's case showed just where they intended to draw the line in granting freedom to slaves.

Lunsford Lane was a slave who, by thrift and industry, bought his own freedom and became a successful small businessman. In 1841, after he had been forced out of Raleigh and gone north briefly to raise money to buy his family's freedom, he was charged with fomenting abolitionism and tarred and feathered by an angry mob. It was a milder treatment than he had feared, and milder than it might have been in other states. But it made Lane's story a cautionary tale, and Lane himself a popular lecturer at antislavery gatherings in the North after he escaped from Raleigh.

Professor John Bassett, in his 1898 book, *Anti-slavery Leaders of North Carolina*, said Lane's story suggested a great might-have-been: a black middle class that could have steadied the course of race relations after the war and emancipation.

"Twenty-five years before the war there were more industrious, ambitious, and capable negroes in the South than there were in 1865," Bassett wrote. "Had the severe laws against emancipation not been passed, the coming of freedom would have found the colored race with a number of superior individuals who in every locality would have been a core of conservatism for the benefit of both races."

Raleigh seemed predisposed to such a development, as a bustling urban center away from the rigors of plantation culture. Sherwood Haywood, in whose household Lane was born in 1803, was apparently an indulgent master, at least to his Raleigh slaves. Haywood was the Raleigh representative of the Bank of New Bern and the owner of plantations in Wake and Edgecombe counties. One of Raleigh's original settlers, Haywood had built a house on the corner of Edenton and Wilmington streets. Lane's mother worked in the kitchen. (His father, who with his wife had been sold in the estate of Joel Lane, worked for a neighbor.)

In the city, Lunsford had special opportunities he wouldn't have had on a plantation. He was not taught to read or write, but he went along with his master to hear the great political orators at the State House. He was baptized as a Baptist—a rare act requiring a special permit. And Haywood showed his favor for Lunsford by sending him to the same tailor as his own sons.

In church, Lunsford heard the stock be-content-with-your-lot exhortations preached for blacks. However, in his wanderings about Raleigh, he was also

In the city, Lunsford had special opportunities he wouldn't have had on a plantation.

NEGRO AUCTION AND COM-
MISSION HOUSE.

ON THE FIRST DAY OF JANUARY next,
at the Store formerly occupied by C. W. D.
Hutchings, on Fayetteville street, in the city of
Raleigh, the subscribers will establish an

AUCTION AND COMMISSION HOUSE
for the sale of SLAVES.

We have provided SAFE and COMFORTABLE
quarters, and will be as moderate in our charges
for board, &c., as the times will permit.

With an experience of twenty years in the
trade, and the advantages of an extensive acquain-
tance, we flatter ourselves that we understand the
business; and, with the assurance of quick sales
and prompt returns, respectfully solicit public
patronage.

dec 19 dtf   W. F. ASKEW & CO.

Notice for a slave auction
N.C. Division of Archives and History

*It was a story "not of
what slavery is under its
most revolting features, but
of what it is to be a slave,
with a sensitive nature,
under the most favorable
circumstances."*

exposed to the liberal views of the Presbyterian minister Dr. Heath, whose freed slaves
still worked for him, and of "Pastor of the
City" McPheeters.

On Sunday afternoons, Lunsford joined
other free blacks and slaves at a mineral
spring outside Raleigh to discuss politics.
The debates were said to be so lively that
whites attended, too, and masters were soon
encouraging their slave boys in the competition—until slavery itself became the over-
riding political issue, and slave gatherings
were forbidden.

Meanwhile, Lunsford was proving himself
an enterprising capitalist. He started by col-
lecting tips from visitors (including a silver
dollar from Lafayette) and sneaking off at
night to cut wood. Later, he and his father developed a fragrant smoking tobacco
and a long-stemmed pipe to smoke it in. Both the tobacco and the pipes became
great favorites with the legislature. It was the beginning of a business.

In 1828, Lane was married to Martha Curtis, a slave owned by William Boylan, publisher of the *Minerva* newspaper. Boylan, the conservative, became one
of Lane's stoutest friends.

When Haywood died in 1829, Lane saw his chance for freedom. Mrs. Haywood hired out her slaves to pay the heavy load of debts her husband had left
her, and Lane asked if he could buy his own time and keep whatever earnings he
made on top of that, "a practice that was contrary to the laws of the state, but in
Raleigh sometimes winked at."

When he had accumulated a thousand dollars, he asked Mrs. Haywood to let
him buy his freedom, as Haywood had promised him he could. She agreed. But
there were obstacles. First, only a freeman could make a contract. Benjamin
Smith, a merchant who had bought Lane's wife and children from Boylan, agreed
to take Lane's money and buy him from Mrs. Haywood. But, that achieved,
Lane's petition foundered on a state law that allowed freedom only for slaves
who had shown "meritorious service," usually war service. Finally, Lane received
his manumission papers in New York City, where Smith had taken him on a
business trip.

Smith wasn't so agreeable to Lane's offer to buy his wife and children. He set a
steep price of $3,000, coming down eventually to $2,500, to be paid in five
annual installments of $500 each. (Eight years earlier, Smith had paid $560 for
Mrs. Lane and two children.)

Lane was doing well enough, however, to sustain confidence that he would
make all the payments. His tobacconist's shop flourished. Agents were selling
"Edward and Lunsford Lane Tobacco" in Fayetteville, Chapel Hill, and Salisbury.
And onto the tobacco shop Lane soon added a lumber and dry-goods business.

In 1839, Lane bought a house and lot on Cabarrus Street, into which he moved with his family.

Lane's was not an isolated case. Other slaves were working their way to freedom, and as their numbers grew, they roused the resentment of the white working class. Lane had paid his first installment to Smith and was about to pay the second when he was charged with breaking a state law forbidding "free Negroes from another state" from migrating to North Carolina. He was given twenty days to leave town.

Although many leading citizens, including Boylan, petitioned the legislature, Lane failed to win a delay. To raise the rest of his debt, he set off for Philadelphia and Boston, picking up letters of introduction from former *Raleigh Register* editor Joseph Gales, then in Washington, D.C., on the way.

With the money soon in hand, Lane wrote Governor John Motley Morehead and asked if he could return to complete his transaction with Smith. Morehead reassured him that he could "in perfect safety come home in a quiet manner, and remain twenty days."

Lane arrived on a Saturday. On Monday, he was on his way to Smith's shop when he was arrested and taken to a "called court" to answer a trumped-up charge of giving abolitionist lectures.

Lane defended himself successfully and was released without charge. But as he left the building, he was warned that the crowd that had gathered outside wanted his blood. He tried to board a train, but the mob followed him there and blocked his way.

With the help of a guard, Lane escaped and hid out in the city jail. In the middle of the night, when he stepped out, he was accosted and carried off to the hanging ground southeast of the city, where he was tarred and feathered.

The next day, shaken from his ordeal but unharmed, Lane escaped Raleigh, avoiding another crowd at the railroad station by hiding in a different car from his wife and family. Lane became a popular antislavery lecturer in Massachusetts and other Northern states. His autobiography was published in 1842, and twenty-one years later, as the war rumbled, he cooperated with a Boston minister to produce a biography, *Lunsford Lane, Or, Another Helper from North Carolina*. It was a story, as the author put it, "not of what slavery is under its most revolting features, but of what it is to be a slave, with a sensitive nature, under the most favorable circumstances."

At the outset of the war, two of Lane's children were Union troop carriers in South Carolina. Where and when Lane died is not known.

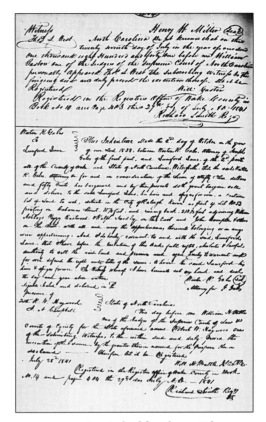

Lane's deed for a lot on Cabarrus Street in 1838

N.C. Division of Archives and History

'Death had passed by'

FROM THE WRITINGS OF LUNSFORD LANE

In The Narrative of Lunsford Lane, *published in Boston in 1842, Lane tells of his near-lynching at the hands of a Raleigh mob. The story is picked up after Lane is released from a court hearing, at which he was charged with delivering abolitionist lectures in New England.*

Voices

from

the

Capital

It now became evident that I should be unable to get off in the cars; and my friends advised me to go the shortest way possible to jail, for my safety. They said they were persuaded that what the rabble wanted was to get me into their possession, and then to murder me. The mob looked dreadfully enraged, and seemed to lap for blood. The whole city was in an uproar. But the first men and the more wealthy were my friends: and they did everything in their power to protect me. . . .

The guard then conducted me through the mob to the prison; and I felt joyful that even a prison could protect me. Looking out from the prison window, I saw my trunk in the hands of Messrs. Johnson, Scott and others, who were taking it to the City Hall for examination. I understood afterwards that they opened my trunk; and as the lid flew up, Lo! a paper! a paper!!

Those about seized it, three or four at once, as hungry dogs would a piece of meat after forty days famine. But the meat quickly turned to a stone; for the paper it happened was one printed in Raleigh and edited by Weston R. Gales, a nice man to be sure, but no abolitionist. The only other printed or written things in the trunk were some business cards of a firm in Raleigh—not incendiary.

Mr. Smith now came to the prison and told me that the examination had been completed, and nothing found against me; but that it would not be safe for me to leave the prison immediately. It was agreed that I should remain in prison until after night-fall, and then steal secretly away, being let out by the keeper, and pass unnoticed to the house of my old and tried friend, Mr. Boylan.

I was discharged between nine and ten o'clock. I went by the back way leading to Mr. Boylan's; but soon and suddenly a large company of men sprang upon me, and instantly I found myself in their possession. They conducted me sometimes high above the ground and sometimes dragging me along, but as silently as possible, in the direction of the gallows, which is always kept standing upon the Common, or as it is called "the pines," or "piny old field."

At length I observed those who were carrying me away, changed their course a little from the direct line to the gallows, and hope, a faint beaming, sprang up within me; but then as they were taking me to the woods, I thought they intended to murder me there, in a place where they would be less likely to be interrupted than in so public a spot as where the gallows stood. They conducted me to a rising ground among the trees, and set me down.

Lunsford Lane

"Now," said they, "tell us the truth about those abolition lectures you have been giving at the North."

I replied that I had related the circumstances before the court in the morning; and could only repeat what I had then said. "But that was not the truth—tell us the truth." I again said that any different story would be false, and as I supposed I was in a few minutes to die, I would not, whatever they might think I would say under other circumstances, pass into the other world with a lie upon my lips.

Said one, "You were always, Lunsford, when you were here, a clever fellow, and I did not think you would be engaged in such business as giving abolition lectures."

To this and similar remarks, I replied the people of Raleigh had always said the abolitionists did not believe in buying slaves, but contended that their masters ought to free them without pay. I had been laboring to buy my family; and how then could they suppose me to be in league with the abolitionists?

After other conversation of this kind, and after they seemed to have become tired of questioning me, they held a consultation in a low whisper among themselves. Then a bucket was brought and set down by my side; but what it contained or for what it was intended, I could not divine. But soon, one of the number came forward with a pillow, and then hope sprung up, a flood of light and joy within me.

The heavy weight on my heart rolled off; death had passed by and I unharmed. They commenced stripping me till every rag of clothes was removed;

and then the bucket was set near, and I discovered it to contain tar. One man, I will do him the honor to record his name, Mr. WILLIAM ANDRES, a journeyman printer, when he is anything, except a tar-and-featherer, put his hands the first into the bucket, and was about passing them to my face.

"Don't put any in his face or eyes," said one. So he desisted; but he, with three other "gentlemen," whose names I should be happy to record if I could recall them, gave me as nice a coat of tar all over, face only excepted, as any one would wish to see.

Then they took the pillow and ripped it open at one end, and with the open end commenced the operation at the head and so worked downwards, of putting a coat of its contents over that of the contents of the bucket. A fine escape from the hanging this will be, thought I, provided they do not with a match, set fire to the feathers. I had some fear they would.

But when the work was completed they gave me my clothes, and one of them handed me my watch which he had carefully kept in his hands; they all expressed great interest in my welfare, advised me of how to proceed with my business the next day, told me to stay in the place as long as I wished, and with other such words of consolation they bid me good night.

After I had returned to my family to their inexpressible joy, as they had become greatly alarmed for my safety, some of the persons who had participated in this outrage, came in (probably influenced by a curiosity to see how the tar and feathers would be got off) and expressed great sympathy for me. They said they regretted that the affair had happened—that they had no objections to my living in Raleigh—I might feel perfectly safe to go out and transact my business preparatory to leaving—I should not be molested. . . .

In the morning Mr. Boylan, true as ever, and unflinching in his friendship, assisted me in arranging my business, so that I should start with my family "that day" for the north. He furnished us with provisions more than sufficient to sustain the family to Philadelphia, where we intended to make a halt; and sent his own baggage wagon to convey our baggage to the depot, offering also to send his carriage for my family. But my friend, Mr. Malone, had been before him in this kind offer, which I had agreed to accept.

Brief and sorrowful was the parting from my kind friends; but the worst was the thought of leaving my mother. The cars were to start at ten o'clock in the morning. I called upon my old mistress, Mrs. Haywood, who was affected to weeping by the considerations that naturally came to her mind. . . .

And now, "with tears that ceased not flowing," they gave me their parting blessing. My mother was still Mrs. Haywood's slave, and I her only child. Our old mistress could not witness the sorrow that would attend the parting with my mother. She told her to go with me; and said that if I ever became able to pay two hundred dollars for her, I might; otherwise it should be her loss.

Sisters of charity

Dorothea Dix Hospital and the Governor Morehead School for the Blind

BY JOHN PARRAMORE
The News & Observer
July 1985

The last two decades before the Civil War were a philanthropic era, fueled by unprecedented prosperity and the spiritual ardor of the Great Awakening in religion. They saw national campaigns to rid the country of illiteracy, intemperance, primitive criminal codes, and a host of social evils.

In the South, this ardor was tempered by the fear that reforms would encroach upon the institution of slavery, but the results nevertheless were impressive. Two surviving legacies of that period are the Dorothea Dix Hospital for the Insane and the Governor Morehead School for the Blind.

By 1840, North Carolinians began to look to Raleigh for improvements in the conditions of the state's handicapped citizens and the criminal element. Such humanitarian reforms had been part of state senator Archibald D. Murphey's far-sighted proposals as early as 1817. And interest had been kept alive by such groups as the North Carolina Bible Society and the North Carolina Institution for the Instruction of the Deaf and Dumb, which was organized in 1827 (largely by Wake Countians) to foster the creation of a school.

In 1843, Whig governor John Motley Morehead finally persuaded the state legislature to consider establishing a school for the deaf and blind. In that same year, a Virginia instructor demonstrated techniques for teaching the deaf in the Capitol and so impressed lawmakers that the following year they appropriated five thousand dollars, to be allocated among counties agreeing to put up seventy-five dollars a year for each student.

William D. Cooke, the Virginia schoolmaster whose pupils had performed in Raleigh, was retained as superintendent of the North Carolina Institution for the Education of the Deaf, Dumb, and Blind, which opened in May 1845 in Raleigh. Money for buildings was added in 1847, and the building on Caswell Square—one of the city's original five squares—was completed in 1849. (In that year, students at the school published the first journal of the

The North Carolina Asylum for the Insane

Harper's New Monthly Magazine

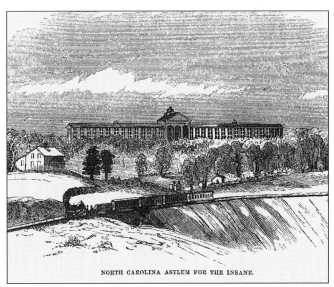

NORTH CAROLINA ASYLUM FOR THE INSANE.

North Carolina School for the Blind on
Caswell Square, around 1905

N.C. Division of Archives and History

deaf for the deaf, the *Deaf Mute*.) A department for blind students was added in 1851. In 1895, deaf children were moved to Morganton, and the school was then called the North Carolina School for the Blind. In 1927, it was moved to a new plant on Ashe Avenue. The school became the Governor Morehead School for the Blind in 1964.

Governor Morehead also had proposed an institution for the insane, which the legislature rejected. New England reformer Dorothea Dix, who was waging a one-woman national campaign for reform of asylums and prisons that eventually took her to every state east of the Rockies, arrived in North Carolina in 1848 and looked into the existing care for the insane. She found it barbaric.

Blocked from appearing before the legislature, Miss Dix came to Raleigh anyway, issued a long "memorial" of her investigation, and lobbied strenuously with lawmakers.

The Whigs were ready to establish the state institution she proposed, but Democrats balked. By coincidence, Miss Dix was staying at a Raleigh hotel with Mrs. James C. Dobbin, the wife of an influential Cumberland County Democrat. The fate of the hospital turned on their friendship.

Mrs. Dobbin suddenly took ill, and was taken care of by Miss Dix. Mrs. Dobbin asked what favor she could do for her in return, and Dix replied that she should ask her husband to support the hospital, according to Elizabeth Reid Murray in *Wake—Capital County of North Carolina*. Dobbin later gave a stirring speech, and the bill funding the hospital passed. The State Hospital for the Insane at "Dix Hill" opened in 1856. In 1859, it was renamed after the woman whose compassion had brought it into being.

PART TWO

Civil War and Reconstruction

General William Tecumseh Sherman in a photograph taken during or shortly after his visit to Raleigh. Note the mourning band for Lincoln on his left arm.

N.C. Division of Archives and History

Sherman's conquest

The long march ends in Raleigh

BY CHARLES SALTER, JR.
The News & Observer
April 8, 1990

In April 1865, Union troops were on their way to Raleigh, and General William Tecumseh Sherman's reputation preceded him like smoke blown downwind. It filled the nostrils of trembling Raleighites, who knew how other Southern capitals in his path had fared. Atlanta had been scorched. Columbia was still smoldering. Raleigh expected the worst. Surely, it would be the next bonfire. It wasn't.

The only matches Sherman lit in Raleigh were for his cigars; he was a chain-smoker. As the Confederates moved toward surrender, he anxiously awaited an end to the fighting. It came in late April when Confederate general Joseph E. Johnston signed a treaty with Sherman at Bennett Place in Durham.

That agreement is overshadowed by the one at Appomattox Courthouse, Virginia, which came first and featured the major figures, Robert E. Lee and Ulysses S. Grant. Because Sherman's occupation of Raleigh was mild compared to what occurred in other capitals, it is often overlooked in Civil War lore. Raleigh was the last stop in Sherman's March, and the treaty at Bennett Place was the largest surrender of the war, easily eclipsing Appomattox.

In his book *Sherman's March Through the Carolinas*, historian John Barrett describes the scene in early April. Exultant from the news of Appomattox, the Union troops tossed their rifles into the air as they approached Raleigh, while in the city, citizens hid their valuables and awaited disaster. The morning of April 13—the date of Sherman's scheduled arrival—broke with dark, foreboding clouds. The last of the Confederate troops were retreating from Raleigh. Desperate for food, they pillaged as they went. One account said the only chicken left behind was on the weather vane at Christ Church.

Several skirmishes with Union men occurred on the outskirts of town, testified to by a trail of bullets, bayonets, and three-pound cannonballs. To protect Raleigh, the governor and the mayor acted fast, according to Burke Davis in *Sherman's March*, his 1980 book which traces the general's route.

On April 12, Governor Zebulon Vance sent a special embassy, including former governors W. A. Graham and David Swain, to meet with Sherman. They were delayed, and, not hearing from them by midnight, Vance left Raleigh, fearful that his embassy had failed. Before he decamped, Vance wrote a second letter to Sherman, which was carried by a second peace party on the thirteenth. The party, including Mayor William Harrison and other city officials, took its white flag a mile south of downtown on Holleman Road, now known as Old Garner

It was the Civil War's largest surrender. About eighty-nine thousand Confederate soldiers laid down their arms.

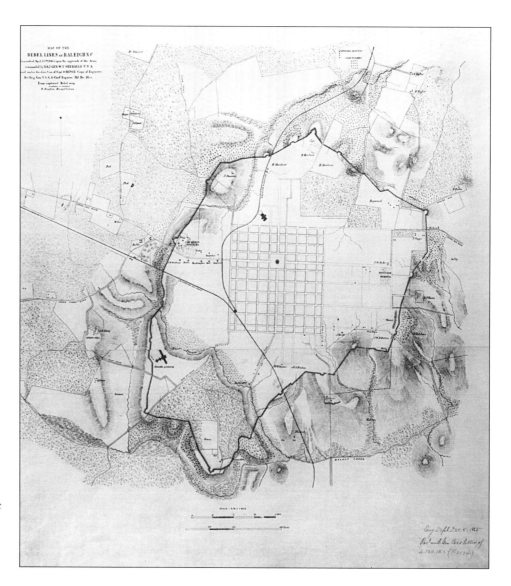

A Yankee engineer made this copy of a Confederate map of the breastworks ordered by Governor Zebulon Vance to protect Raleigh against Union attack.

N.C. Division of Archives and History

Road. There, the group waited in the rain for an hour until General Hugh Judson Kilpatrick, the Union cavalry commander, arrived.

Harrison's group surrendered the city, asking for "forbearance and protection of private persons and private property." Sherman had already agreed to a peaceful occupation on the twelfth. However, if Federal soldiers met any resistance upon entering the city, Kilpatrick said, the agreement was off. In other words, Raleigh would smoke.

In still-heavy rain, Kilpatrick's troops marched up Fayetteville Street with their banners flying and a band playing. The city was quiet and deserted. Newspapers had warned residents to stay home. Businesses were closed. It looked like it would be a peaceful occupation. Then the Federals were fired upon. According to an account by Elizabeth Reid Murray in *Wake—The Capital County of North Carolina*, a Confederate straggler took five hasty shots (none found the target) at the cavalry from a range of a hundred yards. A chase ensued around the Capitol grounds.

The soldier who jeopardized the protection of Raleigh was a young hothead from Texas named Lieutenant Walsh. Twelve Union soldiers pursued and caught him on Hillsborough Street. They took him to Burke Square, the present site of the Governor's Mansion, and strung him up, denying his last request to write a letter to his wife. Walsh, whose first name long ago was forgotten, is buried in Oakwood Cemetery.

It was another dodged bullet for Raleigh, but not the last. Sherman arrived that night and stayed at the Governor's Palace. Soldiers hoisted a United States flag above the Capitol dome and patrolled the streets at night. The occupation was complete.

The end of the Civil War was in sight. Johnston agreed to meet with Sherman at Bennett Place, the midway point between the Union troops in Raleigh and the Confederates in Greensboro, to negotiate a treaty. The morning of April 17, Sherman received a telegram announcing that President Lincoln had been assassinated three days earlier. Concerned about his soldiers' reaction, he kept this information to himself. He boarded a train and made the twenty-minute trip to Durham Station. He arrived at Bennett Place on horseback and met his adversary for the first time. When they didn't reach an agreement, Sherman returned to Raleigh. He would commute daily until his business was complete.

The next threat to Raleigh occurred that night, when word of Lincoln's assassination spread among the Union troops camped around the city. Among the nervous citizens, rumors circulated that the soldiers planned to destroy the city. According to an entry in one Indiana officer's diary, a mob of two thousand angry soldiers charged down from their camp on Dix Hill toward Raleigh to burn it as they had the other Southern capitals. General John Logan learned of their plan and met them at Rocky Branch, according to some historians. He threatened to shoot anyone who wouldn't return to camp. The men turned back. "General Logan saved the City and it owes him a debt it never can pay," wrote the officer. Meanwhile, negotiations between the armies continued, and Sherman had a close call of his own. After the April 18 treaty, he thought he had successfully completed his business. He was wrong. On April 24, Grant arrived unannounced at the door of the Governor's Palace. He surprised Sherman, who appeared in his nightclothes.

The treaty had been rejected. Its concessions to the Confederates were too generous. Sherman, who "would walk on thin ice for Gen. Grant," was crushed, says Dr. Barrett. Determined, Sherman and Johnston went back to work at their usual spot, the small log cabin owned by James Bennett. Following specific instructions, the Union general offered the same terms of surrender that Grant did with Lee at Appomattox. Take it or leave it.

Johnston, who after the war became a close friend of Sherman's and served as a pallbearer at his funeral, signed it. Back in Raleigh, Grant did the same. It was the Civil War's largest surrender. About eighty-nine thousand Confederate soldiers laid down their arms.

The Union troops tossed their rifles into the air as they approached Raleigh, while the city awaited disaster.

'What has befallen us?'

From the diary of a Southern lady

BY CATHERINE ANN DEVEREUX EDMONDSTON
From *Journal of a 'Secesh' Lady,*
The Diary of Catherine Ann Devereux Edmondston, 1860–1866

Catherine Ann Devereux Edmondston was North Carolina's Mary Chesnut. A diarist of literary skill and great passion (if less compassion), Mrs. Edmondston left a memorable chronicle of Southern fortunes during the Civil War—as felt on her own proud pulse. It records her disputes with relatives (not all of them were so strongly pro-secession as she was), her opinions of President Davis's policies and Lee's strategy, notes on her husband's vain attempts to raise a cavalry brigade in Raleigh, and, finally, the arrival of Sherman's army in the state capital.

Catherine was born in 1823 into the planter aristocracy of Halifax County. Her father, Thomas Devereux, raised her and five sisters at Conneconara, his plantation on the Roanoke River, with all the privileges of their class, including private tutoring in the liberal arts. In 1846, she married Patrick Edmondston, the son of a Charleston trader who had done business with her father, and moved to Charleston. Devereux soon induced them back to North Carolina with the offer of a plantation of their own, Looking Glass, adjoining Conneconara. During the war, Mrs. Edmondston often traveled to Raleigh to visit her brother, John Devereux, the chief quartermaster of North Carolina, and his family at their summer home, Will's Forest, off what is now Glenwood Avenue. She also visited George and Margaret Cameron Mordecai at the Cameron mansion, near St. Mary's College.

The war ended in the most humiliating way possible for Mrs. Edmondston, with Union generals Logan, Grant, and Sherman clinking Mrs. Devereux's sherry glasses on the back lawn at Will's Forest. These entries record the news from Raleigh as Sherman's army approached the capital. She died in 1875.

Voices from the Capital

January 10, 1861

Arrived [at Raleigh from Charleston] on the morning of the 10th carrying with us the news of the repulse of the "Star of the West" . . . and Mr. Buchanan's treachery. Every where it was received with surprised dismay, the feeling almost universally being to leave [South Carolina] to herself, give her Fort if she required it, but deny her all benefits of the Government, refuse her all postal intercourse etc. Predictions were freely made that in that event, in a year at most she would if Mr. Lincoln's government should prove an impartial one, petition to return into the Union. . . . Margaret's exclamation when she heard it was "Why Kate, you have been seeing History!" The children all well and already inflamed against the Yankees & "old Lincoln." The North is sowing the wind; see that ere the next generation she does not reap the Whirlwind!

February 3, 1862

Rain! Rain! Rain! again Sunday & today. Went in the pouring rain to dine with Mrs. Mordecai, or rather I should say Mr. and Mrs. George Mordecai. [Union general] Burnside the engrossing topic, what we should do should he come. As to his ever reaching Raleigh, the idea is simply ridiculous. He may make a foray up our river & burn or destroy all he can lay his hands on, but that he will ever make a permanent lodgment even there I doubt. But so the world goes. Mrs. Mordecai thinks of her mirrors, I of my books; & I suppose everyone has some little ewe lamb, some particular hobby that they think he will destroy.

March 24, 1865

Came my Aunt, Mrs. Polk, with my cousins to make us a visit. The anxiety we all suffer prevents our full enjoyment of each other's society, yet it seems to bind us closer together. The arrival of the mail, however, has thrown us into the deepest dejection. Rumour after rumour of the most conflicting character reaches us.

"Raleigh is to be evacuated," says one. "Johnston is falling back on Hillsboro," says another. Sherman ditto on Fayetteville. A heavy raid in the direction of Wilson. Grant moving on Stoney Crk. "Weldon heavily threatened"—& so on. My aunt has determined if the next mail does not bring news of the evacuation of Raleigh to leave & return to her children in Asheville fearing that if she delays she will be unable to reach them.

Catherine Edmondston
N.C. Division of Archives and History

March 25, 1865

Came rumours of another victory, but we fear to rejoice. What is more substantial is the fact that Johnston still remains at Smithfield & the idea of an evacuation of Raleigh seems, from the reports & conduct of those who ought to know, to be abandoned. We hear that Sherman has lost heavily. We have had three engagements with him, in all of which we have been successful. He is reported falling back both to Fayetteville & Goldsboro now held (thanks to Bragg) by Schofield, but which is true, we have not the means of knowing.

We hear sad accounts of the suffering in Fayetteville. Sherman robbers stripped the town of every thing in the way of food & the inhabitants are literally living on parched corn. God help them. . . .

Brother writes from Raleigh, "We are very busy evacuating, indeed are nearly through. . . . Present appearances indicate that Sherman is going to move up the Weldon road & I would advise you strongly to prepare for him."

April 16, 1865

How can I write it? How find words to tell what has befallen us? Gen Lee has surrendered! Surrendered the remnant of his noble Army to an overwhelming horde of mercenary Yankee knaves & foreigners. . . . Noble old man, we almost forget our own loss in sympathy with you. He has been neither out manoeuvred or out generaled but crushed, crushed by mere brute force, force he could no more resist than he could the fall of an avalanche! We but love him the more for his misfortunes. Where Gen Johnston now is, or the President, none know. We hear, however, that they have gone South, leaving Hardee in command.

Sherman's troops entered Raleigh on Wednesday the 12th & rumour has it that they committed no excesses. I fear me, however, that as usual she is but a lying jade, so little faith have I in his wolves.

"Brother writes from Raleigh, 'We are very busy evacuating, indeed are nearly through.'"

April 17, 1865

Pray God we compromise not ourselves in our ignorance. Mr M tells us that the death of Lincoln & wounding of Seward is again reaffirmed, but not one word of the errant tailor. Dr Langdon assures us that he knows A P Hill was killed whilst gallantly fighting his way out of Petersburg but that all the Lees are safe.

April 27, 1865

Yesterday came Capt Langdon back from Warren County, Johnston's capitulation, which sad to say is too true, having put an end to his efforts to join him. Johnston's surrender is true, & the long heads amongst us say that we should be thankful for the terms he has secured. Good God! I cannot write!

April 28, 1865

Capt Langdon has seen a N Y Herald giving the particulars of Lincoln's death & of the attempt on Seward's life. The terrible scene which was reported to us so minutely, of how the cry "Sic Semper Tyrannis" was raised in the Theatre & one hundred & forty pistols discharged at once into Lincoln's box, the immediate extinguishment of the lights & the escape of the conspirators, exists but in imagination. No such coup de Theatre was enacted. The deed was committed by Booth & Booth alone. He made his preparations deliberately & secretly, by barring the door which led from the box to the passage, the proscenium I believe it is called, & taking off the lock of the box and having bored a gimlet hole in the door, watched his opportunity & about the middle of the play entered the box noiselessly & shot Mr Lincoln in the back of the head! . . .

Sherman was most grandiloquent & boastful, not only of what he had done but of what he could & would do! It sickens me to think of his manner, so as humiliation is not a pleasant vale to dwell in I will pass it over. He expressed a hope of being soon able to take his army home (God grant it), that is, should his Government accede to the terms he had offered Johnston. Failing that he intended "to gobble" (such was his elegant expression) "Johnston up," & from the style of his conversation it seemed as tho the whole Confederacy would be but a bonne touch to his Lordship! . . .

It needs no seer to divine his object in his cruel & murderous act. It is to disable and cripple us so much the more & to make us dependent upon the North for our very existence. Would that the women & children who will be starved &

die by his cruelty could haunt every moment sleeping or waking of his future life. He runs ten trains per day between Morehead City & Raleigh & sends out numbers of forage parties daily, three hundred wagons in a party, who forage the country for 50 miles to find food for his army. . . .

Dr H saw brother's grounds, his grove, his yard, and whole premises one camp ground for Yankee soldiers—tents as far as the eye could reach. God help his helpless family! Sherman has 200,000 men in & around Raleigh & for 10 miles around the country seems one vast camp. He saw, too, numbers of negroes, men, women, & children, dressed in their master's & mistress's clothes hurrying from all quarters into Raleigh as to a carnival. Guion's Hotel had been assigned them as Quarters & was packed to overflowing with them.

Andy Johnson has been quietly inaugurated [*sic*] President & made a speech, & such a speech, maudlin drunk. He said amongst other things that "Treason was a crime to be punished, not forgiven," & wound up with the announcement that his "heart was too full" (of Whisky?) to say more—the vulgar old sinner!

May 8, 1865

Howard's corps has gone North, but 130,000 men are still encamped in and around Raleigh. The suffering of some of the people in the country has been terrible, robbed of everything & driven out without a shelter to their heads. Mrs Hinton (Jane Miller), without a moment's warning was surrounded by a gang of thieves who tore off her doors & windows & reduced her house to a ruin to build themselves quarters, robbed her of everything & forced her to seek shelter in the town. She had to walk for three miles through their camp with her children, & lost every thing she had in the world.

Have just read a letter from my niece Nannie which does one's heart good so intensely bitter is it. Such hate as it expresses one does not often read of, but unfortunately for me I am beginning to feel it. She says that at Guion's, the negro headquarters, they have nightly balls & that the Yankee Officers dance with the negro women!

Will's Forest, where Generals Grant and Sherman toasted the end of the war
N.C. Division of Archives and History

The newspaper war

Recollections of a printer's devil

BY C. B. EDWARDS
The News & Observer
June 6, 1907

During the Civil War, Raleigh had eight daily newspapers and seven weeklies coming off presses on Fayetteville and Hargett streets. As the fortunes of war turned against the South, the papers began battling each other over Confederate policy, reflecting the deepening divide between Confederate and Conservative parties.

The State Journal, *the* Daily Confederate, *and the* Raleigh Register *all favored the Davis government's policy of fighting to the bitter end. The* Daily Progress *and the* North Carolina Standard, *edited by the reluctant secessionist and future governor W. W. Holden, urged a negotiated peace. Holden's views were considered treason by many Southerners, and on September 10, 1863, Confederate troops tried to stop his mouth and end the peace movement. A brigade of Georgia troops passing through Raleigh by train marched from the depot to the* Standard's *offices on West Hargett Street. They broke in, dumped the type, and damaged the press.*

The next day, Holden's sympathizers replied by wrecking the offices of the State Journal. *On a third day, further violence was threatened by an Alabama Confederate regiment but was forestalled when Governor Zebulon Vance, who had intervened to calm the rioters on the previous occasions, finally telegraphed Davis to demand that no more troops be sent through the capital.*

On the morning after the Georgia troops' raid, a printer's devil was on his way to work at the Daily Progress *on Fayetteville Street. C. B. Edwards and his partner, Needham Broughton, later founded the printing firm of Edwards & Broughton. In the N&O almost a half-century later, Edwards remembered the events.*

Voices from the Capital

Benning's Brigade of Georgia troops were passing through the city at night on cars from Virginia to someplace south. They were stopped at the old depot (now freight depot of the Southern) for several hours, and before the people were aware of what was going on, about fifty of them had slipped uptown and proceeded to demolish the *Standard* office by dumping all the type and destroying the press as best they could. It was their purpose next to visit the *Progress* office and destroy it also; but Mr. Pennington had learned of the fate of the *Standard*, had the precaution to have all the lights about the office extinguished and office locked up. At that time, the writer and Mr. Broughton, his partner for thirty-six years, were apprentices in the *Progress* office, who alternately had to reach the office very early and open it up, so that people coming to market could obtain their papers, as a great many subscribers preferred to call for their paper while coming to market. Very soon, a large crowd of peace sympathizers had collected in front of the market house, which stood at the present place, and they soon

AN EDITORIAL FACE-OFF

State Journal

June 10, 1863

The editor [of the *Standard*] now seems to doubt the correctness of his former opinion, and he thinks it problematical whether the South can win her independence. He sees a lion in the way, several of them. The first one is failure on account of weakness; the second one is that Davis and Soddon are carrying on the war for themselves and a few favorites; but the biggest one, the one with the longest mane and the loudest roar takes the shape of a picture in which the "Conservatives" are seen leaving office in this state, and some ugly chaps called secessionists are quietly taking their place. Mr. Holden will dissolve this government and erect a despotism in North Carolina sooner than a man who differs from him in politics shall have an office in this state.

North Carolina Standard

June 19, 1863

The people of both sections are tired of the war, and desire peace. We desire it on terms honorable to our own section, and we cannot expect it on terms that are dishonorable to the other section. We believe in fighting as long as we are invaded, and in driving the enemy from our soil . . . but we also hold that the friends of peace in both sections should give utterance to their views, and should thus pave the way for negotiations, to which both sections must at last come, as the only means for closing the contest. If we could negotiate now, so much the better. Thousands of valuable lives would be saved, and much devastation and ruin would be stayed.

began to talk in excited groups. The market bell was rung, and then it was that men came running from every direction and excitement ran high.

It was at this juncture that the writer recognized a tall and familiar figure, who wore a beaver hat, having a red bandanna in one hand and his hat in the other, waving for silence and attention. He soon had both, and mounting something that made him head and shoulders above his hearers, he delivered himself something like this: "My friends, last night a gang of Georgia soldiers destroyed the printing office of our fellow citizen W. W. Holden and threatened to destroy the office of our friend Mr. Pennington across the street for the simple reason that they favored the closing of the war, and now I think it becomes our duty to retaliate and destroy the office of the *State Journal*. Now let every man within the hearing of my voice that believes as I do, follow me," and while mopping his head with his bandanna, and amid a shout that had no uncertain meaning, he led the way in a run across Market Street to the office, and the work of destruction of the *Journal* office was begun.

A Yankee on the dome

A Union soldier signals the end of the war

BY LIEUTENANT GEORGE C. ROUND

George C. Round, a lieutenant in the Signal Corps of the Union army, had perhaps the happiest task of the Civil War: signaling its end.

From atop the Capitol, on which he seems to have had trouble keeping his footing, Round's flag was the vital communications link among the battalions of Sherman's army as it gathered in Raleigh.

In an account published by the United States Veteran Signal Corps Association in 1902, Round recalled his adventure: the claiming of the vacant Capitol, the massing of Sherman's army, the formal review on Fayetteville Street, the troops' near-riot after news of Lincoln's assassination reached Raleigh, and, finally, the joyous signal when Confederate general Johnston and Sherman settled the terms of surrender at Durham Station.

It was the 13th of April, 1865, precisely four years (to an hour) from the capitulation of Fort Sumter. I had been a soldier of the Union for four years lacking seven days. At that time I found myself riding with a small signal detachment in the advance of the armies which had swept from the valley of the Mis-

The Union signalman's announcement of the end of the Civil War was reenacted on April 26, 1990.

The News & Observer

sissippi to the sea and were then turning from the sea toward the mountains. On the afternoon of that day after a march of twenty-one miles, we entered Raleigh, the capital of North Carolina. We found that Kilpatrick's cavalry had been there before us and passed through the city.

Near the centre of the city was a square occupied by the two buildings of the Raleigh Academy, now the location of the Governor's Mansion. I saw an old gentleman on the grounds, who proved to be Professor Lovejoy, the principal. He told me he was a native of Vermont, had come to North Carolina as a teacher, and was concerned for the safety of his family. . . . [He] spoke especially of the burning of Columbia. I told him I was not in that part of the army and did not know the facts about that event, but I could assure him that the most stringent orders had been issued by Gen. Schofield, my immediate commander, for the protection of noncombatants and particularly on the subject of fire. I further told him I was looking for a camping place for the night, and that I would like to pre-empt his grounds for our signal corps before the larger bodies of infantry and artillery came into the city. Professor Lovejoy seemed pleased with the arrangement and readily assented.

I could not be certain but the Capitol was a "Grecian horse," which at any moment might swarm armed men from its halls and corridors to sweep us from the face of the earth.

Exploration

I had pitched a cozy encampment under the trees of the academy and had sent, with my compliments, a small package of "genuine coffee" to Mrs. Lovejoy, and that estimable lady had just reciprocated with a few early vegetables for a supper then impending, when I received an order from the headquarters of General Schofield, then commanding the Army of the Ohio, to establish a signal station at once on the dome of the Capitol, about two squares distant.

I cast a longing glance at the fleshpots boiling under the trees and repaired to the Capitol. A provost marshal's office, under the charge of Capt. John R. Thomas of Illinois, had just been opened on the lower floor, in order to secure to soldiery and citizens the benefits of military law, in the absence of the civil authority. I looked around to find some one who had charge of the building. The provost knew as little about it as I. We found the Senate chamber and Representatives' hall, but no Senators or Representatives. Even the Governor and janitor had stepped out, and not a soul could I find to give me the slightest idea of how I was to reach the dome. It was not without some fear and trembling that I went rummaging around the large, strange edifice.

I could not be certain but the Capitol was a "Grecian horse," which at any moment might swarm armed men from its halls and corridors to sweep us from the face of the earth. I was fortunate enough, however, to find in a closet two bits of candle, which were useful in exploring the dark passages as we worked our way upward. Finally we emerged to the flat roof of the building. I raised my signal flag, placed a man on the lookout and went to inspect the dome. I expected to find some steps, or at least an iron ladder, by which I could reach the top: but not the slightest thing could I see to suggest that such a trip was ever made by visitors. I then went down into the building again and endeavored to find an inside passage to the dome, but I failed for the best of reasons—there was none. . . .

It was after dark when I returned to the roof, tired, hungry and discouraged. I found there my orderly, William Cobb, whom I had left with our horses at the camp. He was a bright, beardless boy of eighteen, still living in Oxford, N.J., and I was much attached to him. The supper which he brought me worked a wondrous change in my feelings. . . .

In order that you may clearly understand the events which are detailed hereafter, and which to me were of the greatest possible importance, I ask your careful attention to a brief description of the Capitol. It stood at the junction of the four main avenues of the city, built of a light-colored stone in the massive style usual for good public buildings, well proportioned and surmounted by a beautiful dome. Its shape was that of a Grecian cross, and in the centre, reaching from the ground floor to the summit of the dome, was the lofty rotunda.

The dome rose from the roof, first in heavy stone abutments or steps, and from the highest of these in a graceful curve to a small circular stone on top, above and around which ran a light iron railing.

On the dome

After watching a time in silence, I again made a circuit of the dome, this time on the projection from which the curve began. I watched and felt in the darkness for notches which would support the footsteps of a climber, but found the dome covered by a smooth copper roofing. Suddenly in my circuit I ran against something. It was the lightning rod. I grasped the rod firmly. It was about an inch in diameter, rough and rusty. I got a good grip, one that would not slip. I began to raise myself, and the blood tingled through my veins as I felt myself on my upward journey. It went hand over hand till I reached one of the iron supports which held rod to the dome. . . . I easily shot upward till, in less time than I write it, I stood where the dome was nearly horizontal, and straightened up beside the stonework which encircled the top. Here I halted to take breath and observations.

I found the stonework ten or twelve feet in diameter and about the height of my sword-belt. The iron railing on top was about as high as my head. I put my hand through the railing and felt the inside edge of the stone, beyond which was a descent as far downward as where my feet rested, and I could discern the dim outline of a cone-shaped roof on the inside by the light of the red moon which was just rising. I seized the railing with my left hand and the lightning rod with my right, and both appearing firm, I pulled myself up on the

The Yankee signalman's takeover of the Capitol may have been re-enacted in this shot, c. 1902.
N.C. Division of Archives and History

HAYWOOD HOUSE

The Civil War brought about an unusual class reunion. Richard B. Haywood, a Raleigh surgeon, and Union major general Francis Preston Blair, Jr., had not seen each other since they graduated from the University of North Carolina (class of 1840). Then, in 1864, when Sherman's army occupied Raleigh, General Blair knocked on Haywood's door and asked if he could use his house as his headquarters. Haywood, a gentleman and a Confederate veteran, took him in.

Haywood's wife, Julia, had been sent north to Philadelphia during the hostilities, and the two men seem to have coexisted easily under the same roof while Sherman negotiated with General Johnston at Durham Station.

Haywood House
N. C. Division of Archives and History

When Union soldiers threatened to riot after they heard the news of Lincoln's assassination, Blair threw a Union uniform on the bed for Haywood. Or so goes the story. Once the peace was concluded, according to another family legend, Sherman joined them for a toast on the front porch.

The Greek Revival house, with its elegant one-story porch of Doric columns and heavy entablature, is one of the few antebellum structures standing in downtown. And of a dozen private homes that survive from the mid-nineteenth century, it is the only one still lived in by members of the original family.

Richard Haywood built the house on a lot his father had given him at the corner of Edenton and Blount streets. It was his wedding gift to his wife, Julia Hicks, the daughter of a wealthy New York import-export merchant. Julia's education in Switzerland had given her a cosmopolitan taste. Reportedly, she asked her husband for the French doors and bay windows.

The bricks, which have helped assure its longevity, were made by slaves at Richard's small plantation off Rock Quarry Road, near the present site of North Carolina Women's Prison. The house was completed in 1854.

stonework, threw my left foot over the railing, and what had appeared impossible was accomplished. . . .

Round and below me lay lovely Raleigh, embowered in a forest of murmuring shade. Through rifts in the leafy clouds, her homes peered here and there in the increasing moonlight. Farther to the right Southwest loomed up a huge asylum, where dwelt the unfortunates of peace, made doubly unfortunate by war.

I swept with my eyes the full circle of the horizon and scanned as closely as possible every field and wood, as the moon, just past its full, beamed fuller and clearer upon them. But I could see no sight and hear no sound that suggested aught of war, save the occasional outbreak for an army mule and the footfall of a single sentinel on the pavement below. I knew that somewhere behind those quiet fields to the North and West, at some distance beyond those glowering forests, to me unknown, crouched the grim hero of Bull Run and Fair Oaks, and that his orders were to "concentrate every available force and drive back Sherman." And I knew he would do it if mortal could. . . . I decided to go down to the room where my men were sleeping, rouse them and move my station to the top at once.

Before descending, however, I desired to explore more carefully the inside of the circle where my station must be located, in order to bring up on my return anything needed for the convenience of the station. So I put my other foot over the railing and leaped gently to what I supposed to be the solid top of the dome. I heard a sudden crash, and the top of the dome gave way beneath my feet. I had actually jumped into the circular glass skylight which lighted the top of the great rotunda. . . .

A narrow escape

The next instant I found myself grasping at railing and stonework and heard the broken glass of the skylight ring sharply on the stone floor of the rotunda, one hundred feet below me. The next day I found that my reckless descent had been interfered with materially by a dark wire netting, which had sufficed first to prevent my seeing the window sash and glass, and, second, to partially support my weight until I could lay hold of something more solid. I did not, however, stop to take any more observations, but pulled myself back to the stonework, drew a long breath and slid down the lightning rod from my lofty perch to the stone below. Here I took an account of stock. I found myself about as before the ascent, plus a terrible fright, a lacerated wrist, and, on the next day, a lame shoulder.

Having failed to establish my station on the dome, I had to content myself with adhering to the spirit of my orders as nearly as possible. I therefore instructed the lookout to walk around the dome every quarter of an hour, and to wake me if anything unusual happened. I then laid down on the roof to sleep.

By daylight the next morning Higgins (the ingenious man of my detachment), had made a raid on a dilapidated fence for boards. He tied the horses' halters together for a rope, and before breakfast we had a platform over the broken skylight. Then we drew up our "signal kit" and tied our station flag to the lightning rod, as notice to the world that we were ready for business.

And we were not a minute too soon, for while regulating the focus of my glass the "lookout" pointed me to a little flag waving at a lively rate. "44!" I shouted, and the flagman waved in a twinkling my nod of recognition. And who do you think sent the message? It was "Old Tecumseh" himself. I copy from my message-book before me, verbatim et figuratim.

"8:45 A.M.

"From Signal Station,

"Near Governor's Palace

"To 2342:

"General Sherman desires that you report to these headquarters all that you see and hear of the moving columns, their distance and direction.

"2314."

My flagman flashed back "14-1434," which means "O.K."

Troops arrive

Soon my new troops came pouring in. With my telescope, conveniently mounted, I could readily distinguish what flags they bore and, generally, to what corps and division they belonged.

Evidently "Tecumseh" had summoned his warriors to meet him here in council. Before the day closed, the Army of the Ohio, the Army of the Cumberland and the Army of the Tennessee filled all the stretch of country around, and at night their blazing camp fires lit up earth and heaven, while their drum-beats and martial airs rolled in from every direction. . . .

During the negotiations for peace, General Sherman reviewed his army in the streets of Raleigh. The review took several days, and on one day General Grant was present. The generals stood on Fayetteville Street, near the market house. It was indeed an historic group that I viewed through my glass from the top of the Capitol, including besides Grant and Sherman all the corps commanders of the various armies. I undertook the job of counting the army as it passed. There were in all 72,343 men, not including Kilpatrick's cavalry, the sick and the guards in the camp, and perhaps a few advanced regiments. If such a feat was ever before attempted I do not know it. I counted the front of each platoon or company division, then counted the number of ranks, did a little multiplying, added a few for the staff and the file closers, and by that time the regiment was gone and another was sweeping on.

Lincoln's assassination

On the 17th of April I was writing a letter in the Senate chamber when a signal lieutenant entered in great excitement and told me that Lincoln and Seward had been assassinated at Ford's theatre. A few weeks before, as Schofield's corps had been passing through Washington on their way from Nashville by rail, I had heard Wilkes Booth play Richard III at Ford's, and the awful tragedy rose distinctly before my vision. The news came by telegraph to Morehead City, as I understood it, and thence by rail and messenger. Soon after, the telegraph line was interrupted and it was several days before we could get any corroboration or details.

Orders were issued by the general to put on mourning for our illustrious chief. The officers attached crape to their swords and the regimental colors were draped in black. Our regular station flag was white, with a red centre. Besides this style we had red flags and black flags, each with a white centre. I took one of my black flags and gave it to a tailor in my detachment and directed him to sew a wide black strip around the station flag.

About a week afterward, Rev. Mr. Pell informed me that I had been the cause of considerable terror in the city, and I found that my attempt to put on

Orders were issued by the general to put on mourning for our illustrious chief.

mourning had been interpreted as the raising of the black flag. Subsequently the provost informed me that Governor Holden, accompanied by a number of women and children, had gone to General Schofield's headquarters, where the staff officers explained the matter to them and laughed away their fears. All this time I was utterly oblivious to what was going on. I cannot think, however, that the consternation was general.

On the thirteenth night after we entered Raleigh I sat at my station to a late hour. The myriad bands had played with unwanted sweetness, closing as if by common consent with "Home, Sweet Home." The "tattoo" had rolled round the wide circle of my vision and 100,000 men had answered to evening roll-call. "Taps" had sounded, the camp fires burned low and the lights had gone out in the homes of Raleigh. . . .

"The war is over!"

I was gazing Westward. I knew that at some point beyond where the sun had set five hours before the two great chieftains were in consultation under a flag of truce. And I felt at that silent hour the prayers of estranged millions ascending to heaven that bloodshed might cease.

Suddenly I heard far out to the front the sharp click of a horse's hoof. "Some drunken cavalry men out of camp," I thought. Clearer and nearer it came. I became impressed that it was no ordinary messenger, and sent word to the provost to look out for the intruder. But straight on toward us it came: nor did it stop till reined up at the Capitol. And when the lookout returned he shouted as he flew up the lightning rod:

"Hurrah! The war is over!"

I wrote at once to Captain Russell, my chief signal officer, and in a few minutes received permission to expend one-half my stock of signal rockets. They were of beautiful colors, some of them changing many times as they floated in mid-heaven. I arranged them in such an order as to announce the glad tidings which would be "of great joy to all people."

Everything now worked smoothly. Rocket after rocket sped away to the zenith. In the silences that intervened I could hear the opening of windows below me and gentle household voices seemed to say, "Watchman, what of the night?" And I knew that for them my answer meant, "The morning cometh." I thought I heard the distant murmur of the camps, as though the army was waking from its slumber and each soldier was pointing his comrade, with whisperings of joy, to the angel of peace hovering over them: and I know that one outpost of the Army of the Tennessee caught the full spirit of the vision, for without the fear of army regulations in mind, they sent such a shout across field and forest as the shepherds might have uttered when, over Bethlehem's plains, they saw the angel convoy of the Prince of Peace, while those skilled in the "cipher code" of freedom thrilled as they read in the fiery heavens: "PEACE ON EARTH— GOOD WILL TO MEN."

Andrew Johnson

A misunderstood native son

BY JONATHAN DANIELS
The News & Observer
October 28, 1958

In Raleigh, no one felt any reason to love him as their own. He had almost made a career of plebeian contempt for Southern aristocracy. A fighting Unionist, he was regarded as a traitor to the South. He had cried loudly for the punishment of treason and the impoverishment of traitors. And before Sherman's troops left Raleigh, Johnson sent General Grant to repudiate the generous terms Sherman had given when he accepted the surrender of General Johnston.

The terms Sherman gave were those he believed Lincoln had wanted. They were terms over which a defeated South could rejoice. In essence, they provided that the South should lay down its arms and then the government would recognize the Southern states "on their officers and legislators taking the oath prescribed by the Constitution of the United States." Andrew Johnson and his cabinet turned them down.

A month later, Johnson chose North Carolina as the state in which he first would outline his policies of Southern Reconstruction, making it the state in which the battle around those policies would first take place. The combative old tailor could have made the meeting to which he called North Carolinians an occasion of special arrogant triumph over the neighbors of his poverty-stricken boyhood.

In wartime anger, Raleigh people had exaggerated the stories about Andy Johnson's running away after throwing rocks at the house of old Mrs. Wells. Those who had hated him as "traitor" made from the obscurity of his background a variety of fables as to whose bastard he had been.

The North Carolinians—though all Unionists—who came to Washington at Johnson's invitation saw its avenues still littered by the debris left by men and horses in the final grand review of the victorious blue armies. Governor Vance was there under lock and key in the Old Capital Prison. The long-lingering Lincoln family had just given up the White House. And in the mansion, Andrew Johnson still must have seemed incongruous even as the legitimate son of Jacob Johnson, the porter at Casso's inn in Raleigh in times when most such labor was performed by slaves.

The clear fact is that at the meeting Johnson was far more generous than many angry Northerners wanted him to be. And the equally clear fact is that his

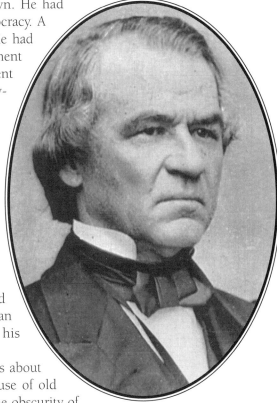

Andrew Johnson
1808–1875

The birthplace of Andrew Johnson was originally part of Casso's inn at the northern end of Fayetteville Street. In 1975, it was moved to Mordecai Historic Park.

N.C. Division of Archives and History

generous terms did not seem generous enough to some of the North Carolinians who had come at his request to discuss them. Johnson's easy amiability reflected his widespread popularity in the North at the time. But the course he took put him historically in the position, worth noticing today, of a moderate in American crisis fated to be damned by extremists on both sides. The proclamation of Reconstruction which he showed to his North Carolina visitors was to be swiftly and furiously damned by such a Northern radical as Wendell Phillips.

Surrender to North Carolina

"It would have been better, far better," cried that famous orator and abolitionist, "for Grant to have surrendered to Lee than President Johnson to North Carolina."

But Bartholomew Figures Moore of Raleigh, at the first conference with Johnson, took an exactly opposite view. Moore, one of the great lawyers in North Carolina history, had walked erect in his Union views on Raleigh's streets throughout the war. He had declined to take the oath of allegiance to the Confederacy, though that limited his practice as an attorney. Now, however, he rejected Johnson's plan to let most white North Carolinians who would take the oath of allegiance to the Union hold a convention and set up a state government. That was unconstitutional, announced Moore.

Andrew Johnson stuck to his terms, which Wendell Phillips regarded as capitulation and history recognized as remarkably generous to the South. Moore held to his objections. The next day, at another meeting, Johnson accepted the recommendation of a majority of the other North Carolinians whom he had called to Washington and named as provisional governor W. W. Holden, who had risen from origins as lowly as Johnson's. As an editor, Holden had led to power the democracy which old Whigs like Moore opposed. Old Bart Moore got up in anger and left the room.

Yet it was Moore who most quickly recognized that Southern division over Johnson's plans might bring on the furies, which did come when Johnson's plans were swept aside by the radical Reconstructionists in Congress.

A man of two voices

Moore did not trust Holden, and subsequent events perhaps proved him right in that. Holden had been an extreme secessionist in 1861. His newspaper beat its drums for the fire-eaters. Yet he as editor became such an advocate of peace and return to the Union during the war that his bold assent was singled out for Union praise by the orator Edward Everett on the same occasion when Lincoln made his Gettysburg Address. Then, in the election ordered under Johnson's plan, those who hated Holden brought out a candidate against him. Undoubtedly, the election of Jonathan Worth over Holden seemed to Johnson a swift show of defiance.

Other things were happening in the South to embarrass him in the North, where political power lay. Not so much in North Carolina, but in other states, the Black Codes passed by some of the all-white governments Johnson recognized seemed to give credence to Northern fears that they were devices to perpetuate slavery.

Johnson's plan came under mounting assault from such men as Thad Stevens of Pennsylvania and Charles Sumner of Massachusetts. And in the South, Johnson's suggestion that suffrage be extended to a few highly qualified Negroes was disregarded. Around him in the White House rose not only the angers of old-time abolitionists but now determined Republicans.

They faced the fact that while emancipation increased the Southern population counted for representation in Congress (slave population was only counted at two-thirds its number), only the whites who had waged the war could vote. That, said Whitelaw Reid, on a tour of the South, "would be putting a reward on treason that we can hardly afford to pay." Other Northerners still had a vindictiveness they wanted to spend. It rose in increasing fury around Andrew Johnson, whose hopes of peace and conciliation were being slashed away.

Slowly, his home people came to realize that. In May 1867, after a radical Congress had passed the Military Reconstruction Act over Johnson's veto, he was invited to come back for the first time to the town which he had left so long ago as a poor young tailor. In Raleigh's City Cemetery, grateful citizens had erected a little monument over the grave of his father, Jacob Johnson. It was to be unveiled on June 4. Governor Jonathan Worth and Mayor Dallas Haywood invited Johnson to attend. Worth regarded the president, he wrote, as "a patriot" at a

Ten Dollars Reward.

RAN AWAY from the Subscriber, on the night of the 15th instant, two apprentice boys, legally bound, named WILLIAM and ANDREW JOHNSON. The former is of a dark complexion, black hair, eyes, and habits. They are much of a height, about 5 feet 4 or 5 inches. The latter is very fleshy, freckled face, light hair, and fair complexion. They went off with two other apprentices, advertised by Messrs Wm. & Chas. Fowler. When they went away, they were well clad—blue cloth coats, light colored homespun coats, and new hats, the maker's name in the crown of the hats, is Theodore Clark. I will pay the above Reward to any person who will deliver said apprentices to me in Raleigh, or I will give the above Reward for Andrew Johnson alone.

All persons are cautioned against harboring or employing said apprentices, on pain of being prosecuted.

JAMES J. SELBY, Tailor.
Raleigh, N. C. June 24, 1824   26 3t

Notice of young Andrew Johnson's flight in the *Raleigh Star*
N.C. Division of Archives and History

time when "partisan rage North and South, has been heretofore and is now, entirely regardless of moral rectitude."

A president comes home

Johnson wrote on May 22, "I accept the invitation of my native city to be her guest and, deeply grateful for the respect in which they hold my father's memory, I will be present."

It was a happy occasion for the boy returning as president, though Governor Worth noted at the time that Johnson seemed "sad and taciturn" even in the friendly place of his youth. He had a right to be. In Washington, to which he hurried back, the angry radical forces were crowding around him. They were to bring about his impeachment less than a year later, for "high crimes" which were constituted only of his efforts to stem the extremist furies. He was to escape conviction by only a single vote.

Andrew Johnson never came back home to Raleigh after that June in 1867. After he left the presidency, his Tennessee people sent him back to Congress. But it was a long time after his death before his courage as the great moderate in the darkest American crisis began to make a growing place for him in the honor of his countrymen, North and South.

At a time when extremists North and South roar again, he is entitled to recognition as an American who, perhaps with courage unequaled in American history, declined to be intimidated. He stood steadfast in his time against those extremists who are always, as old man Bart Moore said, "the most dangerous to the quiet and prosperity of the state."

Peace College

For 'the thorough education of young ladies'

BY DAVID PERKINS

The records of the Spring Garden Presbyterian Church include this note for 1847: "Be it resolved that the Rev. William N. Mebane and Elder Alfred M. Scales respectfully bring to notice . . . the importance of establishing a female institution of learning to be under the direction of the Orange Presbytery."

Thus the seed was sown.

The presbytery began looking for subscribers and found something more, a benefactor, in William Peace, an eighty-six-year-old Raleigh pioneer and an elder in the First Presbyterian Church. With his brother Joseph, Peace had opened a general store on Fayetteville Street in 1798.

Peace came up with eight acres at the foot of Wilmington Street plus ten thousand dollars, enough to pay a third of the cost of Main Building, the grand classical structure on which work began in 1858. Then came war. The Confederate government, needing a hospital in Raleigh, took over the half-complete Main Building. Contractor T. H. Briggs hastily put down floors; cloth was hung over glassless windows; and the first casualties were admitted in June 1862.

After the war, Main Building housed the Freedmen's Bureau. From the classical portico, Federal agents handed out hardtack and white potatoes and administered health care to crowds of free blacks.

The institute's directors took control again in the late 1860s. But facing a large debt, they decided to sell the property. It took a bid from Henry Tupper, the founder of Shaw Institute, to galvanize white Raleighites into forming a stock

Main Hall in 1906
N.C. Division of Archives and History

And in the 1980s
The News & Observer

corporation, mostly of Presbyterians, to buy the land and building. Bankers who had snubbed Tupper wrote a large mortgage.

Main Building was completed, and the school was leased to the Reverend Robert Burwell—who had run a school in Charlotte—and his son, John. Peace Institute opened its doors, finally, in 1872, and was developed along the lines dictated by the Presbyterians. "The Female Seminary will have for its object," ran the original charter, "the thorough education of young ladies, not only in the substantial branches of knowledge, but also in those which are elegant and ornamental." To the traditional liberal arts were added a School of Cooking and a Department of Needle and Fancy-work.

The institute's first students ran from kindergarten (the first in the South, opening in 1879) to college level. The precollege program was gradually phased out, the eleventh and twelfth grades finally closing in 1967 and 1968. Peace Institute was renamed Peace Junior College in 1940 and Peace College in 1943.

Briggs and Sons, Inc.

A memoir of a Raleigh burgher

BY THOMAS H. BRIGGS III

Enter Briggs and Sons, Inc., on Fayetteville Street and the nineteenth century becomes palpable. The old skylight has been covered with a tin ceiling, but the visitor can still buy nails by the handful, a new iron, cutlery, sleds, and popcorn at the door. In the rear of the store, as if keeping track of things, glowers the founder, Thomas H. Briggs, the very model of a postwar businessman.

The oldest Raleigh business to remain in the same family's hands, the Briggs store opened on the 200 block in 1865 as a hardware store and general contracting and building-supply firm. Briggs and his partner, James Dodd, rode the postwar recovery to prosperity, and in 1874, they raised the present four-story building—in its day, the tallest building in eastern North Carolina. The fancy pressed brick and iron facade was ordered from a catalog.

After coming to Raleigh and working as a carpenter on the new state Capitol, among other buildings, Briggs set up a contracting business. In partnership with Dodd, he built much of Oakwood, a speculative suburb, as well as several institutional buildings, including Main Hall at Peace College and an earlier structure for the Edenton Street Methodist Church.

After Briggs's death in 1886, the store was inherited by two of his sons and the contracting business by a third, John D. Briggs. One of John's sons, Thomas Briggs III, born in Raleigh in 1877, became a schoolteacher and later a professor at Columbia University. Thomas III wrote this profile of his grandfather and namesake shortly before his death in 1971.

Thomas H. Briggs
1821–86

Although I was only nine years old when he died, I remember Grandfather very well. He was about five feet eight inches tall and on the "chunky" side. He wore a close-cropped beard, already graying; on one cheek near the nose was a mole; and he had blue-gray eyes, usually serious, but they would often twinkle with the fun that was in him. He wore a heavy gold watch chain across his waistcoat and attached to a Hamilton watch, which Grandmother gave to me as a reward for not smoking until I was of age.

I was told that he came to Raleigh from Fayetteville with his tool chest his only possession. (His father, John Joyner Briggs, also a carpenter and a storekeeper,

Briggs Hardware in the early 1900s
N.C. Division of Archives and History

had preceded him, coming to Raleigh about 1800, when the town had only five houses. It is recorded that he helped lay out the first streets.)

Grandfather set up as a carpenter, and gradually became a contractor in whom everybody had complete confidence that his work would be honest and substantial. At the time of the War Between the States, he was not in the army, but he was employed by the Confederate government to make supplies for the forces in the field. Grandfather had little schooling, just how much I do not know; but inasmuch as there was no educational system in North Carolina when he was a boy, he probably attended a poorly taught country school for only a few short winter sessions.

In 1867, his fortunes had so far improved that he was able to erect for a hardware store a building four stories high extending from a front on Fayetteville Street through the block to Salisbury Street. At that time, it was the largest building in Raleigh. How he managed to finance this venture when the South was financially bankrupt I have never been able to find out. The clerks in the store when I was a boy were named Womble, Whitfield, Sherman Pierce, Lindsay Lancaster, and Guy Bush. Mr. Spruill was the bookkeeper.

Before the war, Grandfather had built a large shop, a woodworking factory, on South West Street, where my father, John D., his assistant there, learned the building trade, inheriting the business when Grandfather died.

The hardware store supplemented the building business. In charge of it he placed his two older sons, Thomas H. Briggs, Jr., and James A. Briggs.

Needing banking facilities, Grandfather made a considerable investment in the Raleigh National Bank, the "Round Steps Bank," at the corner of Fayetteville and Halifax streets, in which he placed his youngest son, Fabius H. Briggs, who later became cashier.

Grandfather was the patriarch of the family in the old sense. Besides taking three of his sons into business with him and setting up the other in the bank that he partly owned, he strictly controlled all of them. As I recall, my father's salary, and probably that of my uncles, was twenty-five dollars a week; but there were occasional overdrafts, certainly in my family, which were met. In addition to the salaries paid the sons, there was a general account for all of the sons' families at the leading dry-goods store of W. H. & R. S. Tucker.

My grandmother and the daughters-in-law charged everything there that they needed; and at the end of the year an itemized bill, which I remember as being of many pages of legal-sized paper, was submitted. First Grandmother and then the four daughters-in-law in turns of seniority checked the items that they had bought, and then the bill was paid. . . . No hard feelings of any kind [were] engendered. This is a high tribute to all of them, who lived in entire amity and affection all of their days.

Grandfather was apparently fond of his grandchildren. Every Christmas, he gave each of us two silver dollars, which in those days was munificent. He also called on his sons' families on Sunday afternoons. He sometimes took me in the buggy with him when he made inspection of the buildings that he was constructing. The buggy, the leather of the strut holding up the top, worn off in one place where Grandfather habitually held his right hand, was drawn by Quixie, a gray mare, driven by Uncle Arthur and later by Uncle Paul.

Being a somewhat reticent man, Grandfather sometimes made criticisms of his workmen in a dramatic way. I remember that once while I was with him he noticed that unseasoned weatherboarding had been used on a house that he was building on Blount Street. Without a word, he took a hatchet and chopped the boards so that of necessity they had to be replaced. Then he climbed back into the buggy and was driven off.

In the shop itself, there were only white employees, among them several relatives. Cousin Billy Briggs, a nephew, was general superintendent, and Cousin Jim Parham worked at a bench. In 1891, their weekly wage was twelve dollars. The other workmen were paid at the rate prevailing at the time, from seventeen and a half cents an hour downward. The workweek was fifty-four hours in the winter and sixty in the summer. Among the workmen was Sam Ruth, so old that he had St. Vitus's dance. It was said that he was the only man who could use a lathe which had become eccentric; its wobbles and the St. Vitus's dance trembles synchronized.

Outside, there were two crews, one white under H. S. Keith as foreman, the other colored under Uncle Tom Williams, a superior man in every respect. One of his sons became a doctor, another a prominent teacher, and two were successful in business. Both crews worked together outside on buildings. So far as I overheard, there was never any conflict of any kind between the two racial crews.

Grandfather's sense of humor was inherited by all of his sons. Once at Christmas, Uncle Henry sent Aunt Lucinda, then very old, some towels. Hearing of the gift, Uncle Jim gave her some washcloths; my father sent some soap; and Uncle Fab some cologne. The old lady was much offended, saying that the boys must have thought that she smelled bad.

One Sunday afternoon as Grandfather was leaving our home after his customary call, I, perhaps five years old, ran down in politeness to open the gate for him. Instead of going through it, he stepped over the low picket fence, chuckling as he went.

"He sometimes took me in the buggy with him when he made inspection of the buildings that he was constructing."

A spectacle for progress

The North Carolina State Fair

BY DUANE PARIS
The News & Observer
October 8, 1968

When the first North Carolina State Fair opened in October 1853, the newspaper reported that hotels were crowded to capacity and the avenues were blockaded "with vehicles of every description."

Afterward, the *Raleigh Register* enthused, "Nearly every section of the State, and every industrial pursuit within its borders, was represented. The East sent its fine staples and its blooded stock; the West its splendid cattle and its rich minerals. The farmer poured in his agricultural products, the mechanic brought forward splendid specimens of his skill, the native artist exhibited the products of his pen or his pencil, and the ladies of the State, never behind in any good work or beneficial object, crowned the excellence of the whole with the multiplied beauties which nature had yielded to their culture, and the varied and tasteful attractions which had sprung from their handicrafts."

Tomorrow, October 9, North Carolina will kick off her hundredth State Fair, using the theme: "A Hundred Fairs of Progress." During the 115 years of the

The Great North Carolina Exposition of 1884, Grand Stand

N.C. Division of Archives and History

State Fair's history, in only 15 were exhibitions not held. These were during war years and periods of financial uncertainty.

The North Carolina State Fair was a product of the Agricultural Society of North Carolina from its beginning until 1927. For the next ten years, the society worked with the state and city governments. The fair was taken over by the state in 1937.

Theodore Roosevelt speaks at the 1905 State Fair. (left)
N.C. Division of Archives and History

Wake County Exhibit, 1884 (right)
N.C. Division of Archives and History

The first fairgrounds were a sixteen-acre site off New Bern Avenue, now the location of the state Department of Motor Vehicles building. Many of the display materials were brought up the "Blackwater," presumably up the Neuse River to the falls, and other materials were brought in by rail. All were transported free of charge.

As the years went by, the attractions grew in number and interest. One of these was the celebrated "Carolina Twins." The Siamese twins Millie-Christine were born near Whiteville in Columbus County. They were joined at the back; above this, they were perfectly developed females. They entertained the crowds with their soprano and alto voices, singing Southern songs and plantation melodies. After touring Europe for several years, the twins were able to speak French, German, and other languages.

A feature article in the *News & Observer* from October 1899 stirred interest in women's suffrage by asking if Millie-Christine would be entitled to one or two votes. No solution to the problem was reached.

In 1895, chicken incubators were of great interest at the fair. Spectators watched up to two hundred chickens being hatched at one time. Many practical men went into the business of raising orphan chickens, and many comments were provoked among them: "Mothers [were] laying eggs and grieving after those whom they could not gather under their wings. . . . These chickens may not have any manners, growing up without home training, but they will eat well if they do not have the flavor of kerosene oil that helps to hatch them."

The 1895 papers mentioned a list of the baldheaded and gray-headed gents who visited the "men only" shows, adding that the list may be printed after the fair was over.

Soldiers' dress march at the race-track, now the Rose Garden

N.C. Division of Archives and History

In 1873, the State Fair was moved to Cook's Hill, about one and a quarter miles outside the city limits, across from North Carolina State University and near what is now the Raleigh Little Theater. The fairgrounds then covered about 55 acres, and were used until 1926. The first fair on the present 250-acre site was held in 1929.

Around the turn of the century, the order of the day seemed to be public speeches. In 1905, President Theodore Roosevelt was the speaker, and two years later, William Jennings Bryan spoke for two hours.

James E. Briggs, a Raleigh businessman, says he remembers the fair of 1919 or 1920, when General Pershing was to speak. An opening salute to the general was fired, and the noise caused two mules pulling the cannon to run away. The army broke ranks, and one soldier shot at the mules, but missed. The general's opening remark that day amounted to a royal chewing out of the army for running.

Horse racing was always a popular sport at the fair. Professional horsemanship, with hunters, jumpers, and three- and five-gaited saddle horses, was introduced by Mrs. George K. Vanderbilt in 1925. The thrills, spills, and chills of the automobile races were introduced to the fair of 1936.

The year 1948 brought more entertainment than ever, some of which has returned year after year. It was that fall that the James E. Strates Shows arrived.

The exhibition has continually reflected the interests of the people and has kept abreast of the state's agricultural and industrial progress.

Oberlin

The village freedom built

BY GLENN ROBERTS
The Raleigh Times
January 1971

A freed slave from Edgecombe County and a carpetbagging sheriff from Brooklyn, New York, were key figures in the founding of Raleigh's Oberlin community. When it started in the late 1860s, though, Oberlin was described as a "village near the city of Raleigh." It was a rural farming area, separated from the city by several miles of woods.

James E. Harris fled from slavery in Edgecombe County in the 1830s and made his way to the abolitionist center of Oberlin College, in Oberlin, Ohio. Educated at that school, he came to Raleigh in 1865 and became one of the most famous black politicians the county had, serving two terms in the state House of Representatives and being elected a state senator in 1872.

Harris was a leading figure in the Oberlin area, serving as an official of both the National Freeman's Savings and Trust Company and the Raleigh Co-operative Land and Building Association. The area probably got its name from Harris's college, but no one is certain.

The first land to become available in the area came from the farm of Lewis W. Peck, who sold 1.75-acre lots for eighty dollars in 1866. On one of these original lots, a man named Thomas Williams built a home. In 1948, his grandson still lived in that house. Now, there is a bank on the site, at Oberlin Road and Clark Avenue.

The largest chunk of land to go on the market at the time came from the farm of politician and former editor William Boylan. Harris's land cooperative association bought five acres. Wake sheriff Timothy F. Lee bought thirty-four lots of the Boylan land, which he resold. A Union soldier from Brooklyn, Lee is referred to in some records as the only Northerner to become active in Wake politics.

Another patron of the area was St. Mary's College rector Dr. Aldert Smedes, who assisted servants at the school to purchase homes in the nearby village of Oberlin.

By 1870, the road to the village was known as Oberlin Road. By 1900, Oberlin ran from Hillsborough Street all the way to Glenwood Avenue. To the west, it reached to Beaver Dam Branch and what is now Brooks Avenue. A street that is probably named for Harris is nearly four miles west of Oberlin Road.

Along Beaver Dam Branch were farms owned by James Dodd and the Reverend M. L. Latta. A street named for Dodd—Dodd Lane—was legally closed to make way for a lawyers' office building. Latta, who also has a street named after him, began Latta University in 1892, a school formed "to solve the race problem."

The combination of assessments, taxes, and the Depression were just too much for some of the residents, and Oberlin land went up for sale at the courthouse door.

Oberlin Road
The News & Observer

Latta, by the way, claimed to have been born a slave on Cameron family lands along the Neuse River. It was the wooded Cameron estate—now Cameron Village—that separated the village of Oberlin from growing Raleigh.

Although Latta University soon failed, an elementary school in the area thrived. First built by residents of the area, the school was taken over by the Raleigh Township School Committee, which expanded the plank building to six rooms.

The Raleigh schools have a deed for part of the school site, signed in 1883 by Needham Broughton, school committee chairman. A brick school was built on the same site in 1916, and stood for fifty-three years.

Although a rural community at first, Oberlin soon found a city growing around it. Nearby North Carolina State University was a major source of jobs for the residents.

According to some Oberlin residents, the extensive community first began to shrink in the late 1920s, when the recently annexed area got a paved street from the Raleigh commissioners. The combination of assessments, taxes, and the Depression were just too much for some of the residents, and Oberlin land went up for sale at the courthouse door.

But by 1948, the area was still extensive. According to a newspaper article by Willis G. Briggs, the Oberlin community included a thousand people in 175 houses. With the opening of Cameron Village a year later and Wade Avenue, the Oberlin area began to shrink quickly, from twelve blocks along Oberlin Road in 1948 to less than half that today. Many of the residences are now zoned for office use. The area is dotted with empty lots and For Sale signs.

W. W. Holden

The career of an enigma

BY HORACE W. RAPER
The News & Observer
July 1985

William Woods Holden was a dominant figure in mid-nineteenth-century North Carolina, a figure about whom few people had, or could afford to have, neutral feelings.

A progressive editor and secessionist before the Civil War, he led a peace movement calling for a negotiated peace and was rewarded with appointment as the provisional Reconstruction governor. Later elected to the governor's office, he overreached his powers and became the first United States governor to be impeached.

Born out of wedlock in Hillsborough in 1818, and without traditional family benefits or formal education, Holden rose to become an influential newspaper editor, a leader in the formation of three political parties, and twice the state's chief executive. At the age of ten, he was apprenticed to the printing trade, working with the *Hillsborough Recorder* and later the *Raleigh Star*. During the latter job, Holden studied law, receiving his license in 1841.

But journalism was his real love, and in 1843 he became owner and publisher of the *North Carolina Standard*, the Democratic organ. As editor, he had a brilliant record and won the popular support of the people throughout the state. A strong advocate of the "common folk," he championed equal suffrage, universal education, internal improvements, labor reforms, and a balanced economy for the state.

By the early 1850s, Holden had become the tactical leader of the Democratic Party, which he led to power by directing the successful gubernatorial campaigns of David S. Reid and Thomas Bragg.

In 1858, having "elected" men of lesser ability, he sought the party's nomination. When it and the United States senatorship were denied because of his vigorous reformist stance, he began to break with the party. But the break did not become final until after the secession crisis of 1860–61.

Earlier, as a Calhoun Democrat, Holden had supported the Southern views on the expansion of slavery to the west and on secession, but by 1860 he had shifted his loyalties to the Union. He had the support of most of the people in clinging to the Union, but the outbreak of hostilities at Fort Sumter forced Holden and the people into the secession. In 1862, he engineered the formation of the Conservative Party and the election of Zebulon Vance as governor.

Sensing the futility of the Civil War, however, he worked for an honorable

W. W. Holden
1818–92

W. W. Holden's house at the corner of McDowell and Hargett streets

N.C. Division of Archives and History

peace rather than unconditional surrender. For such views, he was denounced as a traitor, his *Standard* office was destroyed by Georgia troops, and he was defeated in the 1864 gubernatorial election.

His peace-movement activities led President Andrew Johnson to appoint him provisional governor of North Carolina at the end of the war. Although his administration restored federal authority and some prosperity, he lost in the November election. Later, as radical Republicans gained control of Reconstruction policies, Holden believed it would be disastrous to resist further congressional control. Thus, he not only embraced Republicanism but organized the party in the state, leading it to victory in 1868 by winning the governorship.

As governor, Holden faced many problems in reorganizing local governments, establishing an integrated public-school system, enacting penal reform, rebuilding and expanding the railroads, and obtaining equal justice for all persons. Personal animosities prevented political harmony in his administration, his critics charging him with being an opportunist and a tyrant. Although opponents accused him of financial excesses and favoring blacks, he was never proved to be dishonest or lacking personal integrity.

When civil rights, suffrage, and rights to hold office were extended to blacks, resistance developed throughout the state, and the Ku Klux Klan was organized to restore white supremacy. Holden was forced to take strong measures, with President Ulysses S. Grant's endorsement, in maintaining law and order. These measures culminated in confrontation, or the so-called Kirk-Holden War. In 1870, Holden declared Alamance and Caswell counties in insurrection, organized two regiments of state troops led by Colonel George W. Kirk, and began arresting leading Klansmen, including Josiah Turner, Jr., the strident editor of the *Raleigh Sentinel*, which had criticized Holden and the "carpetbagger assembly." Before the Klansmen were brought to trial, they were released by Judge George W. Brooks of Salisbury. Holden was impeached, convicted, and removed from office. He is the only North Carolina governor with that distinction.

In 1871, he was named political editor of the *Washington* (D.C.) *Chronicle*, although he was never happy in the position. He returned to Raleigh in 1872 to serve as postmaster, a position he retained until 1883. In retirement, he devoted his energies to local civic affairs, church work, and writing. His home, at the corner of Hargett and McDowell streets, became the focal point of lively discussions among politicians and professionals from all persuasions, but his political disabilities were never removed.

Holden suffered several paralytic strokes which left him a virtual invalid. He died in 1892 and was buried in Oakwood Cemetery.

The freedman's 'mania'

Shaw University and St. Augustine's College

BY DAVID PERKINS

"The Freedman has a disease of learning. It is a mania with him," wrote the *Journal of Freedom*, a pro-black journal published in Raleigh in 1865. It might have added that Northern missionaries were equally feverish to teach him.

Postwar Raleigh was, as the *Daily Progress* put it, "a seething, rushing, boiling cauldron . . . the streets being entirely filled with soldiers, negroes, men and women, and strangers from the four quarters."

In the backwash of Sherman's army, hundreds of freed slaves had thronged into the city. One visitor to the Guion Hotel on Capitol Square, which the Yankee generals had designated as a Negro headquarters, counted three hundred to four hundred blacks crowded into eight to ten rooms.

Within weeks, doughty men and women from the North were arriving at the rail depot, determined to teach the freedmen and -women.

Some old Raleighites reacted to the visitors, it may be supposed, with the coolness of Kemp P. Battle, a lawyer and future president of the University of North Carolina. Of one Yankee schoolteacher, he wrote, "His duties, as he believed, required him to receive in his home visits from colored people. He had my sympathy and I met him courteously but did not think it my duty to call on him." Many freedmen's schools lasted only a few months. But the city's two his-

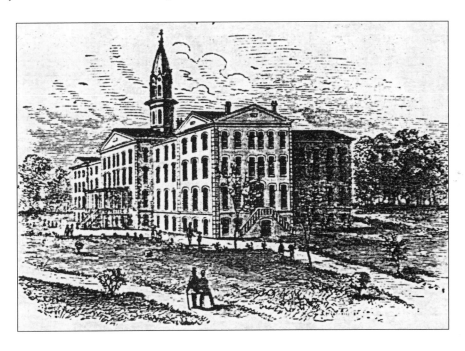

Shaw Hall was built by the students with handmade bricks.

Branson's North Carolina Business Directory, 1872. North Carolina Collection, UNC-Chapel Hill

torically black colleges founded in the postwar years have survived: Shaw University and St. Augustine's College.

They were as unlike each other as were the denominations from which they sprang. Shaw was the fruit of a single man's vision, ambitious in scope, and embroiled in city politics from the beginning. St. Augustine's was closely tied to its sponsoring church, narrower in ambition, and more aloof from the city. It was from Shaw's gates that sit-down strikers emerged in the 1960s, but the sedate St. Augustine's has been financially more secure.

One of the first of the Northerners to arrive was a thirty-four-year-old

Henry Tupper

Union veteran, a graduate of Amherst College and Newton Theological Seminary, Henry Martin Tupper.

Shaw University

Tupper was still in uniform when he appeared before the American Baptist Home Mission Society in New York and asked to be sent south. His assignment was to train talented blacks to become ministers and leaders in a Baptist Church that was splitting along racial lines.

Arriving in October 1865, he and his wife were the first ticket holders on the revived Portsmouth, Virginia–Raleigh railroad. Tupper found the black congregation of the First Baptist Church still meeting in the church basement. He asked permission to preach to them, but was denied. In December 1865, Tupper held his first Bible classes, instead, in the Guion Hotel on Edenton Street. If one takes that as the founding date of what became Shaw University, Tupper's school is perhaps the oldest higher-education institution for blacks in the United States. A few months later, Mrs. Tupper began classes for women in her home.

In February 1866, Tupper organized his own church, Second Baptist Church, and spent his soldier's savings of five hundred dollars on a tract at the corner of Blount and Cabarrus streets, where he and his students built a two-story structure, with one floor to serve the church, the other Tupper's Raleigh Theological Institute. (The building survives as Tupper Baptist Church.)

By 1870, the institute had several hundred students in day and night classes and needed more room. Tupper bid for the Peace Institute property on Peace Street, then up for sale, but prominent whites were indignant and caused the deal to collapse. Tupper finally bought the South Street estate of Daniel M. Barringer, former United States minister to Spain, for his campus. This was no more welcome to some than the earlier bid, and a crowd hunted Tupper down, apparently intending him harm. Tupper and his wife escaped injury by hiding out in the Barringer estate's cotton fields.

Toward purchase of the Barringer land, a Massachusetts textile manufacturer, Elijah Shaw, gave Tupper five thousand dollars, and the school was renamed Shaw Collegiate Institute.

A four-story main building, Shaw Hall, was built by Tupper's students with bricks they made from the clay on the property. (It was torn down in 1967.) Another large building rose to house the Estey Seminary for Women, paid for with a gift from Jacob Estey and Sons, a Vermont manufacturer.

Always, Tupper's ambitions raced ahead of the money on hand. In 1874, Tupper sold the leftover bricks and took the Shaw Jubilee Singers on a nine-month tour of the North. The next year, "The Shaw University" was chartered by the General Assembly.

Tupper's proprietary relationship to the institute left him vulnerable to charges of "making money off colored people." Some disaffected church members also filed groundless lawsuits and forced him out of the church, impairing his credibility in the North.

ESTEY HALL: 'THE FINEST EDIFICE'

Estey Hall is thought to be the oldest college building for black women in the United States. It was built in 1873 for the Estey Female Seminary, the feminine partner to Shaw Collegiate Institute. On a fund-raising tour in the North in 1872, H. M. Tupper, who founded both, raised eight thousand dollars for the building from Jacob Estey, a Vermont manufacturer. The Shaw Jubilee Singers, on the same tour, raised another four thousand dollars. G. S. H. Appleget, an architect who had arrived from New Jersey after the war, designed what Tupper called "the finest school-edifice in the state." The bricks were made by Shaw students from clay on the property.

In 1874, the seminary was incorporated into Shaw as the Female Department. The building was used continuously by the university until 1967, when it was scheduled for demolition. A biracial citizens' committee saved the hall in the late 1970s. With a federal grant and matching funds from the city and private contributions, Estey Hall was restored and reopened as a community center for south Raleigh in 1993.

N.C. Division of Archives and History

Despite his troubles, Tupper was a tireless teacher. "Up to 1875, the institution was in many respects like the one-room schoolhouse," writes Shaw historian Wilmoth Carter, "in which a single person served as principal and teacher and taught from four to seven grades concomitantly. Tupper was not only the creator and builder but also business manager and teacher. In addition to other chores, he taught from 7:00 A.M. to 5:00 P.M. with an hour's intermission, and had charge of the night school."

Tupper's ambitions were never narrow, and Shaw expanded into professional education. The Leonard Medical School opened in 1881. A law school was added in 1888 and a school of pharmacy in 1890. All three closed by 1919.

St. Augustine's College

The Reverend J. Brinton Smith, the first rector of St. Augustine's Normal School and Collegiate Institute, believed as passionately as Tupper in educating freedmen. "I see no difference between them and white children," he said.

There, however, the resemblance ended. Smith picked his students with care; he did not charge for tuition; and he prided himself on keeping the school out of Reconstruction politics.

"Ours is the one [Negro] school in Raleigh whose teachers are not active politicians," he wrote in the *Spirit of Missions* periodical. "We have the confidence of the White community and the best portion of the Negroes."

St. Augustine's also was founded with a more limited ambition than Shaw: to produce teachers for the freedmen's schools.

A St. Augustine's class in the early 1900s (top)

N.C. Division of Archives and History

St. Augustine's Normal School and Collegiate Institute, 1899 (bottom)

N.C. Division of Archives and History

In 1865, the Episcopal Church called on Smith, then a pastor and head of a school for poor children in Jersey City, New Jersey, to lead a new Freedmen's Commission. Smith believed that what the freed blacks needed most were "teachers of their own color" and fixed on the idea of a normal school.

In 1867, Smith secured a twenty-five-thousand-dollar bequest from a Pittsburgh minister and found an ally in the Reverend Thomas Atkinson, the Episcopal bishop of North Carolina, who had a similar ambition. Smith enlisted the support of prominent Raleigh Episcopalians, including Reverend Aldert Smedes, rector of St. Mary's. And on January 13, 1868, the school opened at the Union army barracks on the original state fairgrounds, then called Camp Russell. It had four students.

Kemp P. Battle, who became the school's secretary, praised Smith for trying to "mitigate hostile feelings between soldiers and citizens of the North and South." At a party at Smith's home, Battle found himself playing blindman's bluff with the general of the Union garrison.

Later in 1868, Smith arranged to buy the former estate of Henry Seawell east of Raleigh, where patriot Willie Jones had once owned a summer home, for a permanent campus. By 1875, fifty-eight St. Augustine's alumni were teaching in the field.

Under Smith's successor, the Reverend John E. C. Smedes, a son of the Reverend Aldert Smedes, the school broadened its mission to include ministerial training. The Reverend Aaron Hunter became principal in 1891. It was the time of Booker T. Washington's self-improvement movement, and Hunter added mechanical and vocational training. When the campus was destroyed by fire in 1883 (the city fire brigade did not serve that part of town), St. Augustine's students rebuilt it.

Toward the end of the century, Mrs. Hunter raised funds to open St. Agnes Hospital, one of the major hospitals for blacks in the Southeast until it closed in the early 1960s.

St. Augustine's discarded its precollege and vocational courses in 1928 and became a four-year liberal-arts college.

Anna Cooper

A critic of all favoritisms

BY DAVID PERKINS

"We take our stand on the solidarity of humanity, the oneness of life, and injustice of all special favoritisms, whether of sex, race, country, or condition."

The year was 1893, and Raleigh native Anna Cooper was waxing eloquent at the Women's Congress in Chicago. The topic before the biracial gathering, timed to coincide with the Columbian Exposition, was the "Intellectual Progress of Colored Women Since Emancipation."

The speakers were so moving that the elderly abolitionist Frederick Douglass, a platform guest, rose to speak: "I have heard tonight what I never expected to hear. I have heard refined, educated colored ladies addressing—and addressing successfully—one of the most intelligent white audiences I ever looked upon."

If the tone was patronizing, the progress had indeed been remarkable. And no one epitomized it better than Anna Cooper. In the twenty-eight years since the end of the war, this freed slave from Raleigh had become a national voice for racial and female equality. She would also become a leading high-school principal, the founder of a night school, and the fourth black American woman to receive a doctorate.

Born about 1859, Anna was the daughter of Hannah Stanley Haywood, a slave in the household of Fabius Haywood, a Raleigh doctor and planter. Her obituaries indicate her father was George Washington Haywood, a slave. However, Cooper wrote in her later years that the man was "presumably" the master himself, "although my mother was too shamefaced ever to mention him."

During the war, she joked later, she served "many an anxious slave's superstition to wake the baby up and ask directly, 'Which side is going to win the war? Will de Yankees beat de Rebs or will Linkum free de Niggers?' "

Perhaps because of the Haywoods' standing, Anna was one of the first recruits for the St. Augustine's Normal School and Collegiate Institute, an Episcopal school founded to train black teachers and ministers. She received a hundred-dollar-a-year stipend for board and tuition from the Freedmen's Bureau. She excelled at her studies and soon became a teacher's assistant or "coach." By 1873, at fourteen, she was regularly employed as a teacher.

Still, she found herself constantly up against the low expectations of the

Anna Cooper
c. 1859–1964

rector, the Reverend John E. C. Smedes. She met one obstacle with the outburst that "the only mission opening for a girl in his school was to marry one of the [ministerial] candidates."

Anna did marry a theology student, George Cooper, a native of Nassau who became the second black ordained an Episcopal priest in North Carolina. When he died two years later, the tragedy opened the way for a teaching career.

Anna finished the teaching course—while continuing to teach for fifty dollars a week. But as St. Augustine's did not yet offer a degree, she headed north to Oberlin College in Oberlin, Ohio, a town at the end of the Underground Railroad that was busy with freed slaves and abolitionists. Oberlin was one of the first Northern colleges to admit blacks. After receiving a master's degree in 1884 (she had once again raised a fuss by refusing to take the non-degree "Ladies Course"), Cooper prepared to return to St. Augustine's. Dr. Smedes had promised her a professorship. However, his successor, the Reverend Robert Sutton, reduced the offer to "teacher in charge of girls," and she took a post, instead, at Wilberforce College in Ohio.

Cooper already had made a name for herself as an author and lecturer. *A Voice from the South,* her 1892 collection of essays on women's rights and higher education, was called by the *New York Independent* "a piercing and clinging cry which it is impossible to hear and not to understand." Cooper was one of three black women invited to address the World's Congress of Representative Women in 1893, and one of a few women speakers at the Pan-African Congress in London in 1900.

In 1901, she was appointed principal of M Street High School, later Dunbar High School, in Washington, the largest "colored" high school in the country. She was one of two female principals in the segregated school system. Defying her white supervisor, who wanted M Street students to follow a vocational course, she pushed her students to prepare for college and eventually boasted of the first black students from a public school to be admitted to Harvard. Her strong personality and some rumor-mongering on the staff led to her dismissal in 1906. She was invited back in 1910 to teach Latin.

In the civic arena, Cooper helped start the Colored Women's YWCA in 1905, in reaction to the Jim Crow policies of the white YWCA. The next year, she was a supervisor at the Colored Settlement House, the first social-service agency for the District of Columbia's blacks.

Anna Cooper was a quiet, scholarly woman who preferred what she called the "lesser limelight" to the soapbox or the march. In midlife, she adopted five children, bought a large house at T Street, and undertook a Ph.D. at the Sorbonne. Defying her principal (it was a habit by now), she took a ship to Paris to defend her dissertation on the medieval epic *Le Pelerinage de Charlemagne*. At sixty-five, she became the fourth black American woman to earn a doctorate, according to her *Washington Post* obituary.

From 1929 to 1941, she was president of Frelinghuysen University, a night school for working blacks which she moved into her villa-style home on T Street. She died in 1964 at 105 and was buried in Raleigh City Cemetery.

John Rex and R. Stanhope Pullen

Bachelors who helped make the town

The News & Observer
June 6, 1907

It is the purpose here to call to mind a brace of Raleigh bachelors, one of them so old indeed that after a diligent search, there could not be found one who knew him in life; the other a wise, eccentric, and kindly man.

The first, John Rex, was one of those who see and feel beyond their time. He was in a sense a pioneer in philanthropy. Though we know nothing of John Rex which would not put upon him the brand of mediocrity in life, we have the fact of his greatness of insight.

Before 1839, Rex, living in a time when patients were being bled, when the rule was to "starve a fever and stuff a cold," when the jail was the place for imbeciles, and the indigent sick went to the "poorhouse," devised the bulk of what was for the day a considerable fortune in trust for the establishment of a hospital for the indigent sick of the people of Raleigh.

By another bequest in the same will, he recognized over sixty-eight years ago that slavery was incompatible with civilization; and he recognized, also, the expedient that might once have availed to bring the country through its history without the horrors of war and saved "Reconstruction" and the problem of today—the expedient that even now good men are turning to as the remedy without hope of its being applied—the deportation of the Negroes to Africa!

In the will, the clause providing for this disposition of John Rex's slaves displays the temper of the man—the eccentric habit which was handmaiden to his philanthropy and his genius. One man might have turned loose his slaves and provided for their transportation. John Rex saw a very clear difficulty in the possibility that his Negroes might take their freedom and refuse the journey. He provided against the contingency with what must have been characteristic humor. If any slave should refuse to be transported, such a slave was to be forthwith put upon the block and sold, the proceeds to be turned over to the fund which had been set apart for the deportation and keep of the other servants of the devisor.

Examination of the proceedings with relation to the John Rex estate discloses the fact that his twenty or more slaves were duly settled in Africa, the remnant of the fund of upwards of five thousand dollars after cost of their passage being duly applied to their benefit and keep in Africa.

For years, the Rex Hospital has stood a monument to the man who saw the need in a time that saw it not.

Growth of Rex's gift

All that is known of John Rex is that he was a bachelor, that he was an Irishman, and that he had made a success in Raleigh as a tanner. The fund devoted to

Rex Hospital at its first site, the former home of Governor Charles Manly on South Street

N.C. Division of Archives and History

Rex Hospital consisted of several tracts of land, bank stock in the old antebellum Cape Fear Bank, and other personal securities. The location of the hospital as indicated in his will was to be upon twenty-one acres of land in southwest Raleigh near the lands of the penitentiary. The lands were bounded by what was known as the "Sylvester Smith lands," the "Asylum Road," and the lands of the late William Boylan. With the sale of the lands the board of trustees came into possession of a small fund with which they eventually bought the old St. John's Hospital, and erected an annex, which, with management and some gifts, has now grown to an income-producing fund of about thirty thousand dollars.

Before the fund became sufficiently large to endow the institution, the Civil War intervened, the securities became worthless, and what was a great idea seemed for years to have failed in execution. The present trustees of an estate which is above forty thousand dollars in value entered upon their duties as the guardians of a paltry four thousand dollars. But for years, the Rex Hospital has stood a monument to the man who saw the need in a time that saw it not; and, ever-widening in usefulness, is now upon the point of being placed in a building commensurate with modern ideas and equipped for modern service.

Pullen sketched

Of Mr. Pullen there is a sharper memory, drawn in the lines of his idiosyncrasies, his humour, and his benefactions. And yet, so vagrant is the fancy of the eye, that none can say exactly how he looked, striking as he was. He regarded photographers and the whole cult of painters and portraiturists askance; and not an example of the features of one who, a dozen years ago, was known to every man, woman, and child in the city remains—daguerreotype, photograph, or sketch.

Mr. Pullen did nothing in a hurry—not even the matter of "joining the church," which he accomplished in ripe age and on his own initiative. (He joined Edenton Street Methodist Church.) Who has not seen his striking figure as he walked in the fields and suburbs of the city, alone and meditative, yet keenly alive and observant!

Gifts to the city

His first gift to the city was one in which he himself profited—the opening up of northeast Raleigh, beginning at North Street and running north to the old Mordecai line and east to near the present site of Oakwood Cemetery. This large tract of land, which he purchased of the Raynor estate, he personally cut up into streets and lots, many of which he sold, retaining, however, a considerable tract of land between Oakwood Avenue and Polk Street, which he developed according to his own idea, building thereon a number of substantial brick dwellings and creating a new residence district which, for years, was called "Pullen Town."

A few houses survive in the 1870s development known as "Pullen Town," in Oakwood

N.C. Division of Archives and History

The whole of this development was his own idea and carried out in all its arrangements, including practically the planning of the dwellings. While first and last, his real-estate operations in the north of Raleigh must have been very lucrative, it took the eye of a student and progressive man to see the future and seize it.

When in 1871 he bought the property at the considerable outlay for the period of eight thousand dollars, the old Polk or Raynor mansion, afterwards the Baptist school, stood at North Street looking south and stopping the development of the city. All of Raleigh, therefore, north and east of North and Blount streets, one of the most valuable and desirable of the residential sections of the city, grew from the Pullen idea.

His other gifts of public benefit to the city are included in the tract of land on which the Agricultural and Mechanical College now stands—given by him in aid of that institution and to secure its location at Raleigh—and of the land which afterwards became known as "Pullen Park."

It was in the scheme of the Pullen Park and the A&M College sites that Mr. Pullen took perhaps more abiding interest than in any other of his enterprises. Here, too, he saw far ahead and devised the idea of an avenue or driveway which should divide the grounds of the college from those of the Pullen Park, furnishing easy access to the park by pleasure seekers and an agreeable route for an afternoon's outing.

In the park grounds, Mr. Pullen gave his native genius for landscape gardening full play, and he spent hours upon hours in planting, in terracing, in bringing his mind to see in the uncultivated fields the future which holds so much mature promise of his genius today.

Charitable peculiarities

Among the people, his charities were unnumbered. He gave always of his own motion—and he was always giving. In his later years, he might almost have been said to pass his time watching for needs and listening for distress. His office was

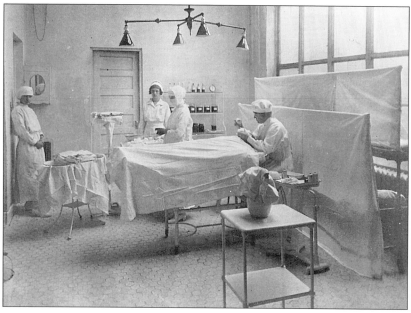

An aerial view of Pullen Park, early 1940s (top)
N.C. Division of Archives and History

An operation at Rex Hospital, early 1900s (bottom)
N.C. Division of Archives and History

on the street. He "hung out." One of his stands was Jones & Powell's feed store. There he would sit and meditate and plan. When something stuck, he went away and sat down and turned it over. Then he acted quickly, positively, and without discussion, frequently anonymously, and always with the desire of avoiding comment.

As he became older and dropped the active pursuit of money, he took rank as a philanthropist. But very speedily, the community learned that it would not do to ask him for money. On this point, he was open to sore offense. Even in the Edenton Street Methodist Church, to which he belonged and of which he was the richest member, it was never thought to put the name of Stanhope Pullen on the assessment list. When the handsome church was building, no one asked him for a contribution. Yet he watched the building and calculated its cost. When the time seemed ripe for mortising with money, he drew his check and turned it in without comment.

It is recalled how he was seen in conversation on the street with a portly preacher larding in the fat of piety and unction, who was engaged in selling a paper published to liquidate the debt of a church; how his high voice was heard in one or two sharp and decisive remarks before he turned on his heel and, his face red with anger, approached a friend with the indignant exclamation, "What do you think that fellow said to me! He asked me for a dollar."

METROPOLITAN HALL

A full block long, three stories high, and made of brick to resist fire, it was an edifice designed to shout that the city was on the rebound after the war. Taxpayers approved a bond issue of fifty thousand dollars to pay for it.

Metropolitan Hall, as it was unofficially known, was built in 1870 on Fayetteville Street between Martin and Hargett streets. For forty years, it was the hub of Raleigh, serving as city hall, police station, town auditorium, and Farmers Market.

Police officers and firemen shared the ground floor with farmers selling produce, city court was held on the second, and parts of the second and third floors were given over to a large auditorium.

On the same site, a market building and a municipal hall, facing Fayetteville and Wilmington streets, respectively, had burned in 1868. The city's first Farmers Market had been nearby, on Hargett Street between Wilmington and Fayetteville streets. But in the 1840s, public outcry against the neighboring "Grog Alley" saloons forced the city to move it to Fayetteville Street.

By 1911, the market was run-down and the auditorium was little used. (The smell of fish from below?) A new city hall and auditorium were built on Fayetteville and Davie streets, where the Branch Bank and Trust Company is today. And a new City Market followed on Martin Street in 1914. Metropolitan Hall was torn down in 1920 and replaced with the Gilmer–Montgomery Ward building and, later, Wachovia Bank.

N.C. Division of Archives and History

N.C. Division of Archives and History

To wake a 'slumbering' state

North Carolina State University

BY GUY MUNGER
The News & Observer
March 18, 1987

The date was March 1, 1887, and the General Assembly was grinding toward adjournment when the showdown came in the House of Representatives. On the calendar was "an act to establish and maintain an industrial school." Opponents, many fearing a diversion of money from the university at Chapel Hill, offered a series of crippling amendments.

The school that was to become North Carolina State University was beginning its hundred-year journey from agriculture to aerospace with a knockdown legislative battle.

The *News & Observer* reported the following day that one of the amendments, sent up by Representative Joel L. Crisp of Graham County, would require that "each farmer have an agricultural college on his own farm, and that his whole family be required to attend twelve months in each year, free of tuition." The amendment, obviously frivolous, was ruled out of order, and other more serious efforts to kill the measure were beaten back. Six days later, on March 7, 1887,

A view of Hillsborough Street with North Carolina A&M in the background, 1909

Carolina Power and Light Company

the legislation was enacted and the North Carolina College of Agriculture and Mechanic Arts became a reality.

The school was to be built on sixty-two acres west of Raleigh donated by R. Stanhope Pullen, a wealthy real-estate developer, and operated in conjunction with an already established agricultural experiment station on nearby land. Income from the sale of public lands under the 1862 federal Morrill Act was transferred from the University of North Carolina at Chapel Hill to the new school, making A&M the state's land-grant college. The cornerstone of Main Building—later renamed Holladay Hall—was laid in August 1888, and the first students began classes on October 3, 1889.

Holladay Hall in the early 1900s
N.C. Division of Archives and History

N.C. State's earliest supporters would be startled by how their hundred-year-old offspring has grown. As N.C. State entered its centennial year last fall, enrollment was a record 24,000-plus, its budget topped $365 million, a State of the Future Endowment Fund had reached a goal of $32 million, and plans had been announced for a 780-acre Centennial Campus expansion on nearby state-owned land.

It is a long way from N.C. State's beginnings in the economic turmoil that followed the Civil War. North Carolina agriculture was devastated, and the state was sharing in none of the industrial expansion of the North or the growth of the Western frontier.

Two widely divergent groups joined to do something about what they called the "slumbering" state—the Watauga Club, an organization of young men formed in Raleigh in 1884 to promote a state industrial school and other projects, and farmer interests led by Leonidas L. Polk, founder of the *Progressive Farmer* magazine and a longtime advocate of agrarian reform.

Inevitably, they ran into conflict with backers of the university at Chapel Hill, which had followed the European tradition of educating young men in the classics, preparing them for such careers as the law or the ministry. Polk was scathing in denouncing what he saw as the university's feeble efforts at providing technical education. When the university announced in 1886 that it was establishing a College of Agriculture and Mechanic Arts, Polk wrote in his magazine that it had been "a long, very long hatching period for such a little chicken." He added, "It is a model of architectural beauty and admirably equipped in all its various departments. It is located on the 49th page of the Catalogue of our

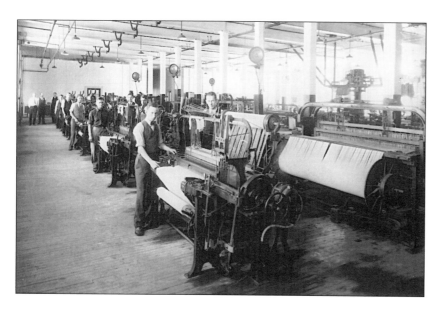

A&M students at the looms in Tompkins Hall, 1920s

N.C. Division of Archives and History

University." Unfortunately, said Polk, not one North Carolina farm boy had availed himself of any of the courses.

When A&M finally opened for classes in Raleigh with Alexander Q. Holladay as president, applicants were required to be at least fourteen years old, and of good moral character, with a knowledge of English, North Carolina history, and arithmetic through fractions. Tuition was set at twenty dollars a year, board fees were eight dollars a month, and room rent was ten dollars a year.

Walter J. Matthews of Asheville, the first student to enroll at A&M, recalled in a 1955 interview how the college not only fed the students and provided a place to sleep, but even supplied the paper tablets on which they wrote and arranged to have their laundry done at the state prison. There was no running water in the residence hall, so each student had a pitcher and washbowl and carried his own water from a well about fifty feet away.

Of the seventy-two students who enrolled as freshmen in 1889, only nineteen graduated in 1893, but by then A&M was a going concern and ready to grow.

Military science was added to the required curriculum in 1894. Then, when George T. Winston became president in 1899, a more stringent code was adopted. All students in the school were called "cadets" and were required to wear blue-gray uniforms with white gloves. Students marched to and from chapel every day and to all meals.

In 1904, when Winston revoked the seniors' privilege of visiting downtown Raleigh once a week, thirty-two of the forty-five members of the senior class rebelled and went home for a month until the president relented. The episode came to be known as the "Thug Revolt," since Winston had called the participants "thugs."

The twentieth century opened with a surge of technical advances—powered flight, radio, discoveries in the basic sciences—and North Carolina A&M shifted its emphasis. Practical work gave way to laboratory science, and in 1917 the school's name was changed to North Carolina State College of Agriculture and Engineering. Off-campus activity increased in 1909 with the formation of a Department of Agricultural Extension to spread new ideas in farm technology and home economics.

Sports shared in the growth, and by 1910 baseball had reached such popularity that the legislature finally declared an official state holiday on Easter Monday, the date of the traditional game with Wake Forest. State's football teams won championships in 1910, 1913, and 1917, but 1918 was a disaster. Military training for World War I and a deadly flu epidemic forced cancellations of most games. For a game against Georgia Tech in Atlanta, State players who were in a nearby army camp were given leave for the afternoon so they could take part. State was crushed 128–0, but an outstanding performance by tackle John H. Riple helped make him State's first All-America athlete.

During World War I, the campus resembled an armed camp. Students wore olive-drab uniforms, bayonet drills were held on Riddick Field, and seven thousand soldiers were encamped in a tent city across Hillsborough Street, training at Camp Polk for tank warfare. The rapid growth in enrollment after the war brought a reorganization of the administration, new degree programs in biology, chemistry, physics, and business, and an independent School of Textiles. The 1920s also saw an effort by religious fundamentalists in three sessions of the legislature to ban the teaching of evolution in biology courses. Fearing such a law would hamper agricultural breeding work and the teaching of biology and geology, scientists at State College joined others to help defeat the proposal.

In June 1927, State College granted degrees to women for the first time. Receiving diplomas were two women who had done much of their academic work elsewhere—Jane S. McKimmon, home demonstration leader, and Charlotte Nelson, daughter of the dean of the School of Textiles—and Mary E. Yarborough, who did all of her college work at State and was a daughter of a member of the first graduating class.

The stock-market crash of 1929 and the Great Depression that followed sent State College (and the rest of the country) into an economic crisis. In 1931, in an effort to cut back on spending, Governor O. Max Gardner, an alumnus, successfully pushed legislation establishing a consolidated University of North Carolina that merged under a single administration the University of North Carolina at Chapel Hill, North Carolina State, and what was then the North Carolina College for Women in Greensboro.

A survey team appointed after the merger recommended that State College become a junior college and that all upper-level courses be offered in Chapel Hill. The proposal would have stripped State of its School of Engineering, School of Science and Business, and graduate school. But Frank P. Graham, who became president of the university system after consolidation, succeeded in getting UNC

North Carolina A&M
N.C. Division of Archives and History

trustees to approve the closing of the engineering school at Chapel Hill and the continuation of N.C. State as a full-fledged college.

From 1940 to 1945, during World War II, the resources of N.C. State were almost totally committed to national defense. Some fifty members of the faculty served on active military duty, and the number of civilian students on campus hit a low of seven hundred.

The military more than took up the slack. There were research projects to develop new diesel engines, to improve materials for radar, radios, and medical equipment, and to find a substitute for the silk used in parachutes. By the end of World War II, more than twenty-six thousand men and women had received either military or industrial training for the war effort at State College. With the coming of peace, N.C. State exploded with activity. Enrollment rose from a high of twenty-five hundred before the war to forty-seven hundred in 1946, with the admissions office processing more than a thousand applications a month from returning veterans.

Temporary classrooms were pressed into service—old two-story wooden barracks with walls so thin that lectures in one classroom could be heard in another. The barracks, however, were favored over metal Quonset huts, where students baked in hot weather and froze in cold weather. If they were assigned a place near the sloping walls, students had to hunch over their desks, unable to sit upright.

Many of the postwar students were married with small children, and for them the college provided trailers and prefabricated housing in little villages with names like Tailwood and Vetville. Totsville, a day-care center, was opened on the western edge of the campus.

Two new schools were established during the period—the School of Architecture and Landscape Design (soon changed to the School of Design) and the School of Forestry.

The School of Design attracted national attention under Dean Henry L. Kamphoefner, drawing such internationally known visitors as Frank Lloyd Wright, Lewis Mumford, and Buckminster Fuller, and having on its faculty men like Eduardo Catalano and Matthew Nowicki.

State College also advanced in scientific research. In 1951, it offered the nation's first bachelor's, master's, and doctoral programs in nuclear engineering, and two years later, the college built a nuclear reactor, the first nuclear pile in the nation to be used exclusively for teaching and research, the first non–Atomic Energy Commission reactor on a college campus, and the first to be open for public inspection.

Research activity grew even more under John T. Caldwell, chancellor from 1959 to 1975. During that time, enrollment also boomed, from 5,300 undergraduate and 700 graduate students to 12,800 undergraduates and 2,600 in graduate schools.

During the mid-1950s and early 1960s, there was growing sentiment to change State College's name to North Carolina State University. State College was one of six land-grant institutions in the country not yet designated a university.

A NORTHERN VISITOR'S VIEW OF THE COLLEGE

From *Harper's Illustrated Weekly*, 1891

Raleigh has several fine educational foundations, but one that interested me very much indeed was the College of Agriculture and Mechanic Arts. The other Southern States possess more or less similar institutions, maintained with Federal aid, and if they are in any great degree as well and even proudly managed as this of North Carolina, it is a grand thing, particularly where men have been too prone to think it undignified to work for themselves. Here we find an expensively housed and well-equipped institution, which, although only four years old, has already graduated one class, two-thirds of whose members obtained situations at once. Both teachers and pupils were alike enthusiastic when I went through the buildings.

I found there a line smithy, a forge-room, a machine-shop (in which stood a steam-engine made by the graduates); a wood-turning department and joiner-work class-room; a very fine chemical laboratory presided over by an ambitious Cornell man; a model barn, a dairy building, a large experimental farm, and an agricultural experiment and State weather station. The young men are here fitted to become intelligent, educated, and practical farmers, horticulturists, cattle and stock raisers, dairymen, as well as machinists, carpenters, architects, draughtsmen, manufacturers, and contractors.

I do not mean to claim too much in saying this; what I do mean is that they learn the rudiments of these occupations, as well as to use their brains and their hands. A full mathematical course is part of the curriculum, and a much more important source of strength to each pupil is the association with the ambitious young fellows of the State, and the daily intercourse with the able and accomplished members of the faculty. Here were some boys from very humble homes, and yet so intent upon becoming masters, instead of dependents, as to be found waiting on the others at the dining table in order to earn their living while they studied. A certain number of pupils are admitted free, subject to an examination in rudimentary studies. They pay eight dollars a month for board and extras. The others pay twenty dollars a year for tuition in addition to the same charge for board and extras.

The Faculty Senate and student government passed resolutions in 1960 in support of the name change, and Caldwell himself liked the idea.

The proponents were challenged, however, by Governor Terry Sanford and by consolidated university officials, including President William Friday. As part of a reorganizing of the entire university system, they wanted to rename the college the University of North Carolina at Raleigh.

This rankled State College boosters, alumni, and students, who felt that the name UNC-Raleigh would portray the college as merely a branch of its sister institution at Chapel Hill. In protest, fraternities picketed the chancellor's residence and the alumni launched a letter-writing campaign. Finally, there was a public debate at which a powerful alumnus, a Spindale textile executive, had what some said was the last word. He said he admired William Friday, thought the world of William Friday, but would never want to be called William Friday at Spindale. Consolidated university officials bent to the wind and sought a compromise. In June 1963, the legislature renamed the college North Carolina State of the University of North Carolina at Raleigh.

That was worse than anyone had hoped, and only prolonged the controversy. The disgruntled alumni began a new letter-writing campaign, and Representative George Wood (State College class of '50) introduced a bill for the NCSU name that passed the House in 1963, although it failed in the Senate. He introduced the bill again, and with the support of Governor Dan K. Moore, and under the threat of making the name an issue in the 1967 elections, it passed in April 1965. In July 1965, the university was officially renamed North Carolina State University at Raleigh.

Outside forces—notably the controversy over the Vietnam War—also were affecting student life. In October 1969, a nationwide call for a student boycott to protest the war was turned into a two-day Vietnam symposium on the Brickyard between the library and Harrelson Hall. The following spring, when National Guardsmen killed four student demonstrators at Kent State University in Ohio, about two thousand NCSU students attended a protest rally in the Brickyard, then marched to the Capitol.

Expansion continued in the 1970s and 1980s, fueled in part by developments in nearby Research Triangle Park, the growth of high-tech industries in North Carolina, and the silicon-chip revolution that made pocket calculators commonplace and slide rules obsolete. Responses of the school included expanded research programs, development of a television course for off-campus studies, and the opening in 1976 of the Jane S. McKimmon Extension and Continuing Education Center, where more than a hundred thousand people gather annually for workshops and meetings.

As its centennial year neared, N.C. State announced an expansion program whose impact is yet to be measured—a Centennial Campus to be developed on 780 acres of state-owned land south of the existing campus. Plans for the Centennial Campus include a mix of public classrooms and laboratories with private corporate research facilities and commercial development.

The school's impact on the state has been obvious. Matthews put it this way in the 1955 interview: "I do believe that if there had been no State College, North Carolina would be bankrupt now. . . . State College is the greatest place in the world."

Much of the material for this article was taken from two histories published in connection with the hundredth anniversary of North Carolina State University—North Carolina State University: A Narrative History, by Alice Elizabeth Reagan, who has a master's degree in history from NCSU, and North Carolina State University: A Pictorial History, by two NCSU faculty members, Murray Scott Downs, professor of English, and Burton F. Beers, professor of history.

In 1914, Dr. and Mrs. A. B. Hawkins (seated middle) drew the best of Raleigh society to their fiftieth wedding anniversary at their Blount Street home. The guests included (to the far right) *News & Observer* editor Josephus Daniels and columnist Nell Battle Lewis, and (far left, seated) William J. Andrews, president of the Southern Railway, another Blount Street resident.

John Bailey

Blount Street

The very best address

BY BETSY MARSH
The News & Observer
December 8, 1968

If you had to ask where Blount Street was, then you missed the point. It wasn't important that it was a maple-shaded avenue one block east of the Capitol, or that a few of its houses were reported to have third-floor ballrooms.

It had huge, imposing houses. It had lawyers and merchants and even a United States senator. It was the center of social life. Here the old families lived; the social determinations were made; the lines drawn. "Blount Street" was not, and still is not, a geographical area. As a symbol, it included a periphery of streets about it. It delineated a mode of life. To this day, it is a synonym for Old Raleigh.

There were reasons for its early success. The Capitol was nearby and easily accessible by foot in days when to have a carriage on Blount distinguished one from the masses. Hillsborough was a broader avenue, but Blount Street had something that Hillsborough didn't have. Maybe it was the Governor's Mansion. Maybe it was the old trees. Maybe it was the great houses with their high ceilings and tricky turrets. Or maybe it was its colorful characters.

Where else would anyone on Christmas paint a great house door red, and leave it? They did at the Josiah Baileys'.

Blount Street in the early 1900s
Steve Massengill

Postcards of Raleigh from the early 1900s
William L. Murphy

"There was," admits Willa McKimmon, "always a rivalry between Hillsborough and Blount streets, but apparently Blount was more fashionable." She herself lived on Blount. As a viable and dominant force in Raleigh society, Blount Street's life spanned two wars. She presided, a great if sometimes less than wealthy lady, from well before 1910 until shortly after World War II, when what had made her dominant in turn made her fall. She was complete. Her residents were growing old, and her sons returning from the war had nowhere to go in the area. Taking their vitality with them, they moved out.

In her day, she could do no wrong. Out of her grew Raleigh's most exclusive clubs. Foremost was The Circle, a club to this day so exclusive as to read like a roster of Old Raleigh. It was strictly patterned. Its business meetings were always combined with cocktail parties, and its dances were always held at the Carolina Country Club after that was built in the 1920s. A Raleigh lawyer remembers coming home from Harvard Law School in 1914 to attend one of these dances. He is still a member.

Its members included the Stanley Winbornes, the John Andrewses, the Hubert Haywoods, the John Mettses, the E.T. Burrs, the Allen Thurmonds, Governor and Mrs. W. W. Kitchin, Mr. and Mrs. Alex Andrews, Mr. and Mrs. Dick Busbee, Mr. and Mrs. Julian Lane—mostly Blount Street residents.

"For a long time, it was thought that it was run by Blount Street," says one lifelong member. And it probably was.

The Nine O'Clock Cotillion, which is only a hair less exclusive than The Circle, was formed ten to fifteen years later and was much larger. It was a Blount Street resident who was instrumental in starting both—Josephine Metts.

Clubs had their ways, and ways had their clubbiness. Blount had its own particular form of snobbishness. At one of the Nine O'Clock Cotillion dances that was held in the book-lined second-floor room of the old Olivia Raney Library, word got out that one of the young men was to bring a certain girl. "There was probably nothing wrong with her," laughs one of the guests who was there. "But I can remember at the time we were horrified. *Nobody* went with her."

Whomever you went with, you went in crowds or groups. And it was such a group that formed the Capital Club, of which Dr. Louis West and Willis Holding were early members. The Capital Club, a forerunner of the Terpsichorean Club, but the same sort of fashionable club for young men, threw three or four dances a year in its own ballroom and clubrooms on the two top floors of the old Capital Club Building.

But its big function was a dance in the clubrooms during the State Fair. A young girl when it happened, one Raleigh woman recalls the year that Mrs. George Vanderbilt of Biltmore, who had arrived with a retinue of maids, threw a party there during the fair: "I was in search of my wrap. There was nothing but this great stack of furs. I finally turned to those. One of the maids snapped at me,

'These are Mrs. Vanderbilt's,' she said. I wanted to tell her I couldn't care less."

Other than the cotillions, the social life revolved around the houses that lined Blount. In its early bloom, it was the day of full-time help and the two o'clock dinner, of high-ceilinged houses with room. While it wasn't the houses that made the people, neither was it the people who made the houses.

The greatest concentration of interest was in the 300, 400, and 500 blocks. And the name and the house that most often came up in conversation were those of Colonel A. B. Andrews. A big man in stature and in accomplishment, Colonel Andrews was almost solely responsible for putting together the Southern Railroad, the nucleus of which was the Richmond and

The Hawkins-Hartness House
The News & Observer

Danville line. Financed almost entirely by the J. Pierpont Morgan banking interests, the venture was masterful, and Colonel Andrews was generally thought to be a man who could have moved to New York and been one of the big railroad men. The line literally opened up the western part of the state.

As a result of his affiliations, Colonel Andrews's house was the scene of entertaining of a largely political and legislative nature. The flamboyance of his lifestyle—his private railroad car with its cook, named Dan Polk, and his carriage, in which there was reputedly a little jump seat for his housekeeper—made him a colorful conversational topic. He had been a colonel in the Confederate army, and children were all told he carried a bullet around in his leg.

Colonel Andrews's house was on the corner of Blount and North streets. In the side yard is a huge oak, the Henry Clay Oak. The story goes that underneath that oak Henry Clay wrote the famous speech in which he said, "I would rather be right than president."

Andrews's sons were William J. Andrews, John Andrews, Graham Andrews, and Alex Andrews. Alex eventually bought the Andrews-Heck House, with its elegant mansard roof and dormers. The oldest house facing Blount Street, it was built in 1870 for Colonel Jonathan Heck.

There were many magnificent houses. The Hawkins-Hartness House had fine mahogany and walnut woodwork, which was executed by a Philadelphia craftsman; bathtubs and lavatories were in walnut frames, with copper lining the tubs and marble lining the lavatories.

The people who lived in these houses and went to their parties were familiar Raleigh names: the McKees, the Gants, the Lees, the Pous, the Mahlers, the Russes, the Spragues, the Strongs, the Haywoods, the Londons, the Tuckers, the Balls, the Laceys, the Joyners, the Andrewses, the Timberlakes, the Boushalls, the McKimmons.

A FORMAL LIFE

BY MATTIE BAILEY HAYWOOD

Mattie Bailey Haywood grew up on Blount Street at the turn of the century. As children, she and her younger brother had left Florida to live with their great-uncle and great-aunt, Dr. and Mrs. A. B. Hawkins, on Blount Street, in the house that Hawkins built for his wife around 1885 as a surprise. (It's said she was not pleased.) The Hawkins-Hartness House is now the office of the lieutenant governor.

In 1926, Mattie Bailey married Marshall DeLancey Haywood, a noted historian who had grown up three blocks away on Blount Street. A year before her death, in 1968, Mrs. Haywood taped her recollections of Blount Street in its prime.

I remember an event in the house of my great-uncle and -aunt where I lived, their fiftieth wedding anniversary. You don't have a chance to go to many fiftieth anniversaries today. On that day, you could not get golden or yellow flowers in Raleigh, so my aunt sent to Washington, D.C., [for] boxes of yellow daffodils, and jonquils, and yellow tulips, and chrysanthemums, everything yellow. The house was just full of them. Then they ordered frozen molded desserts from there, and when the word was passed up the street, the neighbors would stop in. We had callers all day long, and that night the colored choir from the Baptist church came to sing spirituals. All of us stood in the front hall and sat on the stairsteps going all the way up to the landing and had the best time, listening to those voices sing "Swing Low," "All God's Children Got Shoes." Somewhere I have a picture, and it's that picture of some of those people and the family in the parlor there.

We led a formal life. We had five servants. The servants were formal. They'd say "Yes, ma'am" and "No, ma'am." We had a cook. We had Sam who worked in the yard. It was Sam's job to get down on his knees and wipe up the front porch, which was ninety-two feet around, and he did that twice a week. That porch never had any paint on it. It was just oiled. Sam wiped it with no soap in the water. Sam also looked after the flowers. Then in the north garden is where the cistern was. In those days, Raleigh did not have waterworks, they had street pumps. Every few blocks had a pump in the middle of the street, and it was pumped up by the neighbors.

The Governor's Mansion was just to the south of the house. There was a new governor every four years who sent over Uncle David. Uncle David came over with his cedar bucket and toted the water over to the Governor's Mansion for him to drink. And when the governor would end his regime, Dr. Hawkins would call up the next governor and invite him to have water from the cistern.

The machinery of the household ran like a greased wheel. The food we'd have! The breakfast was a gigantic meal. We'd have broiled chicken, egg bread, fish roe, and then sometimes waffles, sometimes battercakes, and the colored man who was the butler would pass all these things around from the kitchen . . . and you'd get the cakes and things right hot from the kitchen. At dinner, you'd have a heavy meal. On holidays, it would be turkey at one end of the table and ham at the other end, and vegetables that were delicious. And figs that grew in the back garden, or maybe raspberries. All sorts of good, fresh vegetables. Then at suppertime, the meal was rather simple, and that was maybe a salad. And we children always had cocoa.

When I was a child, all of us would go down on certain summer afternoons and sit on the terrace of Haywood Hall and watch the practice of the fire department. These engines with the big steamer would start at the Capitol and come dashing down [New Bern Avenue] with four horses pulling them, and when they got to Haywood Hall, the two men would push out this ladder and the men would climb very fast and down again. Oh, it was so exciting.

And the parties were innovative, hospitable, and all-inclusive. Christmas parties were big and smelled of balsam and fir. January the first was another excuse for a big party. And the season halted with a screech during Lent. It could also halt with a screech permanently, for those few who committed the error of trying too hard.

"Old Raleigh," explained a woman who went to Blount Street as a bride before World War I, "has picked up and dropped more people. Why? Oh, for bragging. Old Raleigh," she stated emphatically, overlooking portraits of her grandchildren and antiques of a lifetime, "looked for worth and not money and show." Pushiness was cut. Speaking of her bridge club, she said, "We invited one young bride as a guest several times." She was new in town. But she made it too clear that she wanted to join. "We didn't ask her again."

A bride was an excuse for a party, and one Blount bride of 1910 recalled, "I went to everything from stocking showers upward." For a tea, the new bride was often asked to stand in the receiving line in her wedding gown. Chicken salad and pickled oysters were standard fare at all parties, and though the latter has disappeared from Raleigh's party cuisine, the recipe is still carried in the Christ Church cookbook.

Mattie Bailey Haywood

Bridge clubs were very cliquish, and acceptance in them was a talisman of social acceptance. And book clubs had their own pecking order. Probably at the top of the order was the Fortnightly—"a very learned group," say most—which organized a half-century ago with sixteen or eighteen members and never took in another soul. Among its now-deceased members were Mrs. Charles E. Johnson, Dr. Delia Dixon Carroll, Mrs. James H. Pou, Mrs. Frank Harper, and Mrs. Palmer Jerman. And its only surviving member is Mrs. Hubert Royster. The Fortnightly was followed closely by the Johnstonian and the Tea and Topics.

The story is that the governor's wife was regularly made an honorary member of the Tea and Topics until sometime in the 1940s. Meetings at the Governor's Mansion must have been lively things. In the era of Governor W. W. Kitchin, the furniture-less ballroom was sometimes a roller-skating rink for the Kitchin offspring and friends.

But the elegant mansions of Blount Street mostly stand like empty shells. Some few have made way for Heritage Square, the state's projected building complex. Others are still to go. Many grand old houses have been reduced to two-line ads under "Room for Let."

Rolling out the city

The era of the streetcar

BY PHIL PITCHFORD
The Raleigh Times
August 24, 1987

It was the selling point of the new century. A streetcar would run past an infant subdivision called Cameron Park every fifteen minutes, offering "identical service as is given uptown." In 1910, when going into town meant hitching a horse to a wagon, the trolley tracks were that day's Beltline.

They were hot in summer, cold in winter, and nearly always crowded, but as Raleigh's only source of public transportation, streetcars helped spur the growth of Raleigh's first—and now oldest—suburbs.

"The early suburbs just wouldn't have developed without the streetcars," said Charlotte Brown, curator of art at North Carolina State University and an architectural historian. "Cameron Park had the added panache of the college being on the other side [of Hillsborough Street], but public access was always a selling point." At the turn of the century, Raleigh's population was more homogeneous than today's, and most residents lived downtown. Without streetcars, Brown said, residents would have taken longer to discover "country living."

Once they did, such subdivisions as Glenwood, Cameron Park, and Boylan Heights were born. Developers have expanded the city—most often to the north and west—ever since. "It's not that simple, but once you start a pattern, through no malice aforethought, it's very hard to break," said Brown. "Right now, it would be very hard to break that residential pattern."

The Raleigh trolley system began on Christmas Day 1886, five years after the General Assembly chartered the Street Railway Company to provide service for Raleigh and Asheville. Thousands lined the streets to watch four streetcars drawn by two Texas mules make their rounds along four miles of track in downtown Raleigh.

The first electric streetcar hummed down Hillsborough Street on September 1, 1891, in preparation for the city's centennial celebration in 1892. By 1908, when Raleigh Electric Company merged with several smaller utilities to form Carolina Power and

An early streetcar, c. 1900
N.C. Division of Archives and History

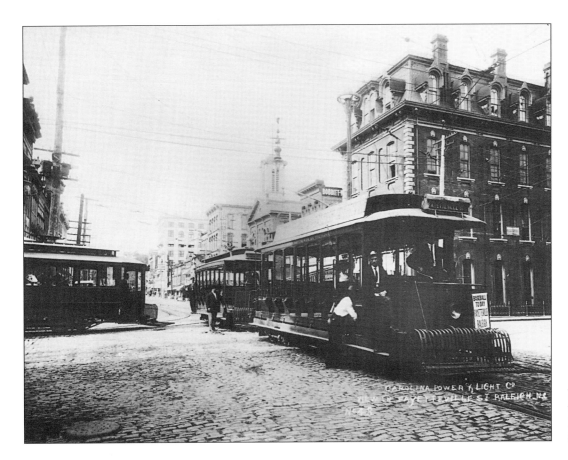

The busy corner of Fayette-ville and Martin Streets, early 1900s

Carolina Power and Light Company

Light Company, there were fourteen cars and fourteen miles of track. The conductor made twelve and a half cents an hour taking tickets and telling the "motorman" when to start and stop the car. Trolleys ran thirty miles per hour, quite a clip in horse-and-buggy days.

The streetcar lines were the arteries of the city. You could take one west onto what was then called Hillsboro Street to the North Carolina State Fairgrounds, north along Blount Street to old Brookside Park, down Fayetteville Street to Cabarrus Street, and west to the railroad depot.

G. Wesley Williams, executive director of the Raleigh Merchants Bureau, rode Raleigh's streetcars as a child, when they were more than just a curiosity. "Many people had to rely on them for transportation, because not many people owned autos," he said. "That was about the only way to get about, other than walk. . . . In areas of the city where there were hills, prankish boys would sometimes put grease on the track and get a kick out of seeing the trolley wheels spin."

"It beat horse-and-buggies," said J. W. "Willie" York, chairman of the board of York Construction and York Properties, "and it was very economical. You could ride all over town for just a nickel."

York's father, C. V. York, may have started the march north in 1914 when he built five houses on White Oak Road and five on Glenwood Avenue to entice CP&L to make hourly streetcar runs there. Willie York remembers using the streetcars to explore Raleigh, and retained his fondness for them in college.

"They [streetcars] encouraged a national trend to occur in Raleigh— suburbanization."

A BOY'S LIFE IN THE 1880S

BY R. C. LAWRENCE
from *The Uplift*
March 11, 1944

It never ceased to pour down rain during fair week. As there were no paved streets in the city, the thoroughfares, especially Hillsboro and Fayetteville, were simply seas of liquid mud through which buggies and carriages slithered and floundered, the hoofs of the horses sending the mud flying in every direction. There was but one sure way to get to the fairgrounds and that was to take the shuttle train which ran from the depot to the grounds every half-hour. I can remember the Centennial Exposition of 1885, which was

Paving East Lane Street, 1906
Carolina Power and Light Company

attended by the famous Seventh Maryland of the Baltimore, and it seemed to me that every citizen of the state crowded into town to see the parade of the regiment.

The first paving in the city was on Fayetteville Street. It was laid with Belgian blocks, and it was while this was being done that I first ascertained that sound required time to travel. I was on top of the Capitol, watching the men do the paving, and would see the heavy mallet hit the stone and then be lifted high in the air before I would hear the sound from the blow. The streets were dimly lit with gas; and I can remember the great curiosity aroused when the first electric streetlights made their appearance. They burned great sticks of carbon, which sizzled and hummed continuously and which attracted swarms of insects of all kinds. Then the first incandescent bulbs appeared, which emitted a feeble yellowish light, and which had a filament so fragile that unless you were an expert the filament would break before the light had been in service but a few hours.

I remember well the appearance of the first streetcars, drawn by mules, with tinkling bells, and the crowds of people who were attracted by the novelty, all of whom took a ride—not that they wanted to go anywhere, but simply for the sake of the ride—for you could ride out Hillsboro as far as St. Mary's; and Blount nearly to the Mordecai place! When electric cars made their first appearance—it was a sensation and a marvel!

"I went to N.C. State from 1929 to 1933, and we rode the streetcar downtown to the California Fruit Store," he said. "That was where all the Meredith girls and Peace girls and St. Mary's girls would go for a soda, and the State guys would go down there to ogle them."

And to Bloomsbury Park, an amusement park opened by CP&L on July 4, 1912, as a ten-thousand-dollar promotion of the streetcar system. Located at the end of the Glenwood tracks, the hundred-acre park featured picnic grounds, a boating pond, a penny arcade, a three-quarter-mile roller coaster, and an elaborately carved carousel.

"It was real common to put a suburban development, a trolley line, and an amusement park in one interlocking deal," said Catherine Bishir, a Raleigh urban historian. The Hillsborough Street line ended at what was then the state fairgrounds, now the site of the Raleigh Little Theater.

"Cause and effect is rarely as simple as A then B, but that is where the first upper-class suburbs were put, and that is where they have continued," said Bishir. "They [streetcars] encouraged a national trend to occur in Raleigh—suburbanization—which has continued ever since. And it focused that suburban growth in a certain direction."

The architect and the 'princess'

The love story of Adolphus Bauer and Rachel Blythe

BY DAVID PERKINS

The tombstone where the legend was born

The News & Observer

In Oakwood Cemetery, one monument shines like a shaft of sunlight amid the gray obelisks and head-stones. It is a little Greek temple of white Italian marble, and sits on a four-foot sandstone base. In the temple door is the photographic image, on a porcelain disc, of a woman with narrow eyes, high cheekbones, a fair complexion, and the expectant radiance of a newlywed. Below it, an inscription reads,

> *In thy dark eyes splendor*
> *Where the warm light loves to dwell,*
> *Weary looks yet tender*
> *Speak their last farewell.*

The little temple was built by Adolphus Bauer, Raleigh's leading architect of the late nineteenth century, as a tribute to, and vindication of, his wife Rachel Blythe. After her early death, Bauer was consumed with guilt for exposing her to Raleigh's race prejudice. Lest anyone miss the point, he had a larger inscription carved on the base, a paraphrase of the state motto: "True value is being, not seeming."

Rachel was a half-Cherokee who had come to Raleigh around 1889 as a stenographer. Her marriage to Bauer in 1895 had caused Raleigh to buzz with speculation. Would they be sued for violating the state law against interracial marriage? That question, and the couple's tragic deaths a few years later, became the basis of a civic legend that for generations drew tourists, lovers, and sentimental newspaper columnists to the monument. It was even said, and some came

Bauer's design for the Baptist University for Women
Meredith College

from afar to test the notion, that Rachel's spirit could be seen flickering in the porcelain face.

Bauer, the son of German immigrants in Ohio, revealed his sense of romantic style early when he ran away to become a gymnast at the circus. After briefly studing to be a clergyman, he found his calling in architecture, and went to work for the Philadelphia architect Samuel Sloan, who brought him to Raleigh in 1883. Sloan was to design the new Governor's Mansion. After some peregrinations abroad, Bauer was called back to Raleigh by Governor Daniel G. Fowle to bid on major state contracts, including the insane asylum in Raleigh (later Dix Hospital).

He met Rachel in a Fayetteville Street boardinghouse where they each had rooms. She was, he wrote his family later, "a young Cherokee maiden pure in thought and pure in character."

After the death of her father, a white farmer and Civil War veteran, in Jackson County, Rachel was sent with her brothers to the Oxford Orphan Asylum in Granville County. She was a bright student, and orphanage director John Mills put her to work in his office. When Mills opened a new orphanage in Thomasville, he brought Rachel along as his secretary.

Her brothers returned to Cherokee, where they became tribal leaders. But Rachel chose the path of assimilation. Sometime around 1889, she moved to Raleigh, studied at Raleigh Business College, worked briefly as a newspaper reporter, and then started a career as a stenographer and typist for the North Carolina Teachers Assembly.

State law forbade interracial marriages, and Bauer and Rachel eloped to Washington for a public wedding. Actually, they had been married already. Letters by

Rachel Blythe Bauer

Bauer discovered by Carmine Prioli of North Carolina State University's English department reveal a clandestine ceremony in Raleigh before that, but Bauer had insisted that everything be kept quiet for fear it would "call forth a clamor from the people of Raleigh and the state, on account of the race prejudice that exists." The elopement was forced, apparently, by Rachel's being pregnant with their first child.

On their return to Raleigh, there was much less fuss than the legend would have it, and perhaps less than Bauer (or the self-dramatizing romantic part of him) had hoped. The *News & Observer*'s wedding notice on June 19 had ended on a friendly note: "Both Mr. Bauer and Miss Blythe have hosts of friends here who wish them all the good gifts that life may bring."

A day later, a letter writer to the *N&O* inquired whether vows made in Washington would be valid in North Carolina, and the newspaper commented darkly about a possible indictment. Yet in a story published the next day, the *N&O* reported that a Waynesville judge had recently thrown out a challenge to a white man's marriage to an Indian after he "noted the respectable appearance of the parties that had been regularly married." And it added, "The young Indian woman who recently went from Raleigh to Washington to marry a white man is, however, half Indian, her mother being a full-blooded Cherokee squaw, and her father a white Confederate soldier, with a good war record."

Indeed, Bauer seemed to relish the attention, even as he exaggerated it: "I don't think there has been a marriage in years over which there has been made such an ado as ours." (He did not mention the pregnancy.)

Then he made a preemptive strike against harsh family judgment: "I hardly believe that Father and perhaps you, too, will approve of this marriage, as he wanted me to marry a rich woman, but I can't help it. In matters of the heart, I do not think mercenary motives ought to enter because it takes all of the soundness out of the relation."

There followed three years of happiness. Bauer had success with big building projects that reflected the city's postwar ambition to be a New South city like Atlanta and Birmingham. He designed the Academy of Music, a multidomed Romanesque-Moorish palace on the corner of Martin and Salisbury streets that served as the city's main auditorium until the Municipal Auditorium opened in 1911. He also drew the plans for the Park Hotel, at the corner of Martin and McDowell streets (later called the Raleigh Hotel), and the Pullen Building, a fancy building with multiple storefronts, cupolas, and domes, on Fayetteville Street. Both buildings have been torn down.

Bauer's masterpiece was the Baptist Female University's "Old Main," a sprawling structure that was completed in 1899, the year after his death. It eventually became the Mansion Park Hotel, and was torn down in 1967.

Of the sixteen buildings commissioned from Bauer in Raleigh between 1883 and 1898, four still stand, according to historian William B. Bushong. They are the Cocker-Capehart House on North Blount Street, the Tabernacle Baptist

Church on Moore Square, the Argo House on Norburn Terrace, and (although attribution is uncertain) the First Presbyterian Church on Salisbury Street.

Bauer's buildings were examples of the florid Queen Anne style, much given to cupolas and turrets and bays, which expressed the exuberance and individualism of Raleigh in the Gilded Age. In his short career, Bauer produced a "body of work that reflected his own romantic and restless spirit and that of the age in which he worked," wrote Catherine Bishir in *North Carolina Architecture*.

It was during this heady time that the first tragedy struck: Bauer was injured when a train struck his carriage in Durham as he was on his way to a church project. His recovery was slow, and business suffered. Bauer's straitened circumstances may also have told on Rachel's health. After bearing a second child, she died of an intestinal inflammation. Distraught, Bauer poured all his energy and his remaining dollars into honoring Rachel's memory. First, the monument. "I am told that it is the most romantic and poetic thing that has been seen in many years," he wrote. Then, after sending his children to live with family (his son Fred became a Cherokee activist), he concentrated on persuading legislators to pass a special bill legitimizing the marriage. After failing at first, it passed with the help of Rachel's "many friends" in the western delegation.

Despite a brief burst of creativity that included the Lucy Capehart House, now on Blount Street, Bauer's mental faculties were failing, and he increasingly holed up with a bottle in his rooms on Fayetteville Street.

On May 11, 1898, Bauer had not been seen for several days when Will Lineham, owner of a clothing store downstairs, went to look for him. As the *News & Observer* wrote on May 13, 1898, "It was not unusual to find Bauer's door

Adolphus G. Bauer
Carmine Prioli

The Lucy Capehart House on Blount Street
The News & Observer

Labor Building in 1900 (above) and 1988 (below)

locked, but when he could gain no response, Lineham climbed into the working room of the apartment. Going to the portiere, which separates the workroom from the sleeping room, Lineham beheld a ghastly sight. There in his bed, half covered in the tumbled bedding, robed in his underclothes and a laundered shirt, the white sheet and pillowcase soaked with blood, lay the unfortunate

The Park Hotel

man. He was stone dead." Beside him lay a .32-caliber pistol and a volume of Shakespeare.

On a side table, a leather memorandum book was found containing a note, according to the *N&O* obituary: "I am just now in sound mind, and before I am otherwise, I wish to say that if I by violence to myself should die, I wish to be buried by the side of my wife, in Raleigh, North Carolina, where I have so long sojourned and among the Southern people I have liked so well."

Bauer was buried next to his wife, but in an unmarked grave. It wasn't until 1986, after Prioli's research had awakened attention, that a reddish marble headstone with Bauer's name, dates, and a summary of his career was erected. At last, the architect was acknowledged in the city he had reshaped, next to the monument that may one day be all that remains of his work.

The author is heavily indebted to two articles in the fall 1983 issue of the North Carolina Historical Review: *"The Indian 'Princess' and the Architect: Origin of a North Carolina Legend," by Carmine A. Prioli; and "A. G. Bauer, North Carolina's New South Architect," by William B. Bushong. Thanks, too, to Dr. Prioli for sharing his research materials with me.*

Thanks are also due to Ruth Brumbaugh of North Canton, Ohio, Adolphus Bauer's granddaughter, for permission to quote from Bauer's letters and manuscripts. Copies of the papers are on file with the state Department of Archives and History.

To redeem the South

The News & Observer and partisan journalism

BY BRUCE SICELOFF
The News & Observer
March 4, 1990

A product of an era in which journalists, political leaders, and the state were "torn between forces of progress and reaction."

The enmity between the governor and his ceaseless tormentor, a prominent Raleigh newspaper editor, was partisan, personal, and deep. One day, in print, the editor blasted the governor as a "pumpkin-faced rascal," a "white-livered miscreant," and a liar, too.

The governor could stand no more. The editor was arrested and held for weeks in a vermin-infested cell. There, he was given stale water to drink, and when he tried to sleep on the floor (there was no bed), he was doused with more water. This episode in 1870 did nothing to quench the partisan fires of North Carolina journalism. Editor Josiah Turner, Jr., freed from jail, was treated as a hero. And within a year, Governor W. W. Holden had been impeached and removed from office.

Now, 120 years later, as North Carolinians absorb Governor James G. Martin's bitter announcement last weekend that he is terminating his bright political career, many in the state surely are puzzling as well over the way he chose to communicate his decision: not in a speech broadcast to all the 6.5 million residents of North Carolina, and not from a podium before an audience of thousands, but in a long epistle Mr. Martin addressed and delivered personally into the hands of one constituent.

His "Dear Claude" letter to the editor of the *News & Observer*, Claude Sitton, raised the specter of a generations-old vendetta between mighty houses. The governor told the editor he had fallen casualty in part to inherited enmity traceable to two of their forerunners: Daniel L. Russell, a Republican, governor from 1897 to 1901, and Josephus Daniels, a Democrat, editor and publisher of the *N&O* from 1894 to 1948.

Democrats, Republicans, journalists, and other North Carolinians can draw their own conclusions about how much political clout any newspaper should have or actually does have in an age of corporate journalism, push-button polling, and video-bite campaigning.

By any gauge, though, the partisan fervor of North Carolina's newspapers, including its most avidly political, the capital-city paper, has cooled since their fiery early days, like lava that has flowed far from its volcanic source.

Most newspapers in North Carolina and elsewhere in colonial and early United States history, started out not as vehicles for sports scores and school lunch menus but as forums where journalistic and partisan interests meshed. Publishers and editors held government or party offices, sometimes while their papers were reporting and editorializing about those governments and parties.

Captain Samuel A. Ashe, chairman of the state Democratic Party, was editor of two papers he merged in 1880 to form the *News & Observer*. After *Charlotte Observer* editor Charles Jones strayed from the party line to criticize some local Democratic officials, Captain Ashe and other Democrats began talking in 1881 of putting up money for a new Charlotte paper with a purer party pedigree.

"Democrats . . . do not want to contribute to the support of a paper that has betrayed their cause," he wrote in the *N&O* in 1882.

But Charlotte would never have as persistently partisan a paper as Raleigh.

"Though future editors and publishers would take vigorous roles in politics, they would continue to publish a business rather than a political paper," Jack Claiborne, an *Observer* associate editor, wrote in his 1986 history of the paper. "Charlotte was a business town, and the *Observer* would remain a business paper."

In 1878, Josephus Daniels, who had moved from Wilson to Raleigh and was publishing the weekly *State Chronicle*, was making a name for himself with relentless attacks on the monopolistic railroads, the "mummified" leadership of the state Agriculture Department, and other targets. He launched a five-month lobbying campaign to persuade the legislature to take the state printing contract away from Samuel Ashe's *N&O* and give it to him.

Josephus Daniels at his desk, 1890s
N.C. Division of Archives and History

"The position of Printer-to-the-State in North Carolina had long been regarded as one of great importance, not alone because it paid the incumbent almost as much as the salary of the Governor, but because for half a century or more the selection of the Public Printer was limited to the editor of a party paper at the Capital of the State, and it was agreed that his selection gave the party imprimatur to his paper," Daniels wrote in his 1939 memoir, *Tar Heel Editor*. "This brought influence and circulation."

The legislature gave Daniels the printing contract in 1887 and again in 1889, 1891, and 1893. With the help of Democratic investors, Daniels took over the *N&O* in 1894.

Besides advancing the Democratic Party, he campaigned for public education, open government, child labor laws, Prohibition, and the virulent, shameful tool employed by Democrats to "redeem" the South from Republicans, blacks, and Reconstruction—white supremacy.

The Southern Railway won influential friends by dispensing free rail passes and other favors to politicians and editors, and shortly after its formation in 1894 it won favorable terms on a ninety-nine-year lease of the North Carolina Railroad, which ran from Charlotte to Greensboro, Raleigh, and Goldsboro. Daniels and others assailed the railroad's discriminatory freight rates, but *Charlotte Observer* editor Joseph P. Caldwell regarded Southern "as the South's lifeline," Mr. Claiborne writes.

Hot-lead typesetters, 1890s
N.C. Division of Archives and History

"Though it was owned and controlled by Northern investors, he saw the railway as a friend of the New South and overlooked its complicity in perpetuating the region's colonial economy."

When Daniels and the Democrats pressed their frenzied white supremacy campaign to destroy the Fusionist coalition of blacks, Republicans, and Populists, Caldwell chimed in. United States senator Marion Butler wrote in his Populist paper, the *Caucasian*, that he was surprised to see the liberal *N&O* and the conservative *Observer* "both in the same bed shouting Nigger."

The Redeemers' 1898 campaign included bands of armed white horsemen in flaming red shirts who paraded three hundred at a time through black neighborhoods and at Republican rallies, discouraging many black voters. Among them were many community leaders and some future state leaders, including future governor Cameron Morrison. "Ordinarily they did not resort to extreme measures," historian Hugh T. Lefler wrote. "A few Negroes were killed, however."

On October 30, 1898, the *N&O* warned of racial violence in Wilmington and urged housewives "not to give up any rifles on orders purporting to be signed by their husbands, as this is said to be one of the schemes of the Negroes to secure arms." Four days later, the *N&O* reported approvingly on "the first red shirt parade on horseback ever witnessed in Wilmington." On November 10, a black newspaper was torched and eleven blacks were killed in Wilmington riots. Many blacks fled the city.

In his 1941 memoir *Editor in Politics,* Daniels admitted that his paper often had reported crime news involving blacks "in a lurid way, sometimes too lurid, in keeping with the spirit of the times."

He gave examples of two inflammatory headlines from the same issue. One seemed to recommend lynching for an accused black man: "Attempted Rape. Another Candidate for the Hemp Road to Glory." The other reported a lynching and effusive approval: "Burned to Ashes, the Black Devil, riddled with bullets first, a righteous Judgment, Ravished and then Killed a White lady, Paid the Penalty for his Crime, an Outraged People Chased the Fiend for Two Days and When They Caught Him Made Short Work of Him." And that's just the headline.

When Democrats celebrated victory at a rally in November 1898, the *N&O* and its cartoonist, Norman Jennett, were praised "for . . . leadership in the fight," Daniels recalled later. "Shouting Democrats came from all parts of the State, a few of them wearing red shirts, and they were welcomed at the *News & Observer* office. Its building was illuminated and decorated with brooms, emblematic of the sweeping victory, and with a rooster in electric lights."

In Charlotte, Caldwell had turned off the rooster lights. He reluctantly endorsed William Jennings Bryan, the Democrats' presidential nominee in 1896, while opposing his free-silver platform plank. But in 1900, when Bryan was again the nominee, the *Observer* blasted him as "dangerous . . . self-willed, headstrong, imperious, determined to have his way . . . not a fit man for President." The paper was no party mouthpiece, Caldwell declared: "It does not speak for the Democracy of Charlotte, of Mecklenburg, of North Carolina, but only for itself."

Daniels, a Bryan devotee, broke with his old friend Caldwell. He charged that Republicans had bought Caldwell's partner and publisher, industrialist Daniel A. Tompkins, by appointing him to the United States Industrial Commission, and that Caldwell was following his orders.

In later years, the *Charlotte Observer* backed Republican candidates in local races. On the national ticket in 1952, it backed Dwight Eisenhower (who carried Charlotte) over Adlai Stevenson (who carried North Carolina). Richard M. Nixon was the one for the *Observer* in 1960 and 1972.

Since the Daniels family bought it in 1894, the *N&O* has endorsed only two GOP candidates in general elections: Robert F. Orr and Donald L. Smith in the 1988 election for court of appeals seats.

Last weekend, in his letter to *N&O* editor Sitton, Governor Martin alluded to Governor Russell and his relationship with the *N&O*: "I knew from experience that your paper has been bitterly hostile to every Republican ever since 1896, when Governor Daniel Russell, the last Republican before Holshouser, took the state printing contract away from you. The great Republican historian Helen Edmonds nailed you on that sorry episode."

It is not clear that Russell was ever involved in the printing contract, however, or that Daniels sought to renew it after the Fusionists took power. Several histories show that the legislature, not the governor, issued the contract. Daniels said in his memoir that he had enjoyed having the contract before the Fusionists won the General Assembly in 1894 and 1896, and that he had decided against seeking it after the Democrats regained the legislature in 1898. He gave no indication that he had entertained hopes of winning the lucrative job from his political opponents.

In a 1951 book identified by a Martin spokesman as the governor's source, Dr. Edmonds cited a speech by a Daniels foe, Dr. Cyrus Thompson, a Populist who served then as Russell's secretary of state. Dr. Edmonds wrote that Thompson contended in 1898, "and perhaps with some justification, that Daniels had grown to regard the job of state printer as a piece of party pie; that now he was angry because the fusion legislatures did not continue to let him reap a rich profit; and that this anger caused him to vilify the Fusionists in his paper." Dr. Edmonds said by telephone last week that she did not recall any evidence that Daniels bore Russell a grudge in the matter.

Daniels certainly was a critic of Russell and his administration on many occasions. But he and Russell found themselves fighting side by side to void the Southern Railway lease. The Democratic editor's backhanded way of complimenting the Republican governor was to laud him, in 1897, as "the first prominent Republican in high position who has not been a creature of corporations since 1896."

In 1932, Virginius Dabney, editor of the *Richmond Times-Dispatch*, offered a mixed appraisal of North Carolina newspapers in his book *Liberalism in the South*.

Josephus Daniels's *N&O*, he said, "has been metamorphosed" since its

Since the Daniels family bought it in 1894, the N&O has endorsed only two GOP candidates in general elections

Composing room, 1890s
N.C. Division of Archives and History

The old *News & Observer* building on
West Martin Street between Salisbury
and McDowell streets, 1938

The News & Observer

shameful role in persecuting John S. Bassett, a Durham professor who dared in 1903 to call Booker T. Washington a great man.

"Its publisher's relationship with the Democratic party causes it to be astonishingly naive at times in its analyses of political issues," Dabney wrote. "On the other hand, the *News and Observer* is probably the most fearless paper in the South in its attitude toward economics and industrial questions. The textile and tobacco interest, the two most powerful commercial groups in North Carolina, are treated as cavalierly by Mr. Daniels as if they controlled no advertising." Daniels's son Jonathan followed him as editor of the *N&O* from 1933 to 1942 (while the elder Daniels served as United States ambassador to Mexico) and from 1948 to 1970. Jonathan Daniels's paper supported Roosevelt's New Deal, advocated equal treatment for blacks, supported busing and the desegregation of the University of North Carolina, and defended the rights of organized labor. W. J. Cash once described him as "sometimes waxing almost too uncritical in his eagerness to champion the underdog."

After World War II, Jonathan Daniels allied with two leading liberals in the state, Frank P. Graham and W. Kerr Scott. He explored the state and the rest of the South in editorials, essays, and books. He saw the Civil War as "a magnificent alibi" for all the South's faults, but as no excuse for its resistance to change.

In 1941, Josephus Daniels looked back "amazed at my own editorial violence at times." But reflecting on his first two decades of fiercely partisan newspapering (1893–1913), he said he had been largely a product of an era in which journalists, political leaders, and the state were "torn between forces of progress and reaction."

"I threw myself with all the zeal of my convictions and strength into the issues and contests of the period," he wrote in *Editor in Politics*. "I imbibed the spirit of the times when political campaigns in North Carolina were more like pitched battles than discussion of issues and when strongly entrenched privilege fought to hold and extend its domain....

"It was a period of personal journalism, and I practiced it to the nth degree. Quarter was neither given nor taken."

Josephus Daniels

Scourge of rum and Republicans

BY JACK ALEXANDER
Saturday Evening Post
April 12, 1947

All Raleigh voluntarily looks up to old Josephus Daniels, who is, by general consent, the capital's leading personage and who, at eighty-four, is the active editor of his daily *News & Observer.*

But while paying him honor, Raleigh often sternly repels his efforts to exercise local influence, and an almost certain guarantee of defeat for a candidate aspiring to town or county office is the *News & Observer*'s blessing. The much smaller *Raleigh Times* is more influential locally. The *News & Observer*, a highly profitable property, lives, as Raleigh itself does, off the farmers and small warehousemen of eastern North Carolina. Six-sevenths of its circulation of more than ninety-three thousand lies in that area, and the farmers' reading is said to consist of the *News & Observer* and the Bible in about equal doses.

As spokesman for the fiercely individualistic farmers, Daniels for half a century has belabored The Interests—the railroads, public utilities, and other corporations—with great fervor, and has ridden herd on North Carolina's ruling politicians. The state government is free of conspicuous graft, and there has not been what natives describe as a "sorry" governor for more than a generation.

Impartial opinion gives the *News & Observer* much of the credit for this happy state of affairs. "It's just as mean as the devil when it gets 'on' somebody," a Raleigh politico says. "Josephus wants Democrats in office, but when they get in, he fights them."

For all the *News & Observer*'s disciplinary power over the state's politicians, it has never been able to bring about a referendum on the liquor question, a project dear to the heart of Josephus Daniels, who has never tasted alcohol and likes to say that he was born a Methodist and a prohibitionist. It is a moral certainty that if the question ever went to a statewide vote, North Carolina, which now has local option, would go dry, so the legislators see to it that the referendum is never held. This necessitates a kind of honored routine every time the General Assembly is in biennial session.

A referendum bill is introduced and referred to committee. During its pendency, Daniels writes blistering editorials against Demon Rum in which he unfailingly refers to the Alcoholic Beverage Control Board as "ABC (Alcohol Brutalizes Consumers)." At the public hearing, the sponsor of the bill orates suitably, representatives of the W.C.T.U. make long speeches, and the climax comes when

Josephus Daniels
1862–1948

Josephus Daniels uncorks an old-fashioned address in support of the referendum. When the speeches are over, the committee votes the bill out onto the floor, where it is respectfully interred. The vote is by voice, with no record kept of who voted which way, as the legislators are mindful of Will Rogers's wry epigram that North Carolina's electors will vote dry as long as they can stagger to the polls.

Despite his age, Josephus Daniels turns up at the *News & Observer* plant at ten o'clock every morning, dressed much as he used to dress when he was Wilson's secretary of the navy—black suit, flat-crown black fedora, black string tie, starched collar, and semi-starched pleated white shirt. Winter and summer—and the summers are hot ones—he wears long underwear; he defends this whim by saying that he detests garters and that he discovered a long time ago that he could keep his socks up comfortably by pinning them to his drawers. In his private office on the ground floor, surrounded by mementos of Wilson and Franklin Roosevelt, his two personal heroes, Daniels slips his suspenders from his shoulders and picks up a pencil. For four hours, he writes editorials in a blind scrawl that only one of the paper's linotypes, a veteran, is able to decipher.

The *News & Observer* is located in a beer-tavern district, and a minor crisis arose a few years ago when one of the taverns installed a blower fan which exhaled beer fumes into Daniels's sanctum. This was one alcoholic challenge to which the *News & Observer* staff was equal; after a week or so of private persuasion, the tavern proprietor relocated the blower.

Around two in the afternoon, Daniels goes home and, after eating a heavy lunch, takes a siesta, a habit which he picked up while serving as Roosevelt's ambassador to Mexico. The rest of the day, up to dinnertime, is given over to the writing of memoirs, some volumes of which have already been published. They are large, fat books, and the writing regimen which the octogenarian editor adheres to would frighten most writers a third of his age.

A widower, Daniels lives alone in a sort of feudal suburban glory, attended by colored servants. Nearby are the homes of three of his sons—Jonathan, a distinguished author in his own right and executive editor of the *News & Observer*; Frank, who is general manager of the paper; and Josephus Jr., its business manager. A fourth son, Worth, is a physician in Washington. The elder Daniels's home, Wakestone, is made of native granite of Wake County, of which Raleigh is the county seat. A pet remark of Daniels's is that he built his home of stones that were thrown at him during an occasionally stormy career as editor. On a concrete base in front of its portico, which is supported by tall white columns, stands a ship's deck gun, a memento of Daniels's tenure as secretary of the navy. After leaving the cabinet, Daniels wrote to his successor, Edwin Denby, asking for a gun of some kind. Denby replied that it was against regulations to allow navy property off a ship or a naval base, but said he was declaring Wakestone a naval base to get around the technicality.

"It's just as mean as the devil when it gets 'on' somebody," a Raleigh politico says. "Josephus wants Democrats in office, but when they get in, he fights them."

'A female seminary of high order'

Meredith College

BY FAYE B. HUMPHRIES
The News & Observer
February 28, 1966

The opening of the Baptist Female University, now Meredith College, in September 1899 was the fulfillment of a long-deferred dream.

Thomas Meredith, an early missionary to eastern North Carolina and founder of the Baptist journal the *Biblical Recorder*, had asked in the early 1830s that a "female seminary of high order" be located at or near Raleigh. A Baptist State Convention committee chaired by Meredith reported favorably in 1838 on establishment of a women's university. What delayed chartering of the school until February 27, 1891, remains uncertain.

It took another eight years to erect the first building. Money was tight and sympathy was weak for the cause. The case of education for women was so weak, in fact, that a series of financial agents forsook it. The man who finally succeeded for the Baptists was Oliver Larkin Stringfield, later called "a champion of forlorn causes." Stringfield was better known in the 1890s as principal of Wakefield Academy near Wendell. He is credited now with the financial impetus for Meredith College and a half-dozen other institutions, including a female college in what is now part of Furman University; Boiling Springs Academy, now Gardner-Webb College; and a home for motherless children in King's Creek, South Carolina.

Meredith College, 1930s
The News & Observer

Meredith students cut up, 1890s
N.C. Division of Archives and History

Many rebuffs

Stringfield faced many of the same rebuffs reported by Charles Duncan McIver, a literature teacher at Peace College who was working at the same time on establishment of what was to become Woman's College (now the University of North Carolina at Greensboro). McIver cited the following 1896 argument from a male teacher: "What is the use of educating a woman, anyhow? If she was educated, she couldn't be sheriff, not a register of deeds, not a clerk of court, nor go to the legislature. . . . The fact is, it ain't her hemisphere to be educated, anyhow, it is us men's hemisphere."

McIver spoke to the legislature in 1896. "Pointing toward the walls of the Baptist Female University, standing exposed, without a workman in sight," says Dr. Mary Lynch Johnson in her *History of Meredith College*, "he said, 'Look there, gentlemen, and see for yourselves the folly of the voluntary principle in education.'" In his memoirs, Stringfield commented, "The legislature made haste to appropriate money for the Normal School at Greensboro. We did this much good by going at a snail's pace."

First students

Nevertheless, Stringfield raised the money from Baptists to pay for the site and the first building, and the fantastic creation by Raleigh architect Aldolphus Bauer was completed at the corner of Edenton and Blount streets. The building later became the Mansion Park Hotel, and was torn down in 1967.

The Baptist Female University was ready by 1899, expecting no more than 125 students. Well over 200 showed up the first day. Many of them could not pay full tuition and board, much less train fare home. All were determined to stay.

The school had eighteen faculty and staff and faced students whose academic qualifications were sometimes no better than the fourth grade. A club was formed for the indigent, where the girls prepared and served their own meals. They were aided by a benevolent Raleighite, John T. Pullen. The first class was graduated in 1902.

Meanwhile, a ten-year debate had begun over whether it should call itself a university, and in 1910, it was renamed Meredith College. During the early 1900s, the college paid off its debts, and by 1920 it overflowed its city block. It needed to move in order to expand. The board of trustees chose a farm on the western outskirts of town. It was wise in that choice; although the farm is now well within the city limits, the land available for expansion is the envy of most colleges in the state.

THE GOVERNOR'S MANSION

BY DAVID PERKINS

When Sherman and his troops decamped, the Governor's Palace at the end of Fayetteville Street, the chief executive's brick, pillared residence since 1816, was the worse for wear. Sherman had used it as his headquarters and had not used it well.

Even if he had, the man who had locked up Governor Zebulon Vance had ruined its symbolic connotations. For whichever reason, governors wouldn't live there after the war. For almost forty years, they lived, instead, in their own homes or in the Yarborough Hotel on Fayetteville Street. The palace was converted to the Centennial Graded School, and then razed for a new school building in 1885. (The school was torn down, in turn, to make way for Memorial Auditorium in 1932.)

The General Assembly, then as now tight-fisted about gubernatorial perks, was in no hurry with a remedy. In 1876–77, legislators appointed a commission to sell real estate, including the land under the old palace, and to use the money to build a "suitable building" on Burke Square, which had been designated in William Christmas's original city plan as "a proper situation for a Governor's House."

The mansion itself was not authorized until 1883, and a year later construction began on Blount Street. Samuel Sloan of Philadelphia and his assistant, Adolphus Bauer, were hired as architects. Their plans were for a strong example of the Queen Anne style, a flouncy, fancy Victorian style that favored elaborate gables and porticos. Relying heavily on convict labor, as the legislature had required, William J. Hicks, warden and architect of the state penitentiary, oversaw the construction until it was completed in 1891.

Along the way, costs rose, and progress was halted often as funds ran out. Instead of sandstone, the mansion was made of bricks. To eke out the original appropriation of $25,000, additional state lands had to be sold, always over protests from some legislators. When finished, the building had cost $58,843, according to historian Beth Crabtree.

On January 13, 1891, Governor Daniel G. Fowle hosted two thousand at a gala opening. Legislators grumbled about "Fowle's folly." Others thought the mansion an ornament to the capital.

"The mansion may well be a source of pride to every North Carolinian," the *News & Observer* reported. "The interior is finished in native pine, which gives a beautiful effect, and the massive pillars, doors, stairway, and other woodwork make it a veritable palace. . . . The whole mansion was illuminated upstairs and down by splendid chandeliers, the gas jets of which were magnified . . . by hundreds of prismatic crystals."

N.C. Division of Archives and History

BLOOMSBURY PARK
Joyride at the end of the line

Bloomsbury Park was a bit of fantasy and fun spun in the early years of the century, when electric lights and streetcars and roller coasters were still new.

The park opened on July 4, 1912, on a hundred acres that now encompass the Carolina Country Club and Country Club Hills. Golfers today bypass the pond—or try to—that once offered boat rides to park visitors.

Carolina Power and Light Company, which ran the city's streetcars, built Bloomsbury as an end-of-the-line attraction for "joyriders" and a promotional gimmick for electricity. At night, the park blazed with eight thousand bulbs.

On opening day, Fourth of July fun-seekers arrived with picnic baskets aboard special open-air streetcars. They stood in long lines to ride the nickel-fare roller coaster, advertised in the *Raleigh Times* as "a one-third-of-a-mile ride on a roller coaster with no hair-raising dips that make such things dangerous." Rides on a twelve-thousand-dollar merry-go-round, "one of the best in the South," also cost a nickel. "It safely carries a hundred passengers, is electrically operated, and the fare is only five cents with beautiful orchestration

N.C. Division of Archives and History

playing high-class music." The carousel was later moved to Pullen Park, where children ride it today.

An orchestra furnished music for dancing in the new pavilion in the afternoon. There was also a penny arcade and an ice-cream parlor. No exact closing date has been found, but by the 1920s the park had fallen into disuse.

THE PULLEN PARK CAROUSEL

It was the great safari before the ice-cream treat, and family outings on Saturday afternoons in Pullen Park could not end without it.

Built in the second decade of the century for Carolina Power and Light Company's Bloomsbury Park, the carousel was bought by the city in 1920 for $1,500 and moved to Pullen Park. It is one of 160 antique wooden carousels in the United States, and as of the early 1980s, one of 25 surviving works by the master carousel craftsmen William and Gustav Dentzel of Philadelphia. The menagerie includes 29 horses, 4 pigs, 4 ostriches, 4 rabbits, 4 cats, 2 chariots, 2 giraffes, a lion, a tiger, a deer, a goat, and a mule.

At a cost of $330,000, paid for with government grants and private contributions, the carousel was restored in the early 1980s by Raleigh artist Rosa Ragan. The original military-band pipe organ was also refurbished.

The News & Observer

Hargett Street

The rise and decline of the black Main Street

BY MICHAEL FLAGG
The News & Observer
May 21, 1985

There used to be eight barber chairs in the Capital City Barber Shop on East Hargett Street. Now there are four, all of them empty on a recent afternoon, a symbol of decline in what was once Raleigh's flourishing black business district.

"You had to dodge the crowds out there," said barber John D. Minter, indicating with a nod the empty sidewalk outside his plate-glass window. "It was one of the busiest sections of Raleigh."

Squeezed into two blocks between Fayetteville and Blount streets by Jim Crow segregation laws, black businesses prospered on East Hargett Street from the 1920s until integration and the automobile dispersed their clientele in the 1960s.

Integration brought new opportunities—and new problems—for black businesses. Many of the problems can be seen in microcosm on East Hargett Street, shabby now from twenty years of decline. And while Raleigh tries to rejuvenate East Hargett Street and nearby Moore Square, no one knows what will happen to the small businesses that hang on amid the vacant storefronts and parking lots.

"After integration, the black market became dispersed," said Lewis H. Myers, an assistant secretary of commerce and director of the state Minority Business Development Agency. "There are now black folk all over town, and I doubt they're going to ride from North Raleigh to go to a black Laundromat downtown when they pass ten or fifteen on the way."

Black shop owners weren't the only ones who watched their market melt away into the suburbs in the 1950s and 1960s. White merchants also suffered as downtowns everywhere went to seed, while shopping malls with acres of free parking sprouted next to suburban neighborhoods. The area around East Hargett Street began to wither after the City Market on Moore Square, which the street opens onto, closed in the 1950s when a new state Farmers Market was built off U.S. 1 North.

Black shop owners in Southern cities such as Raleigh also lost a ready-made customer base after the integration of white stores began in the 1960s. Suddenly, they had to compete with bigger, more convenient white businesses that helped make East Hargett a street leading into the past. The crowds of shoppers and the movie queues outside the Royal Theater, now a parking lot, were gone.

"I don't think that time will ever come back, and I don't want it to come back," said F. J. Carnage, a soft-spoken ninety-year-old black attorney who has practiced law in the same cramped suite over the Capital City Barber Shop since 1932. "But I miss the way this street use to be," Carnage said. "This was a leading area for Negro businesses, and I wonder if we're making as much effort to help Negro businesses as we did then."

Carnage himself contributed to the transformation, as one of the few black lawyers in Raleigh at the time, by defending black college students during the early-1960s sit-ins at downtown businesses.

Before the Jim Crow laws of the 1890s, black businesses were scattered around downtown and were patronized by both races. By the turn of the century, blacks operated most of the downtown restaurants and barber shops. Other blacks ran butcher shops and cobbler shops. By the 1920s, segregation laws hardened, and East Hargett Street—near the black neighborhoods spreading south and east of Raleigh—became the premier business area of local blacks.

In 1940, the street's high-water mark, there were fifty-one black businesses and twenty-seven white, according to *The Urban Negro in the South*, by Wilmoth A. Carter, a Shaw University vice president who has studied the area. By 1959, there were forty-six black businesses on the street and twenty-three white. Now, there are only a handful of businesses—a beauty parlor, a thrift store, a dentist's office, a nightclub, and a drugstore.

A visitor to East Hargett Street on a Saturday night in the 1930s would have seen shoppers crowding the sidewalks, almost all of them black. At number 13 was the Mechanics & Farmers Bank Building, well on the way to becoming one of the largest black-owned banks in the country.

Hargett Street, 1926
Carolina Power and Light Company

Past the cigar stores, cobblers, and cleaners, the visitor would have crossed Wilmington Street to the old Odd Fellows Building, the first commercial building in Raleigh owned by blacks. Here was published the *Afro-American* newspaper, and across the street was the *Carolina Tribune*. Nearby was the Royale Theater, where lines formed on the sidewalk for the movies.

Across the street at the Lightner Arcade Building, the third-floor ballroom of Raleigh's only hotel for blacks would have been crowded with dancers. It was known in those days as the premier hotel for blacks between New York and Atlanta. Black musicians such as Count Basie used it as a home base for performances around the state.

Up the street, at the Mechanics & Farmers Bank's new office, where the old bank and the Yellow Rose Tea Room once stood, bank chairman J. J. Sansom, Jr., discussed the problems of black business. "During segregation, black businesses had a bigger share of the black market, because nobody else wanted it," he said. The Durham-based bank opened its Raleigh branch in 1926, and it has risen to be the nation's ninth-largest black-owned bank, with a modest $63 million in assets. But the problems that nag Hargett Street's smaller businesses also confront Mechanics & Farmers. "We have a limited market, and we still get only part of that market," Sansom said. "Very few whites bank here, but white banks have a substantial amount of black money now."

Big changes loom in the future for East Hargett Street, but few of them may benefit the small businesses that hang on in decrepit buildings along the street. Once problems with acquiring the land are cleared up, the city will scoop out the interior of one block fronting East Hargett and Moore Square and build a bus transfer point and parking deck. If the city, the banks, and the developer can agree on a financing plan, the City Market will be renovated to house smart shops and restaurants. Few will cater to low-income residents in the vicinity.

The biggest change, the bus transfer, is a unique project that will wind through the middle of the block. It is unlike anything in other cities, city planner David A. Betts said. For that reason, Betts said, "no one is sure how the transit area will affect businesses on the periphery of the block."

Said Garland C. Banks, who runs a small restaurant on East Hargett Street across from where the bus station will go, "The buses should be good for business—if I can hang on that long."

A SEGREGATED LIFESTYLE

Audrey Wall and Norma Wall Haywood grew up in east Raleigh in the 1930s and 1940s, when there were not one but two capital cities, one struggling to keep its head high in the shadow of the other. Haywood earned a degree in history and music education from Fisk University, Wall a master's degree in social work from Howard University. Haywood served for thirty-nine years in the Wake County public schools. Wall is director of the social-work program at the University of North Carolina Hospitals in Chapel Hill. They were interviewed in 1988 by Loretta Hicks as part of the "Raleigh Roots" oral-history project of the Raleigh Historic Districts Commission.

HICKS: When you were growing up, what was the center of the community? Was it called east Raleigh?

WALL: They called it east Raleigh, but all of the black activities occurred on Hargett Street at the drugstore and what they used to call the arcade. What you'd do was walk, because more than likely you would not have a seat on the [school] bus, and the bus went all around New Bern Avenue, Tarboro Road. . . . Had one bus to pick up everybody.

HAYWOOD: And then, you see, he couldn't take on any more, and then you'd be late for school. So we just walked, even when it would rain, snow, anything, because schools didn't close when it snowed.

WALL: Every Friday and Saturday, we'd have little parties. That was where we had social activities. There were two theaters. The first one was the State, and you went back in a back alley to go. . . . Had big signs up there to let you know, and we would go only when it was what we thought was something special and my mother thought was special. And that was like Lena Horne in *Stormy Weather* and certain things where they would have blacks in them. You see what I'm talking about. . . . Up on Fayetteville Street where you have the stores, you know, there were stores where you couldn't try on dresses or hats. You could buy a hat but you couldn't try it on. . . . You could not go to the bathroom. To get some water, you had to go to the public fountain marked "Colored." That was after the sit-ins from A&T, because I remember my mother and I rode, and my father, all the way to Nashville, Tennessee, and there's wasn't a place we could stop in a blizzard. It was a long time before the water fountains on Fayetteville Street changed from white and colored. I can just remember so many things. You know, you used to stand and wait for the elevator, and they would get on first. Then they wanted to be at the front of the elevator, and then they couldn't figure out how to get you to the rear.

HAYWOOD: You're supposed to wriggle by and not touch them, and wriggle by and let yourself in the back of the elevator and hold yourself right tight so you wouldn't be touching them.

WALL: And you know, you'd go on Fayetteville Street to shop, they'd wait on all of them before they could wait on you.

HAYWOOD: You had to stand there.

WALL: And we used to do things like, we'd just leave it on the counter and walk on out, you know. We used to do things like that. But I'm so glad things have improved some, and I just think that things eventually will even get better, given time. But it's been a long time.

Curtain up!

The founding of Raleigh Little Theater

BY GUY MUNGER
The News & Observer
January 19, 1986

The fifty-year history of the Raleigh Little Theater has all the ingredients for a first-rate drama—birth in adversity, a struggle through the Great Depression and World War II years, heroes, villains, and enough fragile egos for a season of soap opera, culminating in one instance in the firing of a director after a very bitter and very public debate.

It has been a long road, that journey from the Little Theater's formation in 1936 to today's ambitious plans for expansion of RLT's plant and services. But the theater has endured, the curtain still goes up at the playhouse on Pogue Street, and RLT will celebrate its golden anniversary Friday with a fifty-dollar-a-plate gala at the Raleigh Civic Center.

Looking back, it would be hard to imagine a worse time to start a theatrical venture. The Depression was still on and the first rumblings of World War II were being heard from overseas. In short, money was scarce and the future uncertain.

There had been earlier unsuccessful attempts to start an amateur theater group in Raleigh, but RLT succeeded from the beginning, perhaps because of a "happy coincidence," a phrase used by Donald J. Rulfs in a historical sketch of the theater written for its hundredth production in 1955. He noted that "just at the time the local group was attempting to establish an organization, the Federal Theater was seeking local groups with which to organize technical workers under a professional director."

In the winter of 1935–36, Mary Dirnberger, state director of the Federal Theater, one of many New Deal projects, asked Jonathan Daniels, editor of the *News & Observer*, and Ann Preston Bridgers, a Raleigh playwright, for suggestions on how federal money and theater professionals could be brought together with local amateurs.

The first meeting of the newly organized Raleigh Little Theater was held the night of February 11, 1936, at the old Hugh Morson High School. Sadie Root was elected president, and the speaker was Frederick Koch, famed director of the Carolina Playmakers at the University of North Carolina at Chapel Hill and a regional adviser of

Architectural drawing of Raleigh Little Theater

Raleigh Little Theater

the Federal Theater. Koch's Carolina Playmakers presented a new folk play, *Strike Up a Tune, Sister.*

In March 1936, RLT took a big step forward when the Federal Theater sent Kay McKay to Raleigh as a regular, paid director. He had been working in Chapel Hill as senior supervisor of a Federal Theater production of *Jefferson Davis.* McKay immediately started casting and rehearsing RLT's first play, *The Drunkard,* a venerable melodrama that traced its ancestry back to P. T. Barnum.

The play was presented May 13, 14, and 15, 1936, at Murphey School. The reviewer for the *News & Observer,* identified only as "C. J. P.," was ecstatic: "Don't miss it. Unless you have, or are entitled to, gray hair, you have never seen anything like it."

There followed a series of triumphs for RLT—*Quicksand,* the premiere of a new play by Miss Bridgers which was later taken to Broadway; the state premiere of *Coquette,* another drama by Miss Bridgers which had been a New York hit; *Heaven Bound,* a black morality play that drew more than four thousand people to Memorial Auditorium; *Strike Song,* an original play by Loretta Carroll, former Carolina Playmaker, based on the bitter 1929 Gastonia textile strike; even operas like *Cavalleria Rusticana, Martha,* and *Il Trovatore,* with local singers from the Raleigh Opera Company, which drew favorable comment in feature stories in the *New York Times* and other out-of-state newspapers.

But there were troubles ahead. In the summer of 1938, the Federal Theater project was discontinued and RLT lost its paid director. And work on a permanent home for the Little Theater—on the former site of the State Fair in west Raleigh—was bogged down in bureaucratic red tape. The project was a stepchild of the New Deal's Works Progress Administration.

Enter Cantey Venable Sutton, daughter of University of North Carolina president Francis Preston Venable and wife of Louis V. Sutton, chief executive officer of Carolina Power and Light Company. Mrs. Sutton, a genteel Southern lady of considerable charm, had a whim of iron—as far as the Little Theater was concerned. She knocked a few heads together and got the WPA project moving again. A contemporary RLT account said WPA officials were interested in doing landscaping for the amphitheater, because it provided jobs for many men, but balked at the theater building. The account added, "From Mrs. Sutton's diary, you see day-by-day details of the dragging of WPA work from the very beginning, incompetency, and gruffness of overseers, slipshod methods, small amounts of government materials ordered with frequent delays, peremptory demands for materials and services. Almost at any moment, the slovenly work of laborers stopped on small pretext."

Mrs. Sutton led the drive for completion of the building—which raised more than $30,000, as against $23,885 in materials and $86,000 in labor from the WPA. She remained active in RLT until her death in 1983. The Cantey Awards, given annually by RLT for outstanding performances, are named in her honor.

The amphitheater and theater building were finally dedicated September 11, 1940, and the first play in the new structure opened October 30 of that year. It was *Outward Bound,* and the cast included Isabella Cannon, later mayor of Raleigh.

A method for education

Berry O'Kelly

BY TREVA NONES

Berry O'Kelly
1861–1931

Born the child of a slave in 1861, Berry O'Kelly was the most prominent black leader in Wake County when he died in 1931. He had helped develop Method, a black community that still exists in west Raleigh. His mercantile business, situated on a railroad spur track, included transatlantic shipments of goods. And he was instrumental in giving the community a school that provided black students, even those well beyond its borders, an opportunity for education when most doors were closed to them.

His mother died soon after his birth in Orange County. He was reared by relatives in the Method community, known then as Mason Village.

As a youth, he worked for a white family. In his twenties, he clerked in the Mason Village store. Later, he bought part of the store. Then he bought the whole store. After that, Berry O'Kelly was his own boss.

When the community got a post office, it was renamed Method, and O'Kelly became the first postmaster. He established an investment company and a shoe company and was involved with real estate, life insurance, and banking.

He helped the Mechanics & Farmers Bank of Durham start a Raleigh branch, and later became branch vice president, manager, and board chairman. It was one of only two banks in Raleigh that stayed open during the 1929 bank holiday. O'Kelly owned property, was politically active, and got into newspapering as principal stockholder in the *Raleigh Independent*, a black newspaper published from 1917 to 1926.

His first wife, Chanie Ligon, died in 1902. He married schoolteacher Marguerite Bell in 1923. They had a daughter, Beryl, in 1929.

Education for blacks was a driving force in his life. He upgraded the Method school, giving his time, money, and real estate to improve the campus and curriculum and raising money from contributors and foundations for other improvements. In 1914, the school became one of only three county teacher-training and industrial schools in the state and was renamed the Berry O'Kelly Training School.

O'Kelly helped consolidate it with three other small rural schools and transformed it into a boarding school, with students from around the state. By 1923, it was one of three fully accredited black high schools in the state. When he died

A classroom at the Berry O'Kelly Training School, early 1990s

N.C. Division of Archives and History

in 1931, O'Kelly's funeral was in the school auditorium. He was buried in the St. James A.M.E. Church yard adjacent to the school.

As other schools for blacks improved, fewer boarders attended O'Kelly, and the boarding department was eliminated. After Wake County opened a new black high school in Apex about 1955, enrollment dropped. The high school was closed in 1966, and a year later the elementary school was closed. Now, the city of Raleigh operates Method Park and Method Community Center on the old school site.

Miss Blanche's salon

Tar Heel politics at the Sir Walter Hotel

BY NACK ALEXANDER
Saturday Evening Post
April 12, 1947

Blanche Manor

Mrs. Blanche Manor, who is known around the state as Miss Blanche, is a birdlike and talkative widow of indeterminate age, with red hair and a passion for bright colors, sassy hats, and jangling bracelets.

She is hostess of the only political salon in Raleigh. The salon is her suite in the Sir Walter Hotel, which is the unofficial capitol when the General Assembly is in session. Politicians from across the state flock to Miss Blanche to meet each other, and to unburden themselves of heavy political confidences. As a result, Miss Blanche knows, but won't tell, enough to turn the General Assembly into a riot and upset the political balance of the state.

Through the crowded lobby of the Sir Walter, Miss Blanche sweeps in a series of parabolas, dropping greetings and bits of gossip as she goes. She shepherds green legislators around the lobby and introduces to state department heads bright-eyed young men and women who have come to the Sir Walter in the hope of getting on the state payroll. Miss Blanche, who has never been caught saying an unkind word about anyone, is even kind to lawyers and lobbyists.

A Raleigh journalist, Carl Goerch, who edits *The State*, a weekly magazine, once acted as Boswell to Miss Blanche on a trip around the lobby and came up with the following transcript: "It's certainly hot, isn't it? I never have seen such—Hello, there's Erk Smith from Albemarle. He certainly is a nice boy, isn't he? I think he's—By the way, are you going down to the beach for the weekend? There are a lot of Raleigh folks down at Morehead and Wrightsville this season and—Have you seen Si Copp lately? I haven't see him in—Hey, there, Agnes! . . . Let's see; what were we talking about? Oh, yes; I wanted to tell you about an invitation I had to spend some time up in the mountains with the McKees. I just love the McKees, don't you? And—What do you think of Governor Cherry's latest appointments? . . . I declare, if this weather doesn't get any cooler, I don't know what we'll do."

After a day of this, Miss Blanche, a woman of impressive vitality, is capable of dancing at the Carolina Country Club until three o'clock in the morning and starting the cycle all over again in the early forenoon, perky and voluble.

The little airport that could

Raleigh-Durham International Airport takes off

BY DUDLEY PRICE
The News & Observer
March 5, 1989

There was no throng of spectators that Saturday in May 1943 when the first airliner to take off from Raleigh-Durham Airport—a Miami-bound Eastern Airlines DC-3—roared down the runway and into history.

"It was a military base, and no spectators were permitted," said James W. Goodwin, who was Eastern's station manager at RDU from 1940 to 1974.

Today, sleek jets lift off 184 times a day from RDU, which has added "International" to its name and become the north-south hub for American Airlines, the nation's second-largest airline.

In fifty years, aircraft have progressed from lumbering prop planes to widebody jets, air travel has changed from a dress-up special occasion to a routine necessity, and Raleigh-Durham International Airport, whose first terminal was a wood-frame hut, has grown to a sprawling 5,000-acre complex.

The number of daily departures has climbed from 2 to 243, including a direct flight to Paris. Nearly 3.7 million passengers boarded planes at RDU in 1988.

The airport that started with a handful of workers employs 3,600 and has an annual economic impact of $750 million. The small cities of Raleigh and Durham and the village of Chapel Hill have become a metropolitan area with a combined population of 660,000.

Triangle leaders attribute much of that growth to RDU. "If it wasn't for that airport, we'd still have farmers riding up the streets of Raleigh and Durham on wagons, Research Triangle Park wouldn't have a damn brick in it, and the universities wouldn't have grown," said R. Dillard Teer, a retired paving contractor and airport-authority member from 1949 to 1980.

"It's unbelievable what the airport has done to the community, and, with over three thousand employees, it's a pretty good industry in itself," he said.

Before RDU was built, the area's air service was centered at Raleigh Municipal Airport, established in 1929 by the Curtiss Wright Flying Service at the intersection of

Dedication ceremonies at Raleigh Municipal Airport, 1929

N.C. Division of Archives and History

Tryon Road and U.S. 70-401 south of Raleigh. Eastern Air Transport, the predecessor of Eastern Airlines, began passenger and air-mail service to Raleigh Municipal Airport in 1932 using Curtiss Kingbird biplanes. Durham had no airport.

By the late 1930s, business was outgrowing the old airport. Runways were only 2,100 feet long and could not be expanded, Goodwin said. Although the twin-engine DC-3 carried only twenty-one passengers, it could not take off fully loaded with passengers or cargo, because the runway was too short.

In 1938, Eastern's president, World War I ace Eddie Rickenbacker, told Raleigh and Durham officials they should consider building a new airport.

At the urging of federal officials, and with Durham residents tired of driving to Raleigh to catch flights, the municipalities agreed. In 1941, they paid $200,000 for 891 acres of scrub pine and farmland midway between the two cities, and started building an airport.

Construction did not hit high gear, however, until 1942, when the United States Army Air Corps decided the new airport would be a good base to train pilots. The corps leased the airport, bought another 949 acres, and laid out three runways in a triangular arrangement, each 4,500 feet long and 150 feet wide. The airport opened in early spring 1943. On May 1, Eastern moved its operation from Raleigh Municipal Airport to RDU.

"It really never was used as an active military base, except for one glider outfit," Goodwin said. "Its one claim to fame was that Jackie Cooper, the child actor, was a member of the unit."

The problem for the army was RDU's remote location, Goodwin said. The airport was served by U.S. 70 on the north and what was then called U.S. 70A—now N.C. 54—on the south. Each was a two-lane asphalt highway.

"It was a very isolated area," he said. "It was fourteen miles to Raleigh, the same to Durham, and nothing much in between. The military turned it down because it was so remotely located there was nothing for the troops to do."

Starting out small

RDU's first terminal was "one little twenty-by-forty-foot wood-frame building," Goodwin said. "There were no seats in the waiting room at all, just a pot-bellied stove and small restrooms for men and women."

Next to the terminal was the control tower, a two-story wooden "box on stilts." Controllers, who had no radar, used radios to communicate with pilots. But "with high winds, they'd have to evacuate it," Goodwin said.

In 1947, Capitol Airlines, which merged into United Airlines in 1961, began to serve RDU, followed by Piedmont Airlines in 1948. The airport made terminal space for them, said Teer, by combining two former army barracks buildings.

Newer and larger airliners began to land at RDU. Runway 5-23, which is still in use, was lengthened to 5,500 feet in 1955 to give bigger planes enough room to land. That same year, the airport finished work on a one-story brick terminal building—now known as Terminal B.

AMELIA EARHART BRINGS FIRST AUTOGYRO TO CITY

The News & Observer
November 6, 1931

While a reception committee was coming up double quick to keep its appointment with a woman who was more than prompt, Amelia Earhart literally dropped in on Raleigh yesterday.

A small crowd that expanded with unbelievable rapidity, as the first woman to fly across an ocean circled the airport, was on hand for the arrival, which had been announced for between 11:00 and 12:00. Actually, the autogyro, which always will be best described as a flying windmill, hove into sight at 11:09, and at 11:15 the tousle-topped young lady, who really does look like Lindbergh, swung over the edge of the rear cockpit to be greeted, photographed in the first round of such things scheduled for her first stay here.

Although not scheduled to put the autogyro through its paces in a public demonstration until Saturday afternoon at 2:00, Miss Earhart, or Mrs. George Palmer Putnam, as those who disdain Lucy Stonism would insist, gave a preview of what the rotor ship will do, while state auditor Baxter Durham, representing the governor, and other members of the welcoming committee were rushing into action.

After three steep-angled descents and two swift, steep-angled climbs, she set the ship down easily over the hangar, and the greeting began.

Holder of the altitude record for this kind of ship—and the only woman to pilot one across the continent—Miss Earhart was kept busy answering questions about it.

"It's a very friendly type of airplane," she said. "Not so fast, but it will fly low as you please."

"That really was the turning point, when we moved into the new terminal," Teer said.

The expansion continued a bit at a time: a terminal addition to house Federal Aviation Administration offices in 1958; a new control tower in 1959. "We did everything piecemeal; we didn't have any money," Teer said.

The airport's development has been guided by an eight-member airport authority. Each of the four governments—Raleigh, Durham, Wake County, and

Durham County—appoints two members and chips in $12,500 to the airport, which had a $20-million operating budget in 1988. The rest of the airport's operating revenues come from rent, grants, and landing fees.

Elizabeth C. Crassweller, a former Eastern flight attendant who grew up in Raleigh, remembers flying into Raleigh from Chicago on a four-engine Lockheed Electra in 1961.

"It was just that tiny little airport," said Crassweller, who lives in Baltimore. "A one-story brick building with one entrance and exit and two gates.

"There was one ticket counter and restaurant. You just walked out the glass doors and were virtually ready to board the plane."

Passengers, too, were different from today, Crassweller said. For many, an airplane flight was something new.

"It was a big experience, something people would talk about," she said. "Passengers were always dressed up. You never saw anyone in blue jeans."

W. Eddie Pegram, RDU's assistant director for operations, said things hadn't gotten much more sophisticated when he began working at the airport in 1966.

"There was no security to go through, and you could drive right out onto the field," he said. "We had young boys come out and try to drag race on the runways, and couples would sit right next to the runway and watch planes land.

"We had a farmer that planted the areas between the runways and taxiways with hay. It was a couple of hundred acres. . . . It was a service to us because he maintained the grounds."

Into the modern era

Fast, spacious jetliners were taking over airline fleets. They were too heavy, however, for RDU's one main runway, which had been lengthened to 7,500 feet but was designed to accommodate planes no heavier than the DC-3.

In 1962, the first talks were held on the need for a new runway. Thus began one of the longest-running construction projects in the area: the new airliner runway was not completed until twenty-four years later.

The authority first came up with a plan, called Plan A, for a 10,000-foot runway to be built east of and parallel to the airport's 7,500-foot runway, between the terminal and Umstead State Park. The site was chosen largely because land to the west sloped downward, and the FAA then required parallel runways to be the same elevation and 5,000 feet apart, Teer said.

But in 1968, Wake and Durham county voters turned down a $20-million bond issue, which would have increased their taxes to pay for Plan A.

The runway plan was not dead, but it would have taken a land swap with the state park to make it happen. Park supporters, bearing the relatively new name *environmentalists*, opposed the transfer. They championed Umstead as, among other things, the habitat of the gray squirrel. Plan A died in 1972 when the state vetoed the land swap.

The authority then began Plan B, which called for a 10,000-foot runway parallel to Interstate 40 and perpendicular to the 7,500-foot runway. The problem

was that it would aim the flight patterns of jetliners directly at Research Triangle Park businesses and at residential areas in North Raleigh, western Raleigh, and Cary.

Residents and executives from RTP businesses opposed the plan, demanding noise studies. Later, the residents did their own noise studies, which backed up their assertions that noise would increase significantly if the runway were built.

Frustrated by years of trying to get an acceptable plan, one authority member suggested that the authority buy the Burroughs Wellcome building in order to silence the firm's objection to Plan B. But in 1977, authority support for the plan caved in, and it was tabled.

Willie York, an authority member from 1976 to 1985, said Plans A and B had failed because the authority "never bothered to involve the public" in the planning process. Planning was begun anew, this time by a diverse group of citizens and business leaders whose charge was to come up with the most acceptable plan.

Their work, headed by former authority member Malcolm L. Williams, culminated in a 10,000-foot runway being built parallel to and west of the 7,500-foot runway. It opened April 1, 1986. At York's urging, a $9.6-million terminal, called Terminal A, was built and opened in 1982, housing Piedmont, Delta, and United airlines. Passengers also can thank York for eliminating pay toilets in the terminals.

American Airlines picked RDU as the site for its hub for north-south flights largely because of the increased capacity for landings and takeoffs afforded by the new runway, airline and airport officials said. The hub, which opened in mid-1987, doubled the number of airline flights at RDU.

American spent $122 million on a terminal-and-hub complex and, with 120 daily flights, ranks as the busiest of eight major airlines serving RDU.

The airport has come far, said authority chairman Eugene B. Hardin, Jr., of Raleigh, not just in jet flights and acreage, but also in creating a region out of several neighboring municipalities.

"Air transportation has been such a key to the growth of this area, as well as

RDU International Airport, 1988
The News & Observer

the whole state and country, and the airport has really grown with that," he said. "One reason this area has such a bright future and will continue to grow is the tremendous air service we have."

Even as it celebrates a half-century of airport history, though, the authority is looking ahead. Another committee is drawing a plan to guide growth through the year 2010. Runways are expected to be at capacity in the mid-1990s, and the number of annual landings and takeoffs is expected to nearly double, from 271,000 in 1988 to 463,000 by 2010.

Air cargo also is expected to increase from 30,400 tons shipped in 1988 to 87,700 tons in 2010. To meet demand, the authority is issuing $25 million in bonds to develop a 200-acre air-cargo area.

G. Smedes York, an authority member and chairman of the planning committee, predicted runways would be built during the next twenty to thirty years.

"The impact of the airport is so widespread that it needs to be continually promoted and improved," he said. "The prosperity of the region is so vitally dependent on it."

Clarence Poe

An editor for the common man

The News & Observer
July 1985

Clarence Poe stated his creed, and the problem of the South in his day, in simple words: "The South's greatest fallacy has been the belief that the farmer, the common laborer of every sort, needs no training; educate him and you will spoil him; the poorer you keep him, the richer will be the upper classes."

Poe's own story was a triumph of self-education. He was born on a Chatham County farm, never attended high school or college, became editor of a statewide newspaper at eighteen and its owner at twenty-two, and built it into one of the great publishing empires of the twentieth century. And that was only one of his many achievements.

In 1897, when he was sixteen, he got his first job with the *Progressive Farmer*, a weekly farm newspaper published in Raleigh. He was an avid reader and a quick study. He learned the newspaper business so thoroughly that when editor J. L. Ramsey stepped down in 1899, Poe was the logical choice to succeed him. Beginning with a circulation of about five thousand, Poe built the *Progressive Farmer* into the largest independent weekly farm journal in the world, with a circulation of well over a million.

Poe developed into a forceful writer, a spokesman for the farming community, and a catalyst of change and progress.

Accordingly, he used the *Progressive Farmer* as a schoolroom to overcome old wives' tales and superstitions still rampant in agricultural practices. He joined with Governor Charles B. Aycock and, later, Frank P. Graham in establishing a system of libraries across the state so that farm children would have access to adequate reading materials.

Poe's interest in the well-being of the farm population encompassed the ability to plant crops, preserve the soil, and manage money, on which themes his journal carried innumerable articles. He also became involved in efforts to improve the health and well-being of the farm family, notably in the campaign to eradicate hookworm disease, which in the early 1900s infected 43 percent of the population. There was opposition to this effort, chiefly from those who felt the South was being disparaged by Yankees when the Rockefeller Foundation granted funds to combat the problem.

Poe urged farm wives to adopt better canning methods, testified before Congress on the need for Hill-Burton funds for hospital construction, founded the

Clarence Poe
1881–1964

North Carolina Conference for Social Services, wrote books on a variety of themes and topics, and converted a suburban estate of eight hundred acres into one of Raleigh's most desirable subdivisions, Longview Gardens, setting out many of the crape myrtles that graced its streets.

Meanwhile, the *Progressive Farmer* expanded from a state to a regional, and then a national publication. It eventually moved its headquarters to Birmingham, Alabama.

Poe was married to Alice Aycock, daughter of Governor Charles B. Aycock. He was named chairman of the State Hospital and Medical Care Commission in 1944 and was touted as a candidate for governor in 1940 before withdrawing his name. He died in 1964.

The City Market in the 1930s

'Like family!'

It was the equivalent, in its day, of a new shopping mall—and it opened with fanfare, bunting, and toasts on September 30, 1914, on Moore Square.

The News & Observer account bragged that it "would not bring the blush of shame or the averted head," a not-so-veiled reference to the old market in Metropolitan Hall on Fayetteville Street, with its livestock stalls, flies, and drunks staggering in from Wilmington Street.

The new market was a model of cleanliness. Butchers and fishmongers did their trade in booths, not stalls. "Fish, oysters, spareribs, and round steak will be handed out over porcelain-lined trays . . . just like bonbons at a church festival." Down the center of the building, a pipeline channeled cold air to refrigerators.

The market was a wonder of architecture, too. James Kennedy designed the building in the Spanish Mission style, with a broad, low, hipped roof to cover vegetable and flower stands and fancy parapet walls at either end.

The City Market was a busy community of merchants of both races until the 1940s, when suburbanization, chain grocery stores, and a new Farmers Market on U.S. 1 North took away its clientele.

In the late 1970s, the city council began to look at the City Market as a charm for reviving downtown. In 1988, York Properties, Inc., was hired to manage the property, and has re-created some of its old bustle and charm. Restaurants and arts-and-crafts and clothing shops do a busy trade with downtown office workers. Police patrol on horseback; a streetcar bus cuts a circle to and from the government mall. Moore Square hosts jazz festivals and the North Carolina Symphony.

Ironically, the founder of York Construction Company, C. V. York, had bid second to build the market more than a half-century earlier.

In the 1920s and 1930s, Robert Hodge owned a meat shop at the market. His son, Rufus, remembered the Depression days at the market in a 1988 interview with Frank Ridley and Terri Myers for the Raleigh Historic Districts Commission's oral-history project, "Raleigh Roots."

Voices

from

the

Capital

The City Market, 1914
N.C. Division of Archives and History

Little girls selling flowers at the market
N.C. Division of Archives and History

RUFUS HODGE: My daddy ran away from home when he was fifteen years old, and he went right up to that City Market, and there was a Jew fellow had a key. He'd open it up around four o'clock, four-thirty . . . in the morning. . . . His name was J. Schwartz, Juny Schwartz. He was sitting there on the doorway. This man walked up, Mr. Schwartz who had the key, and my daddy asked him if he needed anybody to work. He didn't tell him yes. He never told him no. My daddy went right on in there behind him. . . . The man I'm named for is named Rufus Knuckles, but Mr. Rufus Knuckles . . .

FRANK RIDLEY: He was a butcher.

HODGE: He was a butcher. . . . Now, he worked for Mr. Schwartz. He was a butcher and he was a grown man, and Mr. Schwartz told my daddy to clean up, wash some trays. . . . Now, he wasn't nothin but a boy. And when Mr. Knuckles came in, and he was a black man, he said, "What have we here?"

"This young fellow seems like he wants to work. Teach him all you can." Well, my daddy hurried up and learned how to cut some meat. I'll tell you why, how he learned. Knuckles would show him and then he would sit down. And getting paid while my daddy did the work. . . .

And so that's when my father went in business. . . . Mr. Schwartz liked him and so he bought that building from Mr. Schwartz in about 1922, 1923, something like that.

TERRI MYERS: Mr. Schwartz had the business and then he had Rufus Knuckles, who was a meat cutter there, who taught your father, and then your father bought the business from Mr. Schwartz?

HODGE: That's right. Now, there were a lot of black businesses in there. After my father back here. There was a fellow in there had a meat business there named Jim Scott. He lived down on South Bloodworth Street.

RIDLEY: These are some of the people who had businesses in the market.

HODGE: These are black ones. White ones were in there, too. . . . C. D. Arthur's white. . . . A man was in there named Mr. Browning, you know. He sold all cured meat, cured ham, cured shoulders, smoked sausage, side bacon. All cured meat. These guys I'm telling you now are white, and I'm telling you what they did. And they all got along like family.

MYERS: White and black?

HODGE: Like family! They were integrated. I can tell you that! They loved each other. Now, you can't tell me they didn't, 'cause my daddy could run over there and say, "Let me have two dollars," or he could run over there and borrow something from my daddy, you know. . . . They were scratching each other's back, so they had to love each other.

MYERS: So all these people had these stalls in the City Market at the same time.

RIDLEY: Each person rented a table. You'd have about thirty on each side. At least twenty on each side.

HODGE: It looked like a fair! It looked like a circus around there, because if you wanted a decent piece of meat you had to go down to the market, and people came from all over.

RIDLEY: Terri, people came from—all the big people in Five Points, Hayes Barton, big judges and lawyers. They bought downtown.

HODGE: That's right. That's where they came to buy a decent piece of meat. Or fresh vegetables. That's where they had to get them.

RIDLEY: There was no Farmers Market in existence then like they have out now.

HODGE: It's like a one-stop situation. It's a big business!

MYERS: Probably more variety than at the supermarket?

HODGE: That's right. Now you see, you didn't have Winn-Dixies. You had a Piggly Wiggly and you might could buy a piece of meat. You might. But they weren't set up with meat like you see down here.

RIDLEY: No, not the choice of meat like you got. . . . And they had a grocery around the market across the street on the other side.

HODGE: And restaurants. Now, a fellow named Herbert Seligson had a restaurant.

RIDLEY: Their family owned the restaurant. Right where they have that Subway [sandwich shop]. That was a restaurant.

HODGE: A big business. See? A big business. And on the west corner of the City Market was a grocery store. And that was Mr. Stronach. And next door to him was Young's Hardware.

RIDLEY: That old hardware store. The inside of the market, Terri—you're going to fall over when I tell you this—Charley Cross worked for his daddy.

HODGE: For Daddy.

RIDLEY: And he worked and delivered stuff for your daddy, 'cause Robert Hodge said he'd pay him a nickel a trip. Charley Cross had an old bicycle. Used to deliver a nickel a trip.

HODGE: Charley Cross's hair struck him right there [indicating shoulder blade]. He had a sister named Charlotte. Charley Cross was a poor boy.

RIDLEY: That's right.

HODGE: And his daddy died. In that City Market. Sat right down in

Men hawking watermelons on Martin Street

N.C. Division of Archives and History

his chair and died. . . . Mrs. Cross just cried, cried, cried. My mama went over there and put her arms around Mrs. Cross. She said, "Lord, I don't know what I'm gonna do." My mama said, "Mrs. Cross, as long as we got skin of meat, you nor none of your children will not go hungry." I'm trying to tell you how people were. That Charley Cross, now, he's rich. . . .

Well, miss, I'm going to tell you the truth. If I tell you anything, it's gonna be the truth or I ain't gonna tell you nothin'. Everything in Raleigh then was just as segregated as it could be. But in that City Market, you wouldn't know it. No segregation existed. That's all I can tell you.

MYERS: And this is the 1920s and on into the 1930s?

HODGE: Thirties, because my father died in 1935, and then my brother and I and my mother, we ran the business.

MYERS: When the market was going full swing and everything, was it open on a daily basis?

HODGE: Every day including Saturday, except Sunday. And it would close a half-day on Wednesday.

RIDLEY: And on Friday and Saturday was the big day. That's when all the vegetable farmers came in.

HODGE: Now, they shut up at the end of the day, but they were there every day, but like you say, on Fridays and Saturdays it was great! Across the street from the market, they would have their stuff on their wagons, horses and wagons, and some of them had trucks.

RIDLEY: The market was the meeting place of Wake County!

HODGE: See, you didn't have all these places you could get this stuff like that. And then, too, it was a common bond among people. A farmer—if he lived in Zebulon and he come to the market, he knew people that had moved from Zebulon to Raleigh, and those people would come up there on Saturday. They'd come and stand around and they'd talk. That'd be the opportunity to get to see . . .

RIDLEY: Like having a family reunion.

HODGE: They had great big groves out there. Moore Square. And you'd see the wives or the mothers and the children, they would spread like a picnic and have the time of their life.

MYERS: So people would come in and it wasn't just shopping. It was also a social event?

HODGE: Oh, sure. You see, you didn't have all this entertainment. People had to make their own fun. And like I say, it was a little bit more closeness with people than it is today.

RIDLEY: Oh, yes. Very close.

HODGE: It seems like people are not so needed today.

RIDLEY: If you see somebody that lives in, say, Fuquay Springs, and if you ever expect to see him, you could see him at the market on Saturday.

HODGE: On Saturday. Because you didn't really have nowhere to go in particular. So what they would do, they would know him and know he worked around there and would sell around there, and so just for an outing they would come to Raleigh, which is not too far away, and then they would bring their picnic baskets and their food. In the grove, they had a fountain out there that you'd step on a little old pedal and it would shoot water up. They didn't have an electric pump.

RIDLEY: And they had things where they'd tie the horses to around the square.

HODGE: In the twenties, you had more horses than you had cars!

RIDLEY: Didn't have cars till about '32, '33, something like that.

Vegetable sellers on Moore Square
N.C. Division of Archives and History

HODGE: Listen, man, it was right up in the thirties pretty good before we had, say, a million cars. See, back in the twenties and the early thirties, you saw a lot of horses! And wagons and carriages and buggies.

RIDLEY: That's right. And they had so many children, Terri, that they couldn't afford to eat in restaurants and things, so they'd bring all their food and sit right down there and eat in the square.

HODGE: That's right! That's right.

MYERS: It sounds like there would be hundreds of people.

HODGE: It could be. It was kinda like a circus, I tell you.

RIDLEY: Old man Moe Watson and them, that string band, they used to play the violins. It was a black group of men. Used to play guitar and washboard.

HODGE: Yeah, yeah, yeah.

RIDLEY: And they used to bring the washboard.

HODGE: Yeah, a little short doctor.

RIDLEY: And Moe? Ken Beatty? Williams up here.

HODGE: And K. C. Another fellow named K. C. played the guitar. They used to be up there on Saturdays.

RIDLEY: Yeah, on Saturdays, and that was the only black string band in existence.

HODGE: And the people would be round them like bees. They would give them a little money. They picked up good change like that, too.

Nell Battle Lewis

Crusader for a reformed South

BY TREVA NONES
The News & Observer
December 1991

Nell Battle Lewis

1893–1957

Battle was her middle name, and for more than thirty years, her credo.
Cornelia "Nell" Battle Lewis was an active social conscience in North Carolina in the 1920s, 1930s and 1940s, fighting inequality and ignorance and crusading for social justice and education through an influential newspaper column.

Her column, "Incidentally," ran in the *News & Observer* from 1921 until her death in 1956, except for a brief period in the 1930s when she was ill and again in 1948, when she worked for the *Raleigh Times*.

Known as "Battling Nell" in the 1920s, by the mid-1940s the liberal had changed her views and become an archconservative, susceptible to the fears of the McCarthy era and afraid that communist infiltrators were involved with the state's university system.

When she celebrated the twenty-fifth anniversary of her column in 1956, she characterized the earlier "Battling Nell" as "a very, very callow, half-baked liberal" who didn't know enough. "I was a South-saver," she said. "I wanted to lift the South up in all directions and was very critical of it in every respect." As for her early women's rights crusades, she decided there was "too much emphasis on equality and too much aping of men" by women.

She was born in Raleigh on May 28, 1893, the daughter of Richard Henry Lewis, a well-known physician and public-health pioneer, and Mary Gordon Lewis, his second wife. She attended Raleigh schools and St. Mary's College and graduated from Smith College in Northampton, Massachusetts, in 1917. After working briefly for a bank, she joined the YWCA canteen service and served the American Expeditionary Force in 1918 and 1919. She began her newspaper career at the *News & Observer* in 1920. She wrote general and society news stories, was literary and feature editor, and produced the column.

A suffragist and feminist in the 1920s and 1930s, she was active in several organizations, including, in the 1920s, the Legislative Council, a clearinghouse for seven major women's organizations that lobbied for passage of laws. She

INCIDENTALLY: ON THE SCOPES TRIAL

BY NELL BATTLE LEWIS
The News & Observer, June 1925

If before the Scopes affray there had been any doubt that Fundamentalism was in politics—which there was not—the mock trial at Dayton would have removed that doubt. Clearly, what the Fundamentalists led by William Jennings Bryan propose to do is indirectly to force their interpretations of the Bible upon the rest of the people of the United States by prohibiting in public schools and colleges the teaching of any subject which they consider contrary to the Scriptures. However they may try to explain it away, this means nothing less than the beginning of ecclesiastical control of legislation. This is the most serious issue connected with the Scopes trial. It is an issue of first importance. The question is perfectly clear: Shall a sect of the Protestant Church control the public educational system of the country in accordance with that sect's interpretation of the Bible?

promoted higher education for women, addressed problems of working mothers, and pushed for changes in women's legal status. She ran for the legislature in 1928 and lost. During textile strikes in Gastonia in 1929 and 1930, she presented the laborers' point of view. The *N&O* editors allowed her a wide berth. When the newspaper was taking the antievolutionist side at the time of the Scopes trial in the 1920s, she fought for scientific honesty in her column.

She read law and was admitted to the state bar in 1929, although she practiced only briefly and concentrated on the defense of a group of female inmates of Samarcand, the state's women's reformatory. She argued that the inmates, who were charged with torching a reformatory building, were mentally defective. The case prompted her to push for legal and penal reform and piqued her concern for the mentally ill and retarded, which she pursued the rest of her life.

From 1937 until 1944, and again in 1954, she taught English and Bible studies at St. Mary's College. After World War II, she renounced many of her earlier efforts for social justice and reform and freedom of expression and thought. "Battling Nell" died November 26, 1957, apparently the victim of a heart attack that struck her just outside her home at 1514 St. Mary's Street.

Jane McKimmon

When We're Green We Grow

BY TREVA NONES
The News & Observer
December 1991

Jane McKimmon
1893–1957

Raleigh native Jane Simpson McKimmon was one of the state's premier how-to experts and an evangelist for a better way of life for its farm women.

In 1911, she became the first North Carolina home-demonstration agent and one of five pioneer agents in the South. Initially, her job was to teach farm girls how to grow and can tomatoes to earn extra income. By the spring of 1912, under her leadership, home-demonstration agents had been placed in fourteen North Carolina counties.

It had all begun, some years earlier, when farm boys had started "corn clubs." Soon, farm girls were starting their own clubs, and then farm women wanted to improve their skills and to make the family's income go farther. Home-demonstration clubs were established and spread until there were agents and clubs in all one hundred counties. In later years, the program was broadened to encourage reading, health, and music appreciation.

McKimmon, daughter of William Simpson and Ann Cannon Shank Simpson, was born in Raleigh on November 13, 1867. She graduated from Peace Institute when she was sixteen. In 1886, she married Raleigh merchant Charles McKimmon. They had three sons and a daughter. She practiced her own gospel of self-improvement and went back to school, earning a bachelor's degree at North Carolina State College in 1926 and a master's degree in 1929.

From 1924 until 1936, at a time when few women worked outside the home, she was assistant director of the North Carolina Agricultural Extension Service. Known by associates as "Miss Jennie," she retired as home-demonstration agent in 1937 and began writing a book about the work. After publication of *When We're Green We Grow*, she left the extension service in 1946. Two years later, she was featured on NBC radio's "Cavalcade of America."

She lived to see home-demonstration club membership total more than seventy-five. Today, the North Carolina Extension Homemakers Association, Inc., has nearly thirteen hundred clubs, with nearly twenty thousand members in the one hundred counties.

McKimmon died in November 1957. In 1976, the Jane S. McKimmon Extension and Continuing Education Center was completed on the North Carolina State University campus at Western Boulevard and Gorman Street.

PART FOUR

The Boom Years

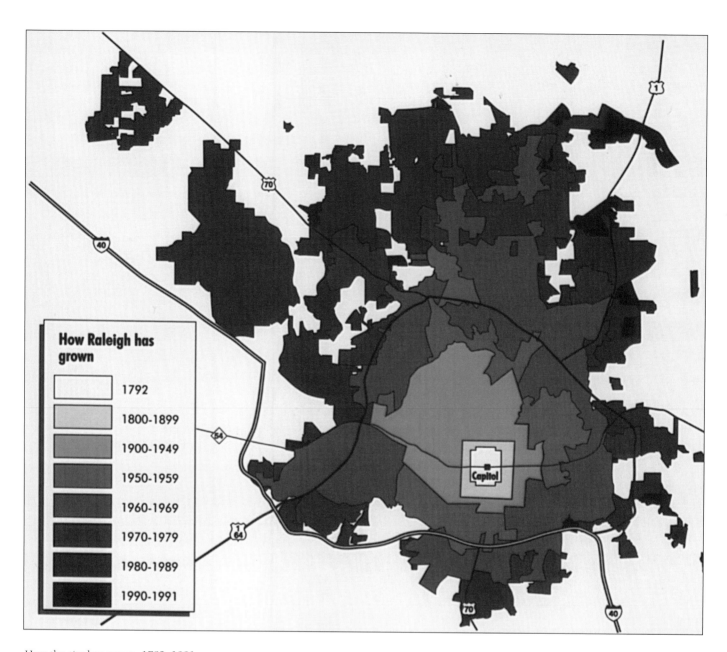

How the city has grown, 1792–1991

City of Raleigh Planning Department

Beyond the Beltline

The rise of North Raleigh

BY STEVEN LITT
The News & Observer
May 4, 1986

In biology, it's called mitosis. A cell grows and splits. In such a fashion, Raleigh has given birth to a sprawling suburban-style sister, North Raleigh.

"It's almost like there are two cities," said Raleigh developer and former mayor G. Smedes York. "I'm not trying to say there's anything wrong with either city. But there is a difference."

Yes, there are differences, underscored by the Beltline, a twenty-five-mile loop of concrete that girds inner Raleigh like the Great Wall of China.

Inside the Beltline, the mood is quiet and historic. The scale is intimate or dense, depending on your viewpoint. Houses, streets, sidewalks, and trees look old and venerable. Historic markers stand sentinel along the thoroughfares leading to the state Capitol. The population varies from black to white, rich to poor, depending on the neighborhood.

Nothing in North Raleigh is old enough to be a landmark. Everything's new, and there's more of it: more space, more shopping centers, more pavement, more Mercedes, and more money. The population is almost uniformly white and well-off. Inner Raleigh is full of families with long connections to the area; North Raleigh has more newcomers. Inner Raleigh has a past; North Raleigh is an instant city.

In twenty years, North Raleigh has filled an area almost as big as Raleigh inside the Beltline—which took two hundred years to develop. But how did North Raleigh take shape, who lives there, and just how expensive is life on the city's cutting edge?

In all of North Raleigh's thirty-five square miles, there are no skyscrapers, no memorable intersections or large public spaces for civic gatherings—nothing on the order of a European piazza or a major square. In short, North Raleigh doesn't seem to have a focus. Instead, its texture is a homogeneous spread of midrange to upscale apartments and houses, sliced by thoroughfares lined with offices, fast-food restaurants, singles bars, and shopping centers. Whatever it may lack in urban attractions, it is exceedingly popular. Otherwise, it wouldn't exist—and it certainly wouldn't have grown so quickly.

Justus M. "Judd" Ammons has built three thousand homes there and has a simple explanation for why North Raleigh looks the way it does: it's what people wanted. "Most people that moved here in recent years still think of North Carolina as more of a rural area," Ammons said. "They picture in their mind having a piece of ground and grass and a tree."

That image sold and still sells. Proof is that real-estate prices continue to

> *"Most people that moved here in recent years . . . picture in their mind having a piece of ground and grass and a tree."*

climb in North Raleigh, Ammons said. "People for a long time got the idea that houses and land appreciate more in North Raleigh than other places," he said. "And they began to believe it, and it happened."

Peter Batchelor, a professor of urban design at North Carolina State University, and one of the region's leading experts on the shape of cities, looks at North Raleigh and dreams of what might have been. Growing up in London made Batchelor a traditional urbanist.

He likes denser cities with bustling sidewalks, prominent intersections, and prominent buildings that announce their importance through sensitive design.

But in North Raleigh, Batchelor sees a generic suburb much like any other in the United States. He misses the landmarks that might give North Raleigh more of an identity. "It could be anywhere in most parts of the country, just about anywhere in North America," he says.

Twenty-five years ago, there was no North Raleigh. The city virtually ended near the current path of the Beltline. From that point, farming fields and pine trees stretched north toward Oxford in an uninterrupted sweep of green.

North Hills was a popular spot for stargazing and viewing downtown Raleigh at night. Crabtree Valley was a glen of trees and pastures where horses grazed by Crabtree Creek. Today, you can drive eight to ten miles north of the Beltline before finding a farm worthy of the name.

Shopping malls have taken over the valley and hills, and Crabtree Valley plays host to the worst traffic jams in the city. Every day, 61,400 cars plow through the Crabtree section of Glenwood Avenue between the Beltline and Leesville Road.

The city's great northward push began just over twenty years ago with the development of North Hills Mall. E. N. Richards, builder of more than ten thousand units of housing and at least a dozen shopping malls in eastern North Carolina, is widely credited with starting it all by building North Hills Mall. Richards, now retired, declined to return phone calls to his office to discuss his role in shaping the North Raleigh boom. "I wouldn't say he was the prime mover," Ammons said. "He was *the* mover."

Others followed. First came a spate of apartments and shopping centers whose names—The Lakes, Woodscape, Sandy Forks, Quail Hollow, Quail Corners, and Quail Ridge—suggested a countrified way of life that was disappearing. Then came a wave of single-family homes.

By the late seventiess and early eighties, North Raleigh's office and shopping booms were well under way. At the same time, Wake Forest Road, Six Forks Road, and Falls of the Neuse Road began to fill with offices, malls, fast-food restaurants, gas stations, and convenience stores.

Statistics don't give the whole story, but they reveal the basic plot. Between 1980 and 1985, the city population as a whole grew 22.8 percent; North Raleigh grew by 58.6 percent. Those are estimates based on the 1990 United States Census. The census itself shows that the people who live in North Raleigh are white (91 percent), have spent more years in school on average than other city residents (93 percent of adults there have completed high school and 41 percent have completed college), and make more money. The mean income of a North

Twenty-five years ago . . . North Hills was a popular spot for stargazing and viewing downtown Raleigh at night.

Raleigh family in 1980 was $28,083 a year, roughly $7,300 more than for the city as a whole.

To shelter North Raleigh's newcomers, 9,600 houses and apartments were built in the past five years, compared with 5,100 for the rest of the city.

"There's been a real explosion in Raleigh, there's no doubt about it," Batchelor said. "It's far in excess of most cities anywhere."

Has North Raleigh's growth come at too high a price? Some experts think not.

City planning director George Chapman has seen what you can get with rapid growth—the cookie-cutter neighborhoods that sprang up in Los Angeles and on Long Island after World War II. "They used to level land and lay out a nice regular pattern of houses," he said. "Then it took thirty to forty years to develop a tree cover." Chapman and Batchelor agree that for the most part, Raleigh developers avoided the slash-and-burn technique. "Trees are almost revered like a religious symbol," Batchelor said. "That's one positive thing about North Raleigh."

But Batchelor is not charmed by the meandering street patterns, numerous culs-de-sac and homogenized appearance. Culs-de-sac make it hard to get from one part of North Raleigh to another, he said, and with the curving streets, some drivers need an on-board compass to know what direction they're headed in.

"If you designed a town like a piece of graph paper, it might be better," Ammons said. "But it's not what people want." Curving roads and culs-de-sacs create a greater sense of privacy on a suburban street. Such features help sell houses and apartments.

To Batchelor, North Raleigh's horizontal spread represents the most expensive kind of urban development. There are more miles of roads and utilities per taxpayer than in a denser type of city. "North Raleigh is where most of America and probably all the rest of the world would probably like to live," he said. "It's their image of the ideal environment. The thing is, we're going to pay for this image. And we're beginning to pay for it already in terms of frustration and inconvenience. It's an urban deficit, and it's building up very rapidly. I don't think people understand the incredible burden of taxes, the fiscal measures that have got to be taken to keep all the infrastructure well maintained."

Ammons agreed with Batchelor. "I expect that he's exactly right," he said. "But that's not the point. People don't want to live stacked up. There's a lot of things we could do cheaper if we wanted to do things the cheapest way."

For Ammons, the weakest points in the appearance of North Raleigh are the area's main through roads—Six Forks Road, Falls of the Neuse Road, and U.S. 1.

"I think they're very bad," he said. "They're not thoroughfares. We've allowed too many signs and driveways. If you drive down Falls of the Neuse Road and you think it's beautiful, we just don't agree. I look back and wonder why I didn't do better. We all just wish we had done better."

David R. Godschalk, a professor of city planning at the University of North Carolina at Chapel Hill, said he was not convinced that North Raleigh's style of development is bad.

Suburban growth—centered on cars, subdivisions, and shopping centers—"is a new aesthetic, and sometimes I think it's pretty exciting," he said. "It's not the old downtown where you saw everything on foot."

> *"It's an urban deficit, and it's building up very rapidly. I don't think people understand the incredible burden . . . of fiscal measures that have got to be taken to keep all the infrastructure well maintained."*

Like a 'life-size pinball machine'

A Yankee experiences Raleigh traffic

BY MATT SCHUDEL
The News & Observer
November 16, 1985

All roads lead to Durham. And there they vanish.

Moving to Raleigh can be, to say the least, an eye-opening experience to someone not accustomed to the ways of the South. Food, driving, speech—all are done in ways that simply do not translate across the Mason-Dixon line.

You could call this the education of a Yankee.

The first clue that not all was right with my new world was the night I was to drive from North Raleigh to east Raleigh to attend a party welcoming me to the city. It was easy, I was told. Just get on the Beltline, get off, and I'd be there. Fifteen minutes, tops.

I followed the instructions, and the fifteen minutes ticked by. After half an hour, I started to feel a little worried. I saw signs that read "64 West/70 East/40 South." I wondered how that was possible, how I could be traveling east, west, and south at the same time. It seemed to contradict the laws of nature or physics or something.

Well, I ended up in Durham, and by the time I got turned around I discovered I was twenty-one miles from Raleigh. I arrived at the party more than two hours late, having gone all the way around the Beltline at least twice. Everyone else had left.

Welcome to Raleigh.

Since then, I've been lost in Durham seven more times. (Isn't Guess Road wonderful for lost drivers? "Where am I?" "Guess." As far as I'm concerned, your Guess is as good as mine.) And what about that concrete moat around Raleigh called the Beltline?

It's like being in a life-size pinball machine with no way out. Newcomers to Raleigh, according to Mary Rudisill, president of the Newcomers Club, have more questions and frustrations about the Beltline than about any other topic. Who's Cliff Benson, they ask, and why would he want a road that is nothing but a circular traffic jam named for him anyway? It's reached the point that I refuse to drive on it for any reason—and a native Tar Heel who has lived here for years says the same thing.

But the Beltline is not alone. All the roads here seem to have been made to cause as much confusion as possible.

This is the only place I have been where the middle lane of three lanes of traffic going the same direction disappears on you. You don't believe me? Then you've never driven on Six Forks Road.

One theory is that Raleigh, for all its talk of being a Southern center of culture and business, is still at heart a dusty country town. The drivers here seem to be country-bred, too, comfortable only when they have plenty of room to move around. Ever notice how everyone turning a corner swings out about a lane and a half before negotiating the turn?

The other turning technique peculiar to North Carolina is "the stop and stop." You know this one. You pull up behind someone at a stoplight and wait for the light to change. The light changes, and the driver in front of you decides to turn on his blinker, usually for a left turn. Both of you sit there and wait. I'm also convinced that there's a state law requiring the tailgate of every pickup to be down, especially when hauling things around.

Backed-up traffic on the Beltline at North Hills
The News & Observer

Southerners often say Northerners are rude and pushy. Northerners sometimes think Southerners are slow and insincerely gabby. It's just that to people raised in different parts of the country, many Southern customs seem, well, a little peculiar. When two people in the same situation—eating boiled potatoes, say, or talking about "the war"—have different expectations, confusion results. Southerners who have been surprised by the barbecue in Kansas City or Dallas know what I mean.

We Northerners and Westerners don't quite know what to do when a barbecue consists of pale, stringy meat and potatoes swimming up from huge vats of grease. Eating hush puppies sounds barbaric, something you'd want to alert the SPCA about.

It comes down to this: in matters of manners, what is normal in one part of the country can be strange or crude in another. In the North, for instance, no one over the age of four says "Daddy." When you come down here, it takes some getting used to when you hear it coming out of the mouths of grown men. The "Yes, sir" and "No, ma'am" so common in everyday Southern speech is unheard of in the North.

Argument is practiced much differently in the South. In the North, it is a way of life. Discussions—heated ones with pounding fists and flashing eyes—are not at all uncommon in families and workplaces. In the South, it seems harder to express an honest difference of opinion without being suspected of sedition.

One of the basic differences is that Southerners, by and large, seem convinced that they live in the best possible place on earth. Every Southerner's favorite topic is the South. Northerners, by contrast, routinely complain about how awful their hometowns or home states are. Where do you think the jokes about New Jersey come from, anyway, Honolulu?

The dukes of York

A family of builders

BY STEVEN LITT
The News & Observer
May 10, 1987

> *"All the buildings are buildings you don't have to be ashamed of."*

James Wesley "Willie" York, the man who built a real-estate empire in the city of Raleigh, will never forget the summer of 1931. He was working for his father, driving a truck on a construction site. One day, his father sent for him.

"I'd like for you to know I have just received your report card and that you have flunked out of school," C. V. York said to his eighteen-year-old son, then a sophomore at North Carolina State University.

Willie stood before his father, holding a straw farmer's hat. Sweat soaked his T-shirt and jeans. He felt sick.

"If you want to go back to school, I'll get you back in," the older man continued. "On probation. But if you decide you want to be a truckdriver the rest of your life, I just want to give you one piece of advice: be a good one."

If any single episode galvanized Willie York, it was that moment in the hot summer of 1931. He learned a lesson he would never forget: he was a York. Yorks were not allowed to take the easy way out.

"The more I drove that damn truck and loaded it and unloaded it, the more I decided I really wanted to go back to school," York says today.

York did return to school. He also went on to inherit his father's small, struggling construction business and make it one of the Triangle's biggest real-estate concerns.

Some fifty-six years later, York, who long ago turned his private ambitions into public realities, is a son his father most likely would be proud of. He is also a man of contradictions.

Despite his drive, York has never expanded his business beyond the Triangle. He loves to throw lavish parties, but he prizes his privacy.

He served on the Raleigh-Durham Airport Authority and the North Carolina Board of Conservation and Development. But unlike his son G. Smedes York, a former Raleigh mayor, Willie York has never run for office.

He is devoted to animals and has a 150-acre horse-breeding farm near Clayton. But he loves to hunt and has traveled on four continents in search of exotic game.

He can appear gruff and abrasive, and yet those close to him say he is sensitive, emotional, and loving. He can also lash out when he's hurt.

As a child, York was stung by taunts about his glasses. As an adult, he has been infuriated more than once by business disagreements or scrutiny of his private life. "I fight back always," he says. "I still do."

C. V. York (left)
Willie York (center)
G. Smedes York (right)

York's volatile nature is so well known that it has become legendary, giving him a larger-than-life reputation as a man used to having his way.

"I think that everyone who has known Willie York may have had words with him," says Raleigh real-estate executive Charles W. Bradshaw, Jr. "He's a dominating, astute, and very brilliant person, and he's nearly always right."

Physically, York radiates power. His body is burly, with broad, thick shoulders and heavy, strong hands. When he walks through a doorway, he seems to fill the space. In a room of people, he controls the atmosphere like a general among enlisted men.

His legacy to the city is a brace of shopping centers, industrial buildings, offices, and housing developments, including Mission Valley, Cameron Village, and the industrial area near U.S. 1 North and the Beltline.

As for the aesthetic quality of his work, York says, "All the buildings are buildings you don't have to be ashamed of." But he has his critics.

York has enriched himself and his family without visually enriching the city, says Henry L. Kamphoefner, the nationally prominent dean of NCSU's School of Design from 1948 to 1972. To Kamphoefner, Mission Valley and Cameron Village "have no aesthetic quality," and York's Velvet Cloak Inn on Hillsborough Street "is vulgar, but not cheap. If it was a little cheaper, it would be tacky."

Others view York's accomplishments more positively.

"Willie York has done a lot for this city," says developer Seby Jones, who along with York and the late Ed Richards formed the city's troika of big builders after World War II. Richards and Jones were as successful as York, if not more so. But it was York, Jones says, "who really was the first big developer we had in Raleigh."

On a bright spring day at York's farm, Whisperwind, the developer stands as the center of a small group watching a show horse called Match Me go through his paces. Sunlight glistens on the three-year-old saddle-bred colt's chestnut flanks. Hoofbeats break the soft breeze rushing through pine trees and dogwood blossoms.

"This horse is coming along real good," York says. "He's a product of our breeding operation, and we're proud of him." When a photographer shoots a picture of York with another horse, the developer will tolerate nothing less than perfection. He wants the ears pointing up. "A horse talks to you through his ears," York says.

For a second, everything focuses on the ears. Three York employees snap their fingers, scratch the pavement, and wave sticks to get the animal's attention. The ears go up. The shutter snaps. York is pleased.

James Wesley York was born September 11, 1912, in an upstairs bedroom of his parents' house at 425 South Boylan Avenue The fourth of five children, he grew up in Boylan Heights.

He had two friends whose first names were William, so York was nicknamed "Willie"—and the trio was known as "The Three Bills." The nickname stuck, and J. Willie York is the name most people still know him by.

York was a somewhat awkward youth who wore glasses from age four. He had amblyopia in his left eye, which wandered inward and made him look slightly cross-eyed.

"Willie was a timid young boy," says Raleigh attorney R. Mayne Albright, one of York's schoolmates. "You wouldn't pick him out to be the success he turned out to be."

Perhaps because of his eye, Willie didn't easily learn to read. He had to repeat first grade, and other boys called him "Four-Eyes." Willie learned to fight back with his fists. It took two more years of regular schooling and a year of afternoon tutoring before he learned how to read.

In 1923, his family moved to 2017 Fairview Road in Raleigh's fashionable Hayes Barton section. "My father had a Cadillac and a Lincoln," he says. "And I said to myself, 'My God, this is something.'"

Charles Vance York, Willie's father, was a self-made man. At the age of twenty-three, he enrolled as an engineering student at N.C. State, where he paid his way for two years by shoveling coal into a dormitory furnace.

In 1901, C. V. York left school to look for work in construction. He got a job with Cobb Brothers Construction Company in Greenville and two years later became a partner. In 1908, York & Cobb won a contract to build the first five buildings at East Carolina University, then known as East Carolina Teachers College. Several years later, C. V. York separated from the Cobbs, moved to Raleigh, bought the house in Boylan Heights, and began erecting buildings at NCSU.

C. V. York's projects include some of Raleigh's well-known monuments: the Bell Tower at N.C. State, the Sir Walter Hotel, Wiley School, the Capitol Apartments, and Memorial Auditorium.

Willie York learned the construction business from the ground up, working summers for his father. On his first job, he worked fifty-five hours a week for

THE CLASSIC LINES OF MEMORIAL AUDITORIUM

BY KATIE MOSHER
The News & Observer
April 4, 1990

There's always some last-minute primping before the big show. For Raleigh's Memorial Auditorium, that means finishing touches on a $10.3-million renovation and expansion, including a new five-thousand-square-foot lobby.

"We're elated," architect Irvin A. Pearce said Tuesday as carpenters and carpet layers, window washers and welders toiled around the building. Workers had been there until 2:00 A.M. Tuesday and planned to burn the midnight oil again to complete the fifty-five-foot-high lobby in time for its premiere tonight with *West Side Story*.

When the limestone-granite auditorium was dedicated in August 1932 as a memorial to North Carolina war veterans, it was described as the "most pretentious structure in North Carolina." Over the years, it has hosted basketball games and symphony concerts, debutante balls and theater productions.

The original cost was $300,000—about the price of three of the fourteen granite columns that surround the new glass-enclosed lobby. In the lobby, skylights and recessed lighting were added to the original facade, an idea the architect got from a museum in East Berlin. "We wanted to preserve the front of the old building," said Pearce.

About $5 million of the project was from the stage line back, including a new rehearsal hall, additional dressing rooms, and an expanded main stage.

Among those who will enjoy the official opening Saturday will be Raleigh builder Willie York. His father's company had the contract on the original building, and he spent the summer of 1932 as "general handyman and flunky" on the project.

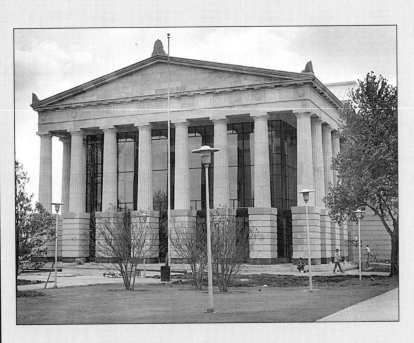

York says Memorial Auditorium still has a long history ahead of it. "The Parthenon in Athens is still there," he said.

The News & Observer

five cents an hour, carrying water for the crew building Wiley School. They loved yelling "Water boy!" to summon a York.

He loved working for his father, and developed a closer rapport with him than his older brother, C. V. York, Jr., had.

"He thought he was smarter than Dad," York says. "For damn sure he wasn't."

If York learned humility from his father, he learned about rivalry from his brother. The pain still echoes in his words. "I was never expected to succeed," York says. "My older brother, they expected greater things from him. I had so much trouble in school."

Throughout much of his freshman and sophomore years, York slept through his 8:00 A.M. classes. The result was his failing report card. But after his dad's lecture the summer of 1931, he buckled down and graduated in 1933 with a degree in civil engineering with a construction option. He went to work for the federal government, surveying roads in North Carolina and Tennessee.

York's father had suffered business losses and was just beginning to make a recovery when the Depression hit. The assignment to build Memorial Auditorium in 1932 was a godsend that temporarily buoyed his business. But when York graduated from college, his father had no work for him.

In 1935, after a two-year construction drought, the elder York got an assignment to build Efird's Department Store in downtown Raleigh. He summoned Willie York home, and his son's apprenticeship began in earnest.

Father and son ran the small construction business without secretarial help. The younger York was in charge of all correspondence. He was clerk, secretary, and factotum. The bond between father and son grew deeper. Willie York was learning the construction business from a man he respected and loved.

And when the workday was done, he was able to party. At one dance in the fall of 1937, he met Mary Smedes Poyner, a member of the prominent Raleigh family that had established St. Mary's College.

He proposed to Mary during the holiday season. She accepted. He bought ten acres of land off Craig Street at three hundred dollars an acre, borrowed fifty-five hundred dollars and built a three-bedroom house. The house was finished in time for York and his bride to move in after their April 30, 1938, wedding.

C. V. York died of heart disease in 1941, leaving his son little more than the family name and an on-the-job education. That was enough for Willie York.

"I can't put a price on that," he says. In late 1941, commercial construction ceased as the United States prepared for war. Willie York, the father of two infant boys, J. W. Jr. and Smedes, was drafted, then rated 4-F when the army discovered his eye problem.

His older brother invited him to work for T. A. Loving Company, which was building a marine air base at Cherry Point. York jumped at the chance.

Within three months, York was promoted to purchasing agent. In the next two years, he was in charge of spending $23 million. It was heady experience for the thirty-year-old journeyman builder.

"That was when I really discovered that the only difference between $2.5 million and $250,000 is moving the decimal point one place," he says. "I started thinking bigger."

He got the inspiration in a flash, acted quickly to assemble land and capital and hired the best people he could find.

In 1944, Raymond A. Bryan of Goldsboro, president of Loving, obtained permission from the government to build fifty houses at Camp Lejeune in Jacksonville. Bryan cut York in on the deal. York's payment was a one-third interest in the project. A year later, York got another "wartime priority" to build fifty houses in Morehead City. He began to accumulate the capital that would propel him in business.

In 1945, York moved back to Raleigh and established the hurly-burly momentum that would make his name.

When the city needed something, York built it. In 1947, the city needed a shopping center and a new housing development. York provided Cameron Village, the first project of its kind in the Southeast.

In 1951, the city needed to diversify its employment base. York bought 560 acres of land near U.S. 1 North and started an industrial center.

In 1956, the city needed a Farmer's Market. York built one. In 1963, the city needed an in-town motel. Willie York built the Velvet Cloak.

The list goes on. It includes Mission Valley Apartments in 1972, Mission Valley Shopping Center in 1973, Cary Village Shopping Center in 1975, Stony Brook Shopping Center in 1977, and more than a dozen industrial facilities.

York surrounded himself with talented lawyers, architects, and associates. And he sparked the careers of a half-dozen of the state's most successful men.

When York built the Morehead City project in 1945, he brought prefabricated houses from a Brooklyn, New York, housing salesman named Ed Richards.

Several years later, York persuaded Richards to move to Raleigh. He rented Richards an apartment downtown and helped him get started. When Richards sold his business several years ago, the price was said to be more than $100 million.

In 1947, Richards introduced York to a young architect from Scarsdale, New York, Leif Valand. York brought him to Raleigh to design Cameron Village, and in the next forty years Valand designed more than two hundred Triangle buildings.

York persuaded a druggist named Banks Kerr to open a store in Cameron Village, the first of what Kerr built into a chain of more than sixty drugstores.

York created a mortgage-financing company in the late 1940s and hired a young Louisiana oil-company engineer named Charles Clifford Cameron to help run it. Cameron went on to become president of Charlotte's First Union National Bank of North Carolina.

Of all the things York has built, Cameron Village is his most characteristic accomplishment. He got the inspiration in a flash, acted quickly to assemble

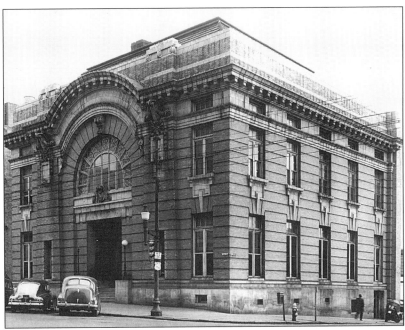

The combined municipal building and City Auditorium, built in 1910. The auditorium served as the city's main public theater until Memorial Auditorium opened in 1933.

N.C. Division of Archives and History

land and capital, and hired the best people he could find to design, build, and operate the stores. The 158-acre development, which has roughly 20 stores, 560 apartments, and 250 homes, still recalls the optimism and burgeoning consumerism of the late 1940s. It is a period piece that sums up the progressive architectural and land-planning ideals of the day.

Wymene Valand, the architect's widow, remembers the York of those years as a blur of action: "He worked hard. All of them did. They all had big dreams. They'd sit around and visualize where their careers were going."

As he looks back on the town he helped build, York says, "There's damn little wrong with the city of Raleigh." He likes the sprawling horizontal development he helped to create. "What's really bad about urban sprawl? It means that people have air and space around them."

For York, being public-spirited meant serving on public bodies. As an appointee, he not only contributed his expertise, he gained a wider arena in which to exert his influence.

From 1957 to 1963, he served on the Raleigh City School Board. He voted against allowing a black student to enroll at Broughton High School during his first year on the board, but he later became a cautious advocate of integration.

"I thought he was a man with a clear and open mind who was trying to do what he thought was best for the city of Raleigh," says Fred J. Carnage, that era's only black school-board member. "He was in favor of moderate change and didn't want to see anything that would hurt the whole school system."

In 1965, York became chairman of the state Board of Conservation and Development. He served for four years and led a drive to raise the interest-rate ceiling for banks. This had the effect of making more capital available for development.

From 1976 to 1984, York served on the Raleigh-Durham Airport Authority and clashed again and again with other members on the location of a new runway. York still grumbles about "hardheaded" R. Dillard Teer, a Durham developer and authority member who opposed him on the runway.

But he earned Teer's respect by fighting for his beliefs. He also got his way. The airport's new runway is where Willie York wanted it to be.

"It wouldn't have been any good if he had been a milquetoast," Teer says. "He's always been tenacious when he knows what he has to do to get things done."

Willie York's tenacity and drive rubbed off on his eight children, four from each marriage. His oldest son, James W. York, Jr., earned a doctorate in physics and is a professor at the University of North Carolina at Chapel Hill. Smedes played basketball for N.C. State and became a popular mayor of Raleigh. Today, he is the president of York Construction and York Properties. Three other York children are in the family business.

As a young family man, Willie York would work hard all day, then come home and help prepare dinner. He loved to cook. And when he was in the kitchen, he was in charge. "He's the boss pretty much wherever he is," says Smedes York.

York and his first wife, Mary, also loved going to parties, and the Valands were among their frequent companions. "Willie was a good dancer, and he was so much fun," says Mrs. Valand. "So was Mary. She was the life of the party."

The Smallwood property in 1947, before its transformation into Cameron Village
N.C.Division of Archives and History

But during the late 1950s, York's marriage foundered. The couple was divorced in February 1962 after a two-year separation, and York was remarried in March 1962 to Elizabeth West Collette, who had been his secretary for the previous eleven years.

"I think they just grew apart," Smedes York says of his parents.

Difficulties with Willie and Mary's third son, Charles Vance York II, who was born with cerebral palsy, also put a strain on the family.

"It was hard for Father to relate to," says Smedes York. "He didn't know what to do. Mother would do anything for Vance. But Dad was so solution-oriented. He said, 'Let's just solve this.' He doesn't have a lot of patience sometimes."

His legacy to his children, Willie York says, is a sense of family identity and continuity—the sense that Yorks will continue to shape the city's growth.

"Even now I'm not known," he says one day in the spacious dining room of his Cameron Village apartment. "Ten years after I'm gone, people will say, 'Who the hell was Willie York?' But I know who I am. And my children will know who I am."

Crossing the color line

William Campbell integrates Raleigh's schools

BY MARY BURCH
The Raleigh Times
May 17, 1979

"I remember the ride seemed to take so long, and there were people on all sides of the street. It looked as if there were a parade, actually.

"When we got to the school, which was only eight or nine blocks from our house, there seemed to be hundreds and hundreds of people. We parked in front of the school and got out."

That day, September 9, 1960, is branded into the memory of William Campbell. The ride and the walk he took with his parents, Ralph and June Campbell, were to enroll in Murphey School. He would be the first black child to attend a white public school here. He was seven years old.

"I remember just about everything about that day," Campbell, said in a telephone interview from his law office in Atlanta, on the eve of the anniversary of the 1954 Supreme Court school-desegregation decision. "I've been over it so many times, and it was part and parcel of what we [the Campbell family] were doing at the time to help bring about integration," he said. Campbell's father was an NAACP official.

Young Campbell had attended first grade at the all-black, private St. Monica's Catholic School. His parents applied to the Raleigh Board of Education to enroll him and his older brother and sister in white schools for the fall of 1960. On September 6, 1960, the school board acted on a motion by Willie York, seconded by LeRoy Martin, to assign young Campbell to Murphey School. At the same time, the seven-member board denied requests by Campbell to enroll his older son, Ralph Jr., and daughter, Mildred, in all-white Broughton High. The older two Campbell children never attended an integrated high school.

"I remember my father telling me that I was going to go to a different school. It didn't seem unusual to me, because we were marching as a family unit almost daily," Campbell said. "I remember we would gather in the evenings at Shaw or St. Augustine's and listen to a couple of speeches and

William Campbell on his way to school, September 9, 1960

The News & Observer

sing a few songs—like 'We Shall Overcome'—and work ourselves up into a fever pitch and march up and down Fayetteville Street."

Campbell said he and a young girl who was about his age were often selected to lead marches. He recalled specifically marches to the Ambassador Theater and the Sir Walter Hotel.

So, to his seven-year-old mind, the day he enrolled in Murphey School was much like just another march, he said. "It just made perfect sense. . . . I remember that day we got up very early, literally the crack of dawn, and there was a lot of hectic activity. I especially recall there were a lot of religious leaders, priests and reverends, who were going to accompany us on the ride over. It took about three or four cars. I was dressed for school as though it were any other day.

"As we were walking, I don't recall anyone shouting epithets, but there may have been," Campbell said. "I was just counting my steps and trying to block out everything. There were crowds and cameras and reporters everywhere."

When he and his parents entered the school, they were met by Principal M. A. Kerbaugh, and the noise seemed to stop, Campbell said. He was assigned to Nell Abbott's second-grade class. But integration didn't come that easy.

The Campbell family received harassing telephone calls and bomb threats. Young Campbell had to be accompanied to and from school by family friends for two months, for his safety. Parents of other children in Murphey School were so upset by integration that they canceled all PTA meetings for two years. "That day, it was one of the worst days of my life," young Campbell's father, Ralph, said in an interview. "There were shouting crowds at the school and there was continued harassment by telephone calls and bomb threats that night. And this went on for months and months. My wife was afraid that Bill would be hurt. But I just had the faith that adults would not do harm to a child seven years old."

William Campbell remembers his teacher, Mrs. Abbott, fondly. "Probably the person who had the biggest influence on me being able to emerge from this unscathed was my teacher, Mrs. Abbott," Campbell said. "She was eminently fair and she was very kind to me. I recall that I really loved that lady, and I went back to see her a number of times after I left the school. After a couple of weeks, I had no concern from anyone in the classroom mistreating me, due to Mrs. Abbott. That was a very secure feeling."

Although his second-grade classmates accepted him, by and large, older boys sometimes jostled him and jeered. His most vivid confrontation came when he was trapped by two older students behind the auditorium curtain after a civil-rights march in which he had participated. "I remember, one said to me, 'Nigger, were you marching with those other niggers last night?' and I said, 'No, not me.'"

Another time, he was playing at the home of a white classmate. The two children were in a bedroom when they heard a knock at the door, Campbell recalled. "The kid said to me, 'If my mother finds you in here, she'll kill us both.

William Campbell on his last day at Enloe High School, May 2, 1971
The News & Observer

You'd better get under the bed.' I was scared—after all I was seven years old—so I jumped under the bed. . . . It turned out it was just someone knocking at the door, but we later learned that the kid's mother just happened to be the woman who was leading a petition drive to try to remove me from Murphey School."

Incidents with adults stick in Campbell's mind as well. "I remember I was walking home one day, and this woman said to me, 'Son, why do you want to go to school with whites? Why don't you want to go to school where the coloreds go? I just can't understand it.' "

As time passed, Campbell, an A student, got along well with most of his white classmates during his school years. "If I had been a marginal student or a poor student, things might have been different," he said.

He was the only black student at Murphey School for five years. He then attended Aycock Junior High and earned a scholarship to the private Taft School in Watertown, Connecticut. He attended Taft for one and a half years, then decided to return to Raleigh and enroll at Enloe for the second half of his junior year and his senior year. He graduated with honors and was inducted into the National Honor Society. After graduation, he received offers of a full scholarship from seven universities. He chose Vanderbilt University in Nashville, Tennessee, because he wanted to remain in the South. He graduated summa cum laude in three years with a triple major in sociology, history, and political science, in addition to being a campus leader.

He attended Duke University Law School on a scholarship, graduated in 1977, and passed the Georgia State Bar the same year. For the past two years, he has been a corporate lawyer with Kilpatrick, Cody, Rogers, McClachey, and Regenstein. In June, he will begin a new job with the United States Department of Justice's antitrust division in Atlanta.

More blacks were admitted to previously all-white Raleigh schools the year after Campbell was enrolled. But substantial integration did not occur until a court-ordered plan took effect in 1971. Murphey School, on Person Street several blocks north of the Governor's Mansion, was closed in 1973 and sold to the state.

In November 1993, William Campbell was elected mayor of Atlanta.

Sit-down strike spreads to stores

The civil-rights movement awakens

BY CHARLES CRAVEN AND DAVID COOPER
The News & Observer
February 11, 1960

The statewide lunch-counter sit-down protest of Negro college students moved to Raleigh Wednesday.

Some seventeen boys and girls took part in the demonstration against white-only food service at eight stores, but the only immediate result of their action was the quick closing of all lunch counters.

The only incidents in connection with the protest movement were the tossing of one egg and the heckling of students by teenagers and other whites.

Ironically, the demonstration came at the same time when Negro church leaders of Raleigh were meeting with white store operators to work out a peaceful solution to the problem.

Further meetings between the two groups were in prospect today.

The sit-down demonstrations began in Greensboro last week and moved to Winston-Salem, Charlotte, Durham, and Fayetteville in subsequent days.

The Raleigh sit-down demonstrations began about 10:30 A.M. Wednesday at Woolworth's downtown store. It moved on to other stores—McLellan's, Hudson-Belk, Kress, Eckerd's Drugstore, Walgreens Drugstore, and Woolworth's in Cameron Village—and in each place the lunch counters were immediately closed when the Negro students asked for service.

Awaiting service at Woolworth's, February 11, 1960
The News & Observer

Ellen Winston

Helping others help themselves

BY NACK AULIS
The News & Observer
May 4, 1986

Ellen Black Winston

1904–84

At her death, at age eighty, in June 1984, one editorial writer said, "No woman in North Carolina—and perhaps no man—understood better than she the complicated ways of social change."

Dr. Ellen Black Winston, a noted North Carolina sociologist, was the first United States welfare commissioner, appointed by President Kennedy in January 1963. For nearly eighteen years before her federal appointment, she was state commissioner of welfare—and the highest-ranking female executive in state government.

She was born in Bryson City in Swain County, in western North Carolina, and received her early education in state public schools. She was a graduate of Converse College in Spartanburg, South Carolina, and received her doctorate in sociology from the University of Chicago.

A long and distinguished career in the field brought her three honorary degrees and service on more boards and commissions than can be listed in a single-spaced typewritten page. "She saw," one writer said, "every social upheaval of the century—Prohibition, the Great Depression and four wars, the civil-rights movement, the women's suffrage movement, and later the ascendancy of women in the political and economic life of America."

Her husband was also a sociologist. Dr. Richard S. Winston was a professor and chairman of the sociology and anthropology department at North Carolina State University for thirty years before he retired in 1963. He died in 1969.

Before entering state government, Winston was head of the sociology department at Meredith College in Raleigh for four years. During her time in the state job, she worked extensively with both national and state social-welfare agencies and achieved wide recognition for her contributions to the public welfare field.

Among her many activities at the national level was a term (1959–61) as president of the American Public Welfare Association.

She wrote extensively about social and economic problems. Her works include hundreds of articles and three books (dealing with rural relief, the social aspects of the plantation system, and population programs), which she coauthored.

Her appointment as the nation's first welfare commissioner came as the result of the reorganization of the federal Department of Health, Education, and Welfare. She resigned that post in March 1967 to devote her time to social-welfare policy matters.

In 1974, she received the North Carolina Award for public service for her work in social welfare. In 1980, she was elected president of the National Council on Aging, a private, nonprofit corporation based in Washington. In 1984, she was one of five women to receive Distinguished Women of North Carolina awards, which were presented for the first time that year.

Winston was a "practical sociologist," one writer said. "She knew how to connect policy to the daily lives of people." Of her work, Winston said, "I simply try to help others help themselves."

Running with the Wolfpack

North Carolina State's sports legacy

BY CHIP ALEXANDER
The News & Observer
December 1991

The score was "small," according to news accounts, but the attendance quite large, at least by the standards of the day. It was March 13, 1892, and the North Carolina Agricultural & Mechanical College engaged in an athletic event with the Raleigh Male Academy. The final score in the competition was 12–6, and a fine time was apparently had by all.

Baseball?

No, it was football—or an imitation of such—being played in March, nearly a century before the Skyhawks would come to town in another spring and do their best to imitate professional athletes. Though the academy boys averaged just 125 pounds and college men a more brutish 160, the game was "interesting and played pleasantly, being free from any disputes or injury," the *News & Observer* reported.

The crowd totaled two hundred interested souls "including an unusual number of ladies," and the game was played at the athletic park in what is now Pullen Park. The *N&O* ended its report with a little editorializing, noting, "We hope this game between the School and the College will be an annual affair."

And it was—for one more year. The college won again in 1893, by a 13–0 count. But another opponent was added that year, the University of Tennessee, which also fell, 12–6, as A&M was 2–0 that season.

A&M, which eventually would be called North Carolina State University, moved on to bigger and better teams. The University of North Carolina was added to the football schedule in 1894—twice—and UNC was the winner in both games. But an athletic trend had been set that has deviated little through the years.

Over the last century, N.C. State has been a chief source of athletic entertainment in the city of Raleigh. Certainly, it has had to share attention with its sister school in Chapel Hill and with that private school in Durham, Duke University, but State has

Wolfpack football team, 1898
N.C. State University

been the big show in Raleigh, especially with the absence of any major-league teams and with marginal competition—and marginal success—by various professional franchises.

State has maintained its entertainment status with its touchdowns and fast breaks from early fall until the spring. State has been the place to go, to see the games and be seen, at Riddick Stadium and later Carter-Finley Stadium, at Memorial Auditorium and Frank Thompson Gym and then Reynolds Coliseum.

"The facilities that were built at State created a big-time athletic aura for Raleigh," said Frank Weedon, State's senior associate athletics director.

Riddick's Field, 1910
N.C. State University

"Because of Reynolds Coliseum, we were able to host the ACC Tournament and NCAA regionals. And, of course, there was the Dixie Classic. The economic impact from the Dixie Classic, from all the people who came to Raleigh for the three days of the basketball tournament after Christmas and spent money in the many post-Christmas sales and who filled the hotels and restaurants, was tremendous.

"Ironically, in some ways Riddick and Reynolds were detrimental, too," Weedon added. "With Riddick available for high-school football games until the late 1960s, the city never saw a need to build a city stadium. And Reynolds, though the prime entertainment center for eastern North Carolina, was upstaged by bigger facilities in Greensboro and Charlotte. Riddick is now a parking lot and Reynolds outdated, and Raleigh has no suitable facilities to contend with the others."

The nicknames of State's athletic teams have varied. In the early years, they were called the Farmers & Mechanics (no, not by students in Chapel Hill; this was an official school nickname). Later came the Aggies, and the Techs, and one that became quite popular—the Red Terrors.

But in 1922, a State fan, disgusted by the team's 3–3–3 record, told athletic officials that the team would never be a winner as long as the players "acted like a wolfpack." State students, being students and thus ever irreverent, immediately tagged the football team the "Wolfpack," and a tradition began.

And what a tradition.

From the starting point, from that primitive football game at the athletic park in 1892, the Wolfpack has provided its fans—and the citizens of Raleigh—so many cherished moments. The names come and go: Beattie Feathers and Earle Edwards, Everett Case and Jim Valvano, Ted Brown and David Thompson, Touchdown Turner and Roman Gabriel, Ronnie Shavlik and Lou Puccillo, Chris Cammack and Mike Caldwell, Tab Thacker and Scott Turner. But the memories last a lifetime and have been woven into the fabric of a city.

Everett Case is no doubt State's most revered athletic figure. Though the school started playing basketball in 1910, the "Old Gray Fox" brought big-time college ball to Tobacco Road in the late 1940s, promoting it and paving the way for others to join a new athletic league created in 1953, the Atlantic Coast Conference.

Case's "Hoosier Hotshots" introduced a fast-paced game that was widely copied, and the Wolfpack soon needed a new arena to pack in the masses aching to see the show—causing problems for the fire marshals. Reynolds Coliseum was built in 1949, the Dixie Classic began a twelve-year run that year, and the ACC Tournament was held there from 1954 to 1966. Case was at courtside until retiring early in the 1964–65 season after 376 wins and a combined ten Southern Conference and ACC championships.

In the spring of 1961, the Dixie Classic was discontinued. Officials of the consolidated university curbed the basketball programs at North Carolina State and the University of North Carolina at Chapel Hill following a game-fixing scandal in which players from the two schools were linked to gamblers.

University president William Friday called for the ban on the Dixie Classic. Friday said the annual tournament, held the week after Christmas, was scheduled when school was not in session and thus exemplified exploitation for public entertainment or commercial purposes.

But venerable Reynolds Coliseum got a coveted addition in 1974, and another in 1983—a pair of new banners raised high in the old gym. They read "NCAA Champions" and are reminders of two special teams that captured the public's fancy, not just in Raleigh or North Carolina but across the country.

The 1974 Wolfpack, coached by Norm Sloan and featuring All-America forward David Thompson, seven-foot-four center Tommy Burleson, and diminutive guard Monte Towe, gave the school its first national championship. Thompson took a terrifying fall in an NCAA game at Reynolds, but he rose to lead the Pack past UCLA and Marquette in Greensboro for the national title.

In 1983, there was another national championship. Jim Valvano was the coach, and his squad was described as a "team that had no All-America, just all of America." The "Cardiac Pack" kept pulling off upsets until Lorenzo Charles's dunk in the final seconds of the final game against Houston thrilled the nation and sent Raleigh into an all-night delirium.

Valvano stepped down as coach in 1990 after the NCAA placed the basketball program on probation and a university investigation uncovered academic deficiencies. It was a controversy that scarred the city and sent many Wolfpack fans into a fury, but Les Robinson took over as State's head coach and helped stem the rage with his unassuming style and exciting offense.

In football, State's 1967 team—known as the "White Shoes" and "Kool Kyoties"—was 8–0 late in the season and number three in national polls, exciting the city as no other team before. It was uncharted territory for the Wolfpack in football, but Penn State ended the Pack's undefeated season in the ninth game, 13–8. "The atmosphere in

Basketball coach Everett Case
N.C. State University

Raleigh was un-matched that fall," said Weedon, who came to State in 1960. "Every-one got caught up in the team, and when it lost at Penn State, the whole town was like a morgue. I've never seen anything like it."

State finished 9–2 in '67 after a Liberty Bowl win. It was the pinnacle of Earle Edwards's seventeen years as coach, an era in which the school canceled any ideas of deemphasizing the

Game time at Reynolds Coliseum
The News & Observer

sport and instead won or shared five ACC championships—with such players as Gabriel, Jim Donnan, and Fred Combs—even though it scheduled many games away from home until Carter Stadium opened in 1966.

Lou Holtz, the little man with thick glasses and sideline genius, added glitz and offensive wizardry to the Wolfpack football program in the 1970s, taking the Pack to the 1973 ACC title and four bowls in his four mercurial years as coach. Ted Brown was Holtz's biggest find, rushing for forty-six hundred yards and gaining All-America status at halfback before heading to the NFL. Bo Rein won the school's last ACC football title in 1979, and there followed a lull in State's on-field success. But Dick Sheridan picked up the reins in 1986, sifting through the ashes and relighting the competitive fires, and the Wolfpack has regained respectability. Sheridan's six years as coach have produced five winning seasons and as many bowl teams, an unprecedented period of sustained excellence in the program.

State's athletic excellence hasn't been confined to its two primary sports. The Wolfpack swimming program has produced Olympic champions, and Pack wrestlers are perennial ACC contenders and often the conference winners. Its baseball team annually ranks among the top thirty in the country and made an appearance in the 1968 College World Series.

The Easter Monday baseball game between State and Wake Forest College attracted such interest in the 1930s and 1940s that the state government was closed. It was a big event long before the Dixie Classic or State-Carolina football games.

"A number of professional teams have tried to cash in on the college athletic atmosphere and success here," State's Weedon said. "I'm not sure any can or will be overly successful, however. Because of the proximity of our Big Four rivals, interest in intercollegiate sports is unique. Nothing can match what Choo Choo Justice did for football in this state and area, or David Thompson and Dean Smith in basketball. And Raleigh is a college town."

Main Street moves indoors

The malling of Raleigh

BY GUY MUNGER
The News & Observer
December 1991

In the unlikely event you should be trapped in one of Raleigh's major shopping centers or malls, you could probably exist for an unlimited amount of time—if you didn't mind a diet heavy on chicken-filet sandwiches and chocolate-chip cookies.

But shopping in Raleigh was not always like this. In fact, it was not until 1949 that the city got its first shopping center.

What has been called America's love affair with suburban shopping centers began in 1927, when developer Jessie Clyde Nichols built a Spanish-style shopping center five miles southwest of downtown Kansas City, Missouri. And in 1949, Raleigh developer Willie York was able to put together the financing, land, and building to bring the shopping-center concept to the Capital City.

His Cameron Village project was the first regional shopping center (over half a million square feet) in the Southeast. It was not universally acclaimed. Two years earlier, the Raleigh Garden Club had asked city officials to postpone action on use of the site for a shopping center pending a survey of park needs. In addition, residents of nearby Cameron Park objected to commercial development so close to a

Cameron Village
The News & Observer

residential area. (Those complaints, incidentally, are still heard today.) But Willie York eventually carried the day and set in motion a revolution in marketing that reshaped Raleigh and the way its people live.

Raleigh's shopping centers range from small neighborhood types—almost random collections of shops that have off-street parking—to the Big Three (in descending order of volume) of Crabtree Valley Mall, North Hills Mall and Cameron Village.

A 1989 market survey conducted for the *News & Observer* by Market Opinion Research found that over a thirty-day period, Crabtree Valley was visited by 239,000 adults, or 47 percent of the Triangle's population. Following behind were North Hills Mall and South Square Mall in Durham with a 37-percent share, Northgate Mall in Durham with 32 percent, and Cameron Village in Raleigh with 23 percent.

If Willie York pioneered the shopping center in Raleigh, developer E. N. Richards is the man who plunged the city into the culture of the enclosed mall when he opened North Hills Mall in the late 1960s. Apart from his retailing ventures, Ed Richards has left his mark across North Carolina with more than ten thousand housing units and more than a dozen shopping malls. He's a blunt-spoken man. A young reporter once asked him why all of Raleigh's development seemed to be on the city's north side. "Because sewage runs downhill," Richards rumbled in reply (only he didn't use the word *sewage*), explaining that gravity is cheaper than building pumping stations.

That bluntness and pioneering spirit were probably a necessity for those who charted this new course in Raleigh retailing, for they were doing nothing less than reshaping a city. Just twenty-five or thirty years ago, Raleigh virtually ended near the current path of the Beltline. From there northward, fields and pine woods stretched in an almost unbroken green sweep toward Oxford.

North Hills was where you went for stargazing and looking at the distant lights of downtown Raleigh. Crabtree Valley was a glen of trees and pastures where horses grazed by Crabtree Creek and entrepreneur Kidd Brewer gazed benevolently down on the pastoral landscape from his baronial mansion high on the hill.

But times change. North Hills Mall now is the center of a mini-city, and Crabtree Valley—especially at Christmas and other peak shopping times—is where you can find almost anything that is sold, along with traffic jams that rival the Jersey approach to the George Washington Bridge on a snowy day.

In 1984, there came what TV sports announcers call "a break in the action." All three of Raleigh's kingpin shopping centers undertook major remodeling at the same time, with a total price tag of $13 million. It was an opportune moment to look at past and future. Time had left Crabtree, North Hills, and Cameron Village looking worn and dated. All three had lighting problems. A series of parking decks built at Cameron Village in the mid-1960s had left storefronts obscured in shadow. North Hills and Crabtree didn't have enough skylights and looked gloomy. What took place in the remodeling says a lot about Raleigh's shopping centers, since things do not happen by accident in this business. Shopping-

Those who charted this new course . . . were doing nothing less than reshaping a city.

Crabtree Valley Mall
The News & Observer

center managers probe and survey and analyze their customers—then they cater to them.

North Hills and Crabtree offer similar environments—boxy and not particularly attractive outside, but inside a different story. Climate is controlled and soft music gently whispers, "Buy! Buy!"

So if the customers wanted more light, let there be light. Crabtree knocked ten skylights in the roof and festooned the ceilings with colorful banners. North Hills added skylights and recessed some of the storefronts to break up the monotonous straightness of the mall. Not to be outdone, Cameron Village installed translucent canopies—again letting in more light—and put up bright blue signs that unified the buildings in the center. In 1991, Cameron Village and Crabtree were taking down the parking decks in another redesign.

A large part of the attraction of shopping centers and malls is only peripherally related to buying merchandise. Thus, while they may have killed downtown retailing and made people more dependent on automobiles, malls also have moved Main Street inside.

Some people come to hang out, meet friends, check out what's happening. Others—some of them oldsters—get their exercise in malls. After all, a brisk walk in a cozy, warm mall is preferable any day to sloshing through city streets and dodging cars. Malls and shopping centers go out of their way to encourage this town-square feeling. Raleigh malls play host to displays by prison artists, Boy Scouts, Girl Scouts, and numerous charitable groups.

Cameron Village regularly provides room for fraternal groups' fish fries and Oktoberfests featuring German music. (It is no accident that residents of Cameron Park know all the verses to "Schnitzelbank.")

Malls and shopping-centers are people magnets, and the people who are attracted come willingly. They want to be at the center of things. But if that fulfillment of an apparent basic human need is a plus, critics say there is also a dark side to the shopping-center phenomenon.

A study at the University of North Carolina at Chapel Hill, for example, found that when shopping-centers are placed close to residential neighborhoods, the crime rate goes up. And that holds no matter whether it's a lower-, middle-, or upper-income neighborhood. (A Cameron Park resident offers anecdotal support for the study. He recalls vividly the night when he was disturbed in his bedtime routine by a police chase—through his home. A suspected shoplifter fled from nearby Cameron Village, broke in the house, raced upstairs—with police in hot pursuit—then hurled himself through a bedroom window. Unlike Superman, he did not soar away. He landed on a porch roof and was taken into custody.) There also, of course, is the broader question of what unchecked commercial growth does to a city's traffic and appearance. It has been said that malls and shopping centers reflect the idea that the best thing land can do is create maximum profit, not serve a public purpose.

A 1984 *News & Observer* editorial offered a scenario of what that attitude brings. The editorial recalled that a Raleigh man, Peter V. Andrews, had told the city council in 1977 "that Falls of the Neuse Road was in danger of becoming a commercial free-fire zone, exploding with drive-in restaurants, shopping centers shoulder to shoulder, neon signs, and endless traffic." By 1984—just seven years later—the two-and-a-half-mile stretch in North Raleigh had six shopping centers, with a seventh on the way, and enough restaurants to satisfy the appetite of Diamond Jim Brady.

How did it happen? Over the years, developers simply got the city council to rezone key locations, and it wasn't long before nearby areas also fell into the developers' laps—like dominoes.

Falling along with these dominoes was an unwritten rule that shopping centers should be at least a mile apart.

There is a footnote. Sometime later, city planners took reporters, editors, and TV journalists on a bus tour of North Raleigh. When they stopped for a coffee break, it was at a fast-food restaurant built where the planners had intended a park to be.

The shopping center–mall phenomenon shows no sign of abating. In fact, business people say that in times of recession, the hard sell will become more common, and that means wooing the customer. What better place to do it than in a mall with seductive music playing softly in the background?

Their environments are boxy and not particularly attractive outside, but inside climate is controlled and soft music gently whispers, "Buy! Buy!"

Fayetteville Street Mall

Letting grass grow on the town's main street

BY GUY MUNGER
The News & Observer
December 1991

Back in 1977 when workers were winding up the job of turning Fayetteville Street into Fayetteville Street Mall, Jimmy Briggs stood in the front door of his venerable hardware store and surveyed the chaos before him.

Two men were laying a brick sidewalk while others were unrolling turf for an instant lawn. Down the block, other workers were planting shrubbery.

Briggs turned to his companions, a couple of reporters taking a shortcut through the hardware store on their way to lunch, then pointed to the gardeners and said, "It's the first time I ever heard tell of expecting to improve business by letting grass grow on the town's main street."

Briggs was not alone in his skepticism, but while turning Fayetteville Street into an open-air mall was not a cure-all for what ails downtown Raleigh, most would agree the overall effect has been positive. And who can say how much impact the mall had on decisions to build the major office buildings that have gone up downtown in recent years?

In its best moments—say, during Artsplosure or the Christmas season—the Fayetteville Street Mall bustles with life and laughter, a whirling blend of music and color and, in the background, the reassuring pulse of commerce.

But at night, the mall is downright spooky. The pools of inky blackness between the cones of illumination from streetlights are frightening, prone to conjuring up images of muggers and other terrors of the night.

There are no people about. Were it not for the occasional cobblestones and concrete barriers, you could roll a bowling ball from the Capitol end of the mall all the way down to the civic center any night of the week and never endanger a human.

In other words, a variety of solutions have been proposed for downtown Raleigh's trouble, and a good many have been tried. But we still got troubles, right here in Capital City.

In a sense, the development of downtown Raleigh and Fayetteville Street as its main artery was haphazard, almost by chance.

Parade down Fayetteville Street celebrating Raleigh's centennial, 1892

N.C. Division of Archives and History

Fayetteville Street happened to be where the road from Fayetteville to Raleigh ended, and Fayetteville was the farthest inland port in times when shipping by water was vital. Hence Raleigh—and Fayetteville Street—flourished.

Over the years, downtown Raleigh grew by fits and starts with little planning or pattern. Fayetteville Street was essentially the Main Street of a small town, complete with all its favorite hangouts and characters.

Old-timers can remember back when it was Fayetteville Street—not the mall—and business was brisk at the California Fruit Store and at Brantley's drugstore, home of heavenly ice cream and honest fountain Cokes. Governor Clyde Hoey, garbed in frock coat, winged collar, and string tie, leisurely strolled from his office at the Capitol down to Brantley's every morning for his Coca-Cola break.

Those were the days when there was head-in parking on Fayetteville Street, and Saturday afternoon downtown was a big deal. But then something happened—first the Depression and then World War II. Downtown withered, and in the euphoria of postwar America, Raleigh, like the rest of America, began to look outward—to the suburbs and the magical new lure of shopping centers and shopping malls.

The suggestions for downtown remedies covered the waterfront. One professor of architecture suggested privately that the best idea might be to level downtown Raleigh and turn it into a park, with perhaps a museum and an auditorium or two set amid the greenery.

Another professor, Peter Batchelor of North Carolina State University, whose speciality is urban design, zeroed in on the need to bring downtown alive at night. He proposed better lighting, nighttime bus service to downtown, and housing in the area. "Office buildings only function between nine and five," Batchelor said. "We've got to have a resident population down there twenty-four hours. People in housing need convenience stores. They need supermarkets, bookstores, clothing stores." Batchelor said the Founders Row condominium complex that opened near the rejuvenated City Market was "a small step in the right direction," but that many more such projects were needed.

Most city planners have ruled out any efforts to restore downtown as a major retail center. That market is gone, flown to the malls and shopping centers in the

Trolley cars on Fayetteville Street in 1913, as seen from the Capitol (top)
The News & Observer

The Yarborough House, the city's grandest hotel from the 1850s until it burned in 1928 (bottom)
The News & Observer

The Mall in 1984
The News & Observer

city's fringes and suburbs. Others working on downtown revitalization have looked for answers in the city's rich history—a sort of "back to the future" approach.

One city program, for instance, encouraged owners and tenants of downtown buildings to rejuvenate the fronts of their buildings by giving them a festive, old-time look, in some cases restoring old facades. Two advantages of the program were its relatively low cost compared to new building and its immediate impact in neatening and brightening up downtown. But such projects are, at best, only nibbling away at the problems of downtown. For long-range, large-scale answers, many are putting their bets on major construction projects—renovation or replacement of the civic center, the skyscrapers that have gone up recently along the mall, and the revived City Market and Moore Square area.

Already in place are two major new buildings—First Union Capitol Center, which cost $65 million and is twenty-nine stories, on the mall's 100 block just south of the Capitol, and Hannover Two, which cost $60 million and is twenty-nine stories, on the mall's 400 block near the civic center.

Plans for a third project, First Citizens Bank Center, a twenty-four-story building across the mall from the downtown post office, have been put on indefinite hold because of business conditions. The recession also has put a damper on a perennial topic of discussion for revitalizing downtown—the expansion, renovation, or replacement of the fourteen-year-old civic center, which lies athwart the mall at its southern end.

The $7-million civic center project is on a city-county want list, along with a $23-million children's museum, a $110-million convention center, and several other big-ticket projects. All would be funded in part with a new tax on hotel rooms and restaurant meals that will be effective in 1992. But their construction is by no means certain.

"It's possible all the projects will be done, none will be done, or just some will be done," said Wake county manager Richard Y. Stevens. None of them is certain at this stage.

Kelly S. King, chairman of the Greater Raleigh Chamber of Commerce, said that he expects to see all the projects built and that the only question is when. "The probability of seeing all of them over an extended period of time is very high," King said. "The probability of seeing them all in the time frame outlined [by 2020] is not as high. It's possible, but it really depends on the recovery of the economy."

For those who wish the best for downtown, there is symbolism in the new skyscrapers that tower over the area. Fayetteville Street and the mall have had their ups and downs. Now—just maybe—things are looking up.

Dorton Arena and its designer

An architect's lonely monument

BY STEVEN LITT
The News & Observer
October 15, 1989

The news clattered across the wires on the last day of August 1950. A four-engine Trans World Airlines Constellation had crashed in the Egyptian desert a half-hour after taking off from Cairo.

Among the fifty-five people killed: Matthew Nowicki, the designer of Raleigh's Dorton Arena and head of the architecture program at North Carolina State University, then called State College. His body, burned beyond recognition, was buried in a mass grave and commemorated with a marker that said simply "Architect." He was forty.

"It was like a good chunk of the world had disappeared," said Nowicki's former student George Qualls, now an architect in Philadelphia. Qualls remembers Nowicki (pronounced no-VIT-ski) as "a movie idol to all of us." With his elegant suits and dignified manner, Nowicki brought a touch of European class to North Carolina State. But he wasn't pompous or remote. Nowicki "just bubbled with enthusiasm," Qualls said. "If you didn't quite produce what you should, he made you feel ashamed of yourself. He had a kind of a hangdog look that would make you want to do anything for him." Today, all that lasts of Nowicki's bright promise—as teacher and architect—is Dorton Arena. With its soaring structure, the building speaks of an America emerging from the Depression and World War II full of energy and optimism and ready to go somewhere in a hurry.

No one was in more of a hurry than Nowicki, whose career streaked like a comet across the late 1940s. He emerged from the Polish resistance to help design the United Nations in Manhattan, to plan a new capital city for the Indian province of Punjab, to design Dorton Arena, and to take over as head of the architecture program at NCSU. He was on his way back to Raleigh from India

The News & Observer

Matthew Nowicki

when he took the flight from Cairo.

Supported by no less an architectural kingmaker than critic Lewis Mumford, Nowicki seemed destined for greatness. He was mentioned alongside the masters of his day—Eero Saarinen, Le Corbusier, Oscar Niemeyer. After Nowicki's death, Mumford wrote a biographical essay on the architect in *Architectural Record*. And Philip Johnson, who popularized the International Style in America with his book of the same title in 1932, organized an exhibition of Nowicki's drawings at the Museum of Modern Art in New York. Mumford reviewed the show enthusiastically in the *New Yorker*. Despite the efforts, Nowicki's name is a footnote.

Le Corbusier put aside other contenders to take over Nowicki's project in India. Eero Saarinen, the architect of the Trans World Airlines terminal in New York, became the name most associated with the bold, sculptural use of engineering Nowicki first explored at Dorton Arena.

All this makes it difficult to think about the arena's origins without a sense of sadness. As much as anything else, the arena is a memorial to a potentially spectacular career cut short.

Matthew Nowicki was born in Siberia in 1910, the son of a Polish diplomat. He studied architecture, design, and engineering in Chicago and Warsaw before graduating in 1936 from the Technological Institute of Warsaw. He practiced and taught for three years before the Nazi invasion. During the occupation, he was allowed to teach bricklaying. But, despite a Nazi ban, he conducted underground classes in architecture and planning.

In 1946, Nowicki came to New York as Poland's representative on the team designing the United Nations. He and his wife, Stanislava, were later introduced to Lewis Mumford at the critic's home in Amenia, New York, where Mumford, now ninety-three, still lives.

"There was extreme friendship between all of us," said Mrs. Nowicki, who moved to Tucson, Arizona, last year after completing a teaching career in architecture at the University of Pennsylvania. "My children felt that Mumford was an adopted uncle."

In 1948, Henry L. Kamphoefner, then the new dean at the North Carolina. State College School of Design, called on Mumford to recommend a chairman for the school's architecture program. The critic recommended Nowicki. On meeting the architect and his wife, the dean was thrilled to find that she, too, was a gifted designer. He hired both of them.

"She said, 'I've never taught in my life,' " Kamphoefner recalled. "I said, 'Well, you have to teach.' "

A year later, J. S. Dorton asked Kamphoefner to recommend an architect for the State Fair arena. The dean suggested hiring Nowicki. Because Nowicki didn't yet have a North Carolina architect's license, Raleigh architect William Henley Dietrick joined the project as the architect of record.

The work of designing the building was roughly one-third finished when Nowicki was killed. But Mrs. Nowicki said the arena was completed substantially as her husband would have wished. "It was," she said, "the beginning of a new way of thinking."

Research Triangle Park

An engine of change

BY GUY MUNGER
The News & Observer
December 1991

The obvious success of the Research Triangle Park has created a stampede of claimants to be its father. But only recently has there been hard evidence of exactly how successful the park has been and its measurable impact on Raleigh.

The documentation is provided by Michael I. Luger and Harvey A. Goldstein, associate professors of city and regional planning at the University of North Carolina at Chapel Hill. This fall, they published their findings in a book, *Technology in the Garden* (Chapel Hill: University of North Carolina Press, 1991).

Luger and Goldstein surveyed the 116 research parks now operating in the United States, then did intensive studies of three of the most successful—Stanford Research Park in California, the University of Utah Research Park, and the Research Triangle Park.

The authors conclude that RTP, like the other successful parks, avoided the pitfalls that have done in many such ventures—poor planning, lack of firm leadership, and bad luck. As for RTP's impact on the Raleigh area, they write,

Research Triangle Park, with Burroughs Wellcome in the center and IBM in the background
The News & Observer

The Research Triangle Park, now 32 years old, has clearly had a significant economic impact on the region. Excluding the area's universities, the park itself represents about three-fourths of the high-tech employment in the area.

Without RTP, almost two-thirds of the 32,000 jobs currently in the park would not be in the region. In addition, we estimate that the park has led to at least another 1,200 high-tech jobs in businesses that have located in the region but outside the park.

Some 31,500 new jobs—both in new firms and in existing companies that have expanded—have been created in the region in response to demands created by RTP.

The total regional employment growth that we attribute to the park is about 52,000, or 12.1 percent of the total number of jobs in the region in 1988.

Luger and Goldstein also note some of the less obvious impacts of RTP—enhancement of the research capacity of the Triangle universities (UNC, State, and Duke University), the projecting of an image that the region is a vital concentration of research and development, and the creation of "a milieu that makes the region attractive for professionals who are not necessarily connected with the park."

The impact of the Research Triangle Park on Raleigh can be measured in many ways. Thack Brown, director of public affairs for Burroughs Wellcome Company, an RTP-based pharmaceutical company, has seen the change in attitudes of Raleigh businessmen as the park has developed. "When I moved to Raleigh in 1964 to work for the chamber of commerce, there was a kind of good old boy network, if you want to call it that," Brown said. "Business people favored development, but it was mostly because the new arrivals would buy more houses or more automobiles or whatever. Now, the maturation of the chamber's approach is an example of change within the business community. There's more than just a desire for growth. There's also a recognition of the need to take care of other problems. Now, business people are concerned about infrastructure, highways, mass transit, education, the arts. As a result of the Research Triangle Park's development, the Raleigh business community has simply become more mature."

James R. Wahlbrink, executive officer of the Home Builders Association of Raleigh and Wake County, sees RTP's impact from the perspective of a newcomer. He moved to Raleigh about a year ago from Sarasota, Florida. "As far as builders are concerned, I think this whole area is unique in the country, with its combination of state government, three major universities, and the Research Triangle Park," he said. "The park provides a solid base for the entire area. Austin, Texas, is the only place that's close, and they don't have the kind of industry we have here."

The Government Mall

A new home on Halifax Street

BY BOB WILSON
The News & Observer
August 17, 1972

Those who are fond of Halifax Street as it is from the state legislative building northward to Peace Street have only a short while longer to enjoy it. By the end of the year, that three-block stretch of Halifax Street will have given way to the state's ambitious plans to construct a tree-lined mall anchored on the north by a fifteen-story office building.

Many old houses in the once-prosperous neighborhood already are under demolition contracts and those still occupied will have to be surrendered this fall.

State property control officer Carroll Mann unveiled last December a long-range expansion blueprint for a twenty-five-block state government center, of which the mall and office building are key components.

It proposes that the state eventually own all the land bounded by Downtown Boulevard on the west, Person Street on the east, Peach Street on the north, and Edenton Street on the south. The new plan was prepared in consultation with A. G. Odell Associates, a Charlotte architectural firm that is designing the mall office building. A. G. Odell said the proposed office building will be 236 feet high. "The exterior may be of white stone or precast concrete," he said. "This building will look like a working building. It won't look like the Washington Monument."

The grassy mall linking the new office building and the legislative building will be lined with trees and eventually flanked by as many as six other government buildings.

To compensate for the loss of Halifax Street, a wishbone-shaped street connecting just north of the new office building will be constructed. It will funnel traffic from Salisbury and Wilmington streets to the proposed Raleigh inner freeway to the north.

View of the State Government Mall from the Cardinal Club
The News & Observer

Old Raleigh vs. New Raleigh

The Raleigh Times
April 13, 1987

Everyone has known for a long time that there are two Raleighs—an Old Raleigh and a New Raleigh.

But the lines between the two are not quite as clear-cut as they once were. The Beltline, long the border between old and new, just doesn't cut it anymore.

Let's face it, Brookhaven and North Hills are getting to be as Old Raleigh as White Oak Road. (Of course, don't tell the people on White Oak Road that.)

No, Old Raleigh vs. New Raleigh is more a state of mind than an address.

Here's how you can tell which one you are:

You're *Old Raleigh* if
Your daughter's middle name is her mother's maiden name.
You have a maid instead of a housecleaning service.
You drive a Mercedes so old the hubcaps are the same color as the body.
You are so determined not to move out of Hayes Barton that you buy a house, tear it down, and build a new one on the lot.

You're *New Raleigh* if
You don't remember the pigeon man who used to sell peanuts at the Capitol.
You know every gourmet takeout place between work and home.
You decided to come to Raleigh over Phoenix, Orlando, and Dallas.

You're *Old Raleigh* if
You remember when Ivey's was downtown.
The clerks at Tyler House call you when a blue blouse that would look good with your blue skirt comes in.
Your one-year-old has his own calling cards.
You think the membership fee at Carolina Country Club should be deductible.
You belong to Indian Guides or Indian Princesses.

The debutantes of the Terpsichorean Club come out, 1972.

The News & Observer

You're *New Raleigh* if

You work for a company that goes only by initials.

You think the famous Armistead Maupin is the one who writes books.

You buy that night's groceries on your way home from work.

You have never met anyone named Williams or Haywood.

You're *Old Raleigh* if

You belong to the health club at the YMCA (needless to say, the one on Hillsborough Street).

You know that the unmarked building at the corner of Oberlin and Fairview roads is a jewelry store.

The Angus Barn is the only place to eat if the dining room at the Carolina Country Club is closed.

You wear only jewelry older than you are.

You're *New Raleigh* if

You think the Milburnie Fish Club is a seafood restaurant.

The only time you go downtown is to show the relatives.

You hang out at Cheers.

You figure the Civil War is ancient history.

You're *Old Raleigh* if

The War Between the States is a common dinnertime topic.

You think Raleigh Little Theater is just as good as Broadway.

You knew the grandmother of all your friends.

You went to first grade with the person you are married to.

Your grandfather is buried in Oakwood Cemetery.

You're *New Raleigh* if

Your grandfather is buried in New Jersey.

You mow your own yard to save money for the health club.

You never drive under forty-five miles per hour and fantasize about running over Old Raleigh drivers.

You have at least one extra phone for adults, preferably in the Saab.

You're *Old Raleigh* if

You use the word *Yankees* even when it's not baseball season.

You belong to the North Carolina Art Society.

You remember when Pete Maravich had a crew cut and played for the city's only high school.

You think Durham is "a city somewhere west of here."

You're *New Raleigh* if

Durham is where you buy your groceries.

You can't wait until they build the Outer Loop.

You think the Terps Club is the alumni organization for the University of Maryland.

You have ski racks on your car two months after you went to the mountains.

You're *Old Raleigh* if

You have had the same yardman for at least six years, and your azaleas are at least three feet high.

You buy at least a hundred dollars'-worth of groceries at a time at Harris Teeter in Glenwood Village.

You pretend not to know what being Old Raleigh means.

FAREWELL

Joel Lane's wilderness of oak and hickory has become a forest of steel, glass, and stone. By 1992, the city's original 1,000 acres had grown to an amoebic 59,021, and the 669 pioneers counted in 1800 had reached 207,951—many of them modern pioneers in the subdivided woods of North Raleigh. The careful planning of William Christmas has become a baling-wire effort to control sprawl. The great houses that gave Raleigh a reputation for elegance are mostly gone, replaced with parking lots and steel-and-glass towers.

Yet a walk through historic Oakwood, or around the City Market on Martin Street, tells a different story—one of resurgent civic pride. Raleigh's four colleges and two universities flourish, more places of higher learning than any other city in the state. The North Carolina Symphony, a resident since 1974, performs in a renovated Memorial Auditorium. Fine artists work in a warehouse that was converted to ateliers with city funds. And healthy public and private investment in city projects—new towers on Fayetteville Street Mall, parks, and citywide greenways—testify that the spirit of Lane, Joseph and Winifred Gales, William Boylan, and the other originators is alive and well.

The News & Observer

Index

A. G. Odell Associates, 191
Abbott, Nell, 171
Abernathie, John, 5
Academy of Music, 114
Afro-American, 131
Albright, R. Mayne, 164
Alcoholic Beverage Control Board, 123
Alford, Warren, 8
Amadas, Phillip, 10
Ambassador Theater, 171
American Airlines, 139, 143
American Expeditionary Force, 152
American Home Mission Society, 84
American Public Welfare Association, 174
Amherst College (Mass.), 84
Ammons, Justus M. "Judd," 157, 158, 159
Andres, William, 46
Andrews, A. B., 105
Andrews, Alex, 104, 105
Andrews, Graham, 105
Andrews, John, 104, 105
Andrews, Peter V., 183
Andrews, Wayne, 24
Andrews, William J., 102 (pictured), 105
Andrews-Heck House, 105
Angus Barn, 193
Architectural Record, 188
Argo House, 115
Army Air Corps, 140
Arthur, C. D., 148
Artsplosure, 184
Ashe, Samuel A., 119
Atkins, Rhoddam, 7
Atkinson, Thomas, 86
Atlantic Coast Conference, 178
Aycock, Charles B., 145
Aycock Junior High, 172

Badger, George, 27
Bank of New Bern, 41
Banks, Garland C., 132
Baptist Female University, 114. *See also* Meredith College
Baptist State Convention, 125
Baptist University for Women, 113 (pictured). *See also* Meredith College
Barlowe, Arthur, 10
Barnum, P. T., 135
Barrett, John, 51, 53
Barringer, Daniel M., 84

Basie, Count, 131
Bass, Vincent, 3
Bassett, John, 41
Bassett, John S., 121
Batchelor, Peter, 158, 159, 185
Battle, Kemp P., 7, 32 (memoir), 83, 86
Bauer, Adolphus Gustavus, 112–17, 126, 127
Bauer, Fred, 115
Bauer, Rachel Blythe, 112–17
Beatty, Ken, 151
Bell, Jack, 25
Beltline, 157, 158, 160, 161 (pictured), 181, 182
Bennett, James, 53
Bennett Place, 51, 53
Benson, Cliff, 160
Berry O'Kelly Training School, 136–37
Betts, David A., 132
Biblical Recorder, 125
Bishir, Catherine, 111, 115
Blair, John, 63
Bloomsbury estate, 3
Bloomsbury Park, 111, 128, 129
Blount Street, 103–5
Booth, John Wilkes, 56, 65
Boylan, William, 9, 13, 15, 42, 43, 46, 79, 90, 194
Boylan Heights, 108, 164
Bradshaw, Charles W., Jr., 163
Bragg, Thomas, 81
Branch Bank and Trust Company, 93
Brantley's Drug Store, 185
Brewer, Kidd, 181
Bridgers, Ann Preston, 134, 135
Briggs, Billy, 75
Briggs, Fabius H., 74, 75
Briggs, James A., 74, 75
Briggs, John D., 73, 74
Briggs, John Joyner, 74
Briggs, T. H. (Thomas), 71, 73
Briggs, Thomas H., Jr., 74, 75
Briggs, Thomas H., III, 73–75 (memoir)
Briggs, Willis G., 80
Briggs and Sons, Inc., 73, 74 (pictured)
Brooks, George W., 82
Broughton, Needham, 58, 80
Broughton High School, 168, 170
Brown, Charlotte, 108
Brown, Thack, 190
Bryan, Raymond A., 166, 167
Bryan, William Jennings, 78, 120, 153
Buchanan, James, 54
Burnside, Ambrose Everett, 55
Burr, E. T., 104

Burroughs Wellcome Company, 143, 189 (pictured), 190
Burton, Governor, 20, 21
Burwell, John, 72
Burwell, Robert, 72
Busbee, Dick, 104
Bushong, William B., 114
Butler, Marion, 120

Cabarrus, Stephen, 6
Caldwell, John T., 98
Caldwell, Joseph P., 119, 120, 121
California Fruit Store, 111, 185
Cameron, Charles Clifford, 167
Cameron, Duncan, 33, 36
Cameron Park, 108, 180, 182
Cameron Village, 80, 163, 167, 169, 180–83
Camp Russell, 86
Campbell, June, 170
Campbell, Mildred, 170
Campbell, Ralph, 170–71
Campbell, Ralph, Jr., 170
Campbell, William, 170–72
Cannon, Isabella, 135
Canova, Antonio, 7
Capital City Barber Shop, 130, 131
Capital Club, 104
Capitol, 2 (pictured), 13, 32, 47, 110, 184, 192; choosing site for original, 5; Civil War activity at, 53, 60, 61–65; construction of second, 22–24, 36; dedication of second, 33; description of original, 7; description of second, 34; fire at original, 25
Capitol Airlines, 140
Capitol Apartments, 164
Carnage, Fred J., 130, 131, 168
Carolina Country Club, 104, 128, 138, 192, 193
Carolina Playmakers, 134, 135
Carolina Power and Light Company, 108, 109, 111, 128, 129, 135
Carolina Tribune, 131
Carroll, Delia Dixon, 107
Carroll, Loretta, 135
Carter, Wilmoth A., 85, 131
Cary Village Shopping Center, 167
Case, Everett, 177, 178
Cash, W. J., 122
Casso, Hannah Stuart, 8
Casso, Peter, 33
Casso's inn, 7, 8, 67
Catalano, Eduardo, 98
Caucasian, 120

Centennial Exposition of 1885, 110
Centennial Graded School, 127
Chapman, George, 159
Charles, Lorenzo, 178
Charlotte Observer, 119, 120
Chavis, John, 29–30
Chavis Park, 29
Cherry, Governor, 138
Christ Episcopal Church, 27, 34, 35, 37, 51, 107
Christmas, William, 5, 127, 194
Circle, The, 104
City Auditorium, 93, 167 (pictured)
City Hall, 93
City Market, 93, 130, 132, 147–51, 185, 194
Civic Center, 184, 186
Claiborne, Jack, 119
Clay, Henry, 105
Cobb, Tom, 20
Cobb, William, 62
Cocker-Capehart House, 114
Cogswell, Joseph, 36
Colored Settlement House, 88
Colored Women's YWCA, 88
Cooke, William D., 47
Cooper, Anna, 87, 88
Cooper, George, 88
Cooper, Jackie, 140
Copp, Si, 138
Crabtree, Beth, 127
Crabtree Valley, 158
Crabtree Valley Mall, 181, 182
Crassweller, Elizabeth C., 142
Cross, Charley, 149, 150
Cross, Charlotte, 149
Curtiss Wright Flying Service, 140

Dabney, Virginius, 121
Daily Confederate, 58
Daily Progress, 58, 83
Daniels, Frank, 124
Daniels, Jonathan, 122, 124, 134
Daniels, Josephus, 102 (pictured), 118–24
Daniels, Josephus, Jr., 124
Daniels, Worth, 124
Davie, William R., 6
Davis, Alexander Jackson, 24
Davis, Burke, 51
Davis, Jefferson, 54, 58, 59
Deaf Mute, 48
Delta Airlines, 143
Denby, Edwin, 124
Dentzel, Gustav, 129

Dentzel, William, 129
Devereux, John, 27, 54
Devereux, Margaret Mordecai, 27
Devereux, Thomas P., 20
Dietrick, William Henley, 188
Dirnberger, Mary, 134
Dix, Dorothea, 48
Dixie Classic, 177–79
Dobbin, James C., 48
Dobbs, Arthur, 4, 6
Dodd, James, 73, 79
Dorothea Dix Hospital, 47, 48, 113
Dorton, J. S., 188
Dorton Arena, 187–88
Douglass, Frederick, 87
Drake, Francis, 12
Dudley, E. D., 33
Duke University, 176, 190
Duke University Law School, 172
Dunbar High School (Washington, D.C.), 88
Durham, Baxter, 141

Earhart, Amelia, 141
East Carolina University, 164
Eastern Airlines, 139, 140, 142
Edenton Street Methodist Church, 73, 90, 92
Edmonds, Helen, 121
Edmondston, Catherine Ann Devereux, 54–57
   (diary excerpts)
Edmondston, Patrick, 54
Efird's Department Store, 160
Eisenhower, Dwight D., 121
Elizabeth I (queen of England), 10, 12
Enloe High School, 171, 172
Episcopal School of North Carolina, 36
Estey, Jacob, 84
Estey Hall, 85
Estey Seminary for Women, 84, 85
Everett, Edward, 69
Experimental Railroad, 13, 32

Farmer's Market, 130, 147, 149, 167
Fayetteville Street Mall, 184–86, 194
Federal Aviation Administration, 141, 142
Federal Theater, 134, 135
Fernández, Simón, 10
First Presbyterian Church, 30, 71, 115
First Union Capitol Center, 186
First Union National Bank of North Carolina, 167
Five Points, 149
Founders Row, 185
Fowle, Daniel, 113, 127

Freedmen's Bureau, 71, 87
Freedmen's Commission, 86
Friday, William C., 98, 99, 178
Fuller, Buckminster, 98

Gales, Joseph, 13–16, 29, 32, 43
Gales, Joseph, Jr., 16
Gales, Weston, 16, 33, 44
Gales, Winifred, 9, 13–16
Gardner, O. Max, 97
George II (king of England), 4
Gilbert, Humphrey, 10
Gilmer-Montgomery Ward Building, 93
Godschalk, David R., 159
Goerch, Carl, 138
Goldstein, Harvey A., 189–90
Goodwin, James W., 139, 140
Governor Morehead School for the Blind, 47–48
Governor's Mansion, 103, 106, 111, 127, 172
Governor's Palace, 9, 127
Graham, Frank Porter, 97, 122, 145
Graham, W. A., 51
Grant, Ulysses S., 51, 53, 54, 55, 65, 67, 68, 82
Greater Raleigh Chamber of Commerce, 186, 190
Green, Lewis, 8
Grenville, Richard, 10
Griffin, Captain, 20
Guion Hotel, 83, 84

Hardee, William J., 55
Hardin, Eugene B., Jr., 144
Hargett Street, 130–34
Harper, Mrs. Frank, 107
Harrington, William, 4, 6
Harriot, Thomas, 10
Harris, James E., 79
Harris Teeter, 193
Harrison, William, 51, 52
Harrod, Willie, 20
Hawkins, A. B., 102 (pictured), 106
Hawkins, Mrs. A. B., 102 (pictured)
Hawkins-Hartness House, 105, 106
Hayes Barton, 149, 164, 192
Haywood, Dallas, 69
Haywood, Elizabeth, 8, 9
Haywood, Fabius, 87
Haywood, George Washington, 87
Haywood, Hannah Stanley, 87
Haywood, Hubert, 104
Haywood, John, 7, 9, 25
Haywood, Julia Hicks, 63
Haywood, Marshall DeLancey, 106

Haywood, Mattie Bailey, 106 (memoir), 107 (pictured)
Haywood, Norma Wall, 133
Haywood, R. B., 20–21 (memoir), 25 (memoir), 32
Haywood, Sherwood, 20, 41, 42, 63
Haywood Hall, 106
Haywood House, 63
Heck, Jonathan, 105
Heritage Square, 107
Hicks, Loretta, 133
Hicks, William J., 127
Hill, A. P., 56
Hillsborough Recorder, 81
Hinton, Jane Miller, 57
Hinton, John, 3, 4
Hodge, Robert, 147, 148, 149
Hodge, Rufus, 147–51
Holden, W. W. (William Woods), 58, 59, 65, 69, 81–82, 118
Holding, Willis, 104
Holhouser, James E., Jr., 121
Holladay, Alexander Q., 96
Holmes, Theophilus Hunter, 39
Home Builders Association of Raleigh and Wake County, 190
Howard, Oliver Otis, 57
Hugh Morson High School, 134
Hunter, Aaron, 86
Hunter, Isaac, 3

IBM, 189 (pictured)
Indian Queen Tavern, 8
Isaac Hunter's tavern, 3, 5
Ives, Levi Silliman, 36, 39

Jacob Estey and Sons, 84
James I (king of England), 12
James E. Strates Shows, 78
Jane S. McKimmon Extension and Continuing Education Center, 100, 154
Jennett, Norman, 120
Jerman, Mrs. Palmer, 107
Joel Lane's inn, 3, 6 (pictured)
Johnson, Andrew, 27, 57, 67–70, 82
Johnson, Jacob, 8, 67
Johnson, Mrs. Charles E., 107
Johnson, Philip, 188
Johnston, Joseph E., 51, 53, 54, 55, 56, 60, 63, 67
Jones, Charles, 119
Jones, Seby, 163
Jones, Willie, 6, 86
Jones and Powell's (feed store), 91

Journal of Freedom, 83
Justice, Charlie "Choo Choo," 179

Kamphoefner, Henry L., 98, 163, 188
Keith, H. S., 75
Kennedy, James, 147
Kennedy, John F., 174
Kent State University (Ohio), 100
Kerbaugh, M. A., 171
Kilpatrick, Hugh Judson, 52, 61, 65
King, Kelly S., 186
Kirk, George W., 82
Kitchin, W. W., 104, 107
Knuckles, Rufus, 148
Koch, Frederick, 134
Ku Klux Klan, 82

Lafayette, George Washington, 20
Lafayette, Marquis de, 7, 20–21, 42
Lane, Edward, 42
Lane, Henry, 26
Lane, Joel, 3, 4, 5, 6, 26, 41, 194
Lane, Julian, 104
Lane, Lunsford, 41–43, 44–46 (memoir)
Lane, Martha Curtis, 42
Lane, Ralph, 10
Latta, M. L., 79, 80
Latta University, 80
Lawrence, R. C., 110 (memoir)
Lee, Robert E., 38, 51, 54, 55, 68
Lee, Timothy F., 79
Lefler, Hugh T., 120
Legislative Council, 152
Lenoir, William, 6
Leonard Medical School, 85
Lewis, Cornelia "Nell" Battle, 102 (pictured), 152–53
Lewis, Mary Gordon, 152
Lewis, Richard Henry, 152
Lightner Arcade Building, 131
Lincoln, Abraham, 53, 54, 56, 60, 63, 65, 67
Lineham, Will, 115, 116
Little, Burke Haywood, 27
Logan, John, 53, 54
Longview Gardens, 146
Lucy Capehart House, 115
Luger, Michael I., 189–90
Lyell, Thomas, 37

Macon, Nathaniel, 15
Main Building (Peace College), 71–72
Mangum, Willie, 30

Manley, Charles, 30
Mann, Carroll, 191
Manor, Blanche, 138
Mansion Park Hotel, 114, 126
Manteo, 10
Marling, Jacob, 2
Marshall, John, 8
Martin, James G., 118, 121
Martin, LeRoy, 170
Mason, Richard, 35
Matthews, Walter J., 96, 100
McIver, Charles Duncan, 126
McKay, Kay, 135
McKimmon, Charles, 154
McKimmon, Jane Simpson, 97, 154
McKimmon, Willa, 104
McPheeters, William, 30, 42
Mebane, William N., 71
Mechanics and Farmers Bank Building, 131, 132, 136
Memorial Auditorium, 127, 135, 164, 165, 177, 194
Meredith, Thomas, 125
Meredith College, 111, 125–26
Method Community Center, 137
Method Park, 137
Method Village, 136
Metropolitan Hall, 93, 147
Metts, John, 104
Metts, Josephine, 104
Milburnie Fish Club, 193
Millie-Christine ("Carolina Twins"), 77
Mills, John, 111
Milner, James, 29
Minerva, 9, 12, 15, 42
Minority Business Development Agency, 130
Minter, John D., 130
Mission Valley Apartments, 167
Mission Valley Shopping Center, 163, 167
Moore, Bartholomew Figures, 68, 69, 70
Moore, Dan K., 99
Mordecai, Ann Willis Lane "Nancy," 27, 28
Mordecai, Ellen, 27, 28 (memoir)
Mordecai, George, 27, 33, 54, 55
Mordecai, Henry, 27
Mordecai, Margaret Lane, 26, 27, 28
Mordecai, Moses, 26, 27, 28
Mordecai House, 26, 27, 28, 110
Morehead, John Motley, 43, 47, 48
Morgan, J. Pierpont, 105
Morrison, Cameron, 120
Mumford, Lewis, 98, 188

Murphey, Archibald D., 47
Murphey School, 170, 171
Murray, Elizabeth Reid, 48, 52
Myers, Lewis H., 130
Myers, Terri, 147–51

National Council on Aging, 175
National Freeman's Savings and Trust Company, 79
National Intelligencer, 15, 16
Nelson, Charlotte, 97
New York Independent, 88
Newcomers Club, 160
Newton Theological Seminary, 84
Nichols, Jessie Clyde, 180
Nichols, William, 7, 23, 24, 27
Nichols, William, Jr., 23, 24
Niemayer, Oscar, 188
Nine O'Clock Cotillion, 104
Nixon, Richard M., 121
North Carolina Agricultural and Mechanical College, 91. See also North Carolina State University
North Carolina Agricultural Extension Service, 154
North Carolina Agriculture Department, 119
North Carolina Architecture, 115
North Carolina Art Society, 193
North Carolina Bible Society, 47
North Carolina Board of Conservation and Development, 162, 168
North Carolina Conference for Social Services, 145
North Carolina Department of Motor Vehicles, 77
North Carolina Institution for the Instruction of the Deaf, Dumb, and Blind, 33–34, 47
North Carolina Railroad, 119
North Carolina School for the Blind. See Governor Morehead School for the Blind
North Carolina Standard, 31, 58, 59 (excerpt)
North Carolina State Fair, 76–78, 104
North Carolina State Fairgrounds, 109
North Carolina State University, 80, 94–100, 154, 176–79, 187, 190
North Carolina Symphony, 194
North Carolina Teachers Assembly, 113
North Hills, 158, 182
North Hills Mall, 158, 181
North Raleigh, 157–59
Northgate Mall (Durham), 181
Nowicki, Matthew, 98, 187–88
Nowicki, Stanislava, 188

Oakwood, 73, 194

Oakwood Cemetery, 40, 82, 90, 112, 193
Oberlin, 79–80
Oberlin College (Ohio), 79, 88
Odd Fellows Building, 131
Odell, A. G., 191
O'Kelly, Berry, 136–37
Olivia Raney Library, 104
Olmstead, Frederick Law, 34–35 (memoir)
Orange presbytery, 30, 71
Orr, Robert F., 121
Oxford Orphan Asylum, 113
Oxford *Torchlight*, 30

Pan-African Congress (London), 88
Parham, Jim, 75
Parish, Charles, 8
Park Hotel, 114, 117 (pictured)
Paton, David, 24
Peace, Joseph, 71
Peace, William, 71
Peace College, 71–72
Peace Institute, 39, 84. *See also* Peace College
Pearce, Irvin A., 165
Peck, Lewis W., 79
Pegram, W. Eddie, 142
Pell, Reverend Mr., 65
Phillips, Wendell, 68
Piedmont Airlines, 140, 143
Poe, Alice Aycock, 146
Poe, Clarence, 145–46
Polk, Dan, 105
Polk, Leonidas L., 95
Polk, William, 20, 21
Porter, John, 8
Pou, Mrs. James H., 107
Powell, William, 6
Progressive Farmer, 95, 145, 146
Protestant Episcopal Church, 86
Pullen, John T., 126
Pullen, R. Stanhope, 89–92, 95
Pullen Building, 114
Pullen Park, 91–92, 128, 129
Pullen Park Carousel, 128, 129
"Pullen Town," 90 (pictured)

Qualls, George, 187

Ragan, Rosa, 129
Raleigh, Walter, 6, 10–12, 33, 34
Raleigh Academy, 13
Raleigh Blues, 20
Raleigh Board of Education, 170

Raleigh Business College, 113
Raleigh City Cemetery, 88
Raleigh City School Board, 168
Raleigh Civic Center, 134
Raleigh Co-operative Land and Building Association, 79
Raleigh Electric Company, 108
Raleigh Garden Club, 180
Raleigh Historic Properties Commission, 133, 147
Raleigh Hotel. *See* Park Hotel
Raleigh Independent, 136
Raleigh Little Theater, 78, 111, 134–35, 193
Raleigh Merchants Bureau, 109
Raleigh Municipal Airport, 139–40
Raleigh National Bank, 74
Raleigh *News & Observer*, 118–22, 123–24, 152, 153 (excerpt)
Raleigh Opera Company, 135
Raleigh Register, 9, 13, 15, 16, 29, 31, 33, 58, 76
"Raleigh Roots" oral-history project, 133, 147
Raleigh Sentinel, 82
Raleigh Skyhawks, 176
Raleigh Star, 69 (pictured), 81
Raleigh Theological Institute, 84
Raleigh Times, 123, 128, 152
Raleigh Township School Committee, 80
Raleigh-Durham Airport Authority, 162, 168
Raleigh-Durham International Airport, 139–44
Ramsey, J. L., 145
Reid, David S., 81
Reid, Whitelaw, 69
Rencher, Abram, 30
Research Triangle Park, 100, 139, 143, 189–90
Rex, John, 89–92
Rex Hospital, 89–92
Richards, E. N., 158, 163, 167, 181
Richmond Times-Dispatch, 121
Rickenbacker, Eddie, 140
Ridley, Frank, 147–51
Riple, John H., 97
Robinson, Les, 178
Rockefeller Foundation, 145
Rogers, Will, 124
Roosevelt, Franklin Delano, 122, 124
Roosevelt, Theodore, 77 (pictured), 78
Root, Sadie, 134
Round, George C., 60–66 (memoir)
Royale Theater, 131
Royster, Mrs. Hubert, 107
Rudisill, Mary, 160
Rulfs, Donald J., 134
Russell, Daniel L., 118, 121

Ruth, Sam, 75

Saarinen, Eero, 188
Samarcand, 153
Sanford, Terry, 98
Sansom, J. J., Jr., 132
Scales, Alfred M., 71
Schofield, John McAllister, 55, 61, 65, 66
Schwartz, Juny, 148
Scott, Jim, 148
Scott, W. Kerr, 122
Seawell, Henry, 86
Second Baptist Church, 84
Seligson, Herbert, 149
Seward, William H., 56, 65
Shaw, Elijah, 84
Shaw Hall, 84
Shaw Jubilee Singers, 84, 85
Shaw University, 71, 83–86, 131, 170
Sheffield *Register*, 15
Sheridan, Dick, 179
Sherman, William Tecumseh, 39, 50 (pictured),
    51–57, 60, 63, 64, 65, 67, 83, 127
Simpson, Ann Cannon Shank, 154
Simpson, William, 154
Sir Walter Hotel, 138, 164, 171
Sitton, Claude, 118, 121
Sloan, Samuel, 113, 127
Smedes, Aldert, 36–40, 79, 86
Smedes, Edward, 39
Smedes, Ives, 39
Smedes, John E. C., 86, 88
Smedes, Lyell, 39
Smedes, Sarah Lyell, 37
Smith, Benjamin, 9, 42
Smith, Dean, 179
Smith, Donald L., 121
Smith, Erk, 138
Smith, J. Brinton, 85
South Square Mall (Durham), 181
Southern Railroad, 105
Southern Railway, 121
Spirit of Missions, 85
Spring Garden Presbyterian Church, 71
St. Agnes Hospital, 86
St. Augustine's College, 7, 83–86, 87, 88, 170
St. James A.M.E. Church, 137
St. John's Hospital, 90
St. Mary's College, 32, 36–40, 86, 111, 152, 153,
    166
St. Monica's Catholic School, 170
Stanford Research Park (Calif.), 189

State Agricultural Board, 13
State Bank of North Carolina, 7, 27, 36
State Chronicle, 119
State Hospital and Medical Care Commission, 146
State Hospital for the Insane. *See* Dorothea Dix
    Hospital
State House. *See* Capitol
State Journal, 58, 59
State, The, 138
Stevens, Richard Y., 186
Stevens, Thad, 69
Stevenson, Adlai, 121
Stony Brook Shopping Center, 167
Stoops, Martha, 39
Street Railway Company, 108
Stringfield, Oliver Larkin, 125, 126
Stuart, Hannah Casso, 8, 33
Sumner, Charles, 69
Sutton, Cantey Venable, 135
Sutton, Louis V., 135
Sutton, Robert, 88
Swain, David, 51

T. A. Loving Company, 166
Tabernacle Baptist Church, 114
Taft School, 172
Tea and Topics, 107
Teer, T. Dillard, 139, 140, 141, 168
Terpsichorean Club, 104, 192 (pictured), 193
Thomas, John R., 61
Thompson, Cyrus, 121
Thurmond, Allen, 104
Tompkins, Daniel A., 121
Tornado, the, 31–33
Town, Itheil, 24
Trinity Church, 35
Tryon, William, 4
Tryon's Palace, 4
Tucker, R. S., 74
Tucker, W. H., 74
Tupper, Henry Martin, 71, 72, 84
Tupper Baptist Church, 84
Turner, Josiah, Jr., 82, 118
Turner, Nat, 30, 41

Umstead State Park, 142
United Airlines, 140, 143
University of North Carolina at Chapel Hill, 94,
    95, 97, 99, 122, 134, 178, 190
University of North Carolina at Greensboro, 97,
    126
University of North Carolina Hospitals, 133

University of Utah Research Park, 189
Upjohn, Hobart, 35
Upjohn, Richard, 35

Valand, Leif, 167
Valand, Wymene, 168
Valvano, Jim, 177, 178
Vance, Zebulon Baird, 51, 58, 67, 81, 127
Vanderbilt, Mrs. George K., 78, 104
Vanderbilt University (Tenn.), 172
Velvet Cloak Inn, 163, 167

Wachovia Bank, 93
Wahlbrink, James R., 190
Wake Agricultural Society, 27
Wake Court House, 3
Wake Crossroads, 3
Wake Forest University, 96, 179
Wakefield Academy, 125
Wall, Audrey, 133
Wanchese, 10
Washington, Booker T., 86, 121
Washington Chronicle, 82
Washington Post, 88
Watauga Club, 95
Watson, Moe, 151
Weedon, Frank, 177, 178, 179
West, Louis, 104
Whisperwind, 163
White, John, 10, 12
Wiley School, 164
Williams, G. Wesley, 109
Williams, Malcolm L., 143
Williams, Thomas, 79
Williams, Uncle Tom, 75
Wills, Archibald, 8
Will's Forest, 54, 57 (pictured)
Wilson, Woodrow, 124
Winborne, Stanley, 104
Winston, Ellen Black, 174–75
Winston, George T., 96
Winston, Richard S., 174
Women's College. *See* University of North Caro-
    lina at Greensboro
Women's Congress (Chicago), 87
Wood, George, 99
Works Progress Administration, 135
World's Congress of Representative Women, 88
Worth, Jonathan, 69, 70
Wright, Frank Lloyd, 98
Wyatt, Henry, 23 (pictured)

Yarborough, Mary E., 97
Yarborough Hotel, 127, 185 (pictured)
Yellow Rose Tea Room, 132
YMCA, 193
York, Charles Vance, 109, 147, 162–69
York, Charles Vance, Jr. (son of Charles Vance
    York), 166
York, Charles Vance II (son of Willie York), 169
York, Elizabeth Collette, 169
York, G. Smedes, 144, 157, 162–69
York, James Wesley, Jr., 166, 168
York, James Wesley "Willie," 109, 143, 162–69,
    170, 180, 181
York, Mary Smedes Poyner, 166, 168
York and Cobb Construction Company, 164
York Construction, 109, 168
York Properties, Inc., 109, 147, 168
Young's Hardware, 149
YWCA, 152